Changing

School

Culture

Through

Staff

Development

1990 Yearbook
of the Association for Supervision
and Curriculum Development

Edited by Bruce Joyce

Printed in the United States of America.

Ronald S. Brandt, Executive Editor
Nancy Modrak, Managing Editor, Books
Al Way, Manager, Design Services
Janet Price, Assistant Manager, Production Services
Editorial assistance provided by Janet Mullaney, Carolyn Pool, Ginger Miller, and Nick Lanni.
Composition by Scott Photographics;‑printed by Jarboe Printing Company.

Library of Congress Catalog Card No.: 44-6213

ASCD Stock No.: 610-90009
ISBN: 0-87120-156-9
ISSN: 1042-9018

$19.95

Changing School Culture Through Staff Development

Part I
Messages from the Knowledge Base

These three chapters come from the staff development research perspective. Chapter 1 is framed from the broad perspective of staff development and the culture of schooling. It identifies the changing of the culture of the school as one of the ultimate goals of staff development. Chapter 2 deals with staff development and the training technology from the perspective of what has been learned about teachers as learners. From this position, learning how to learn becomes a central goal. Chapter 3 focuses on teacher personality and the social climate of the schools, illustrating their interactive effects in a study of the implementation of the content of a staff development program.

Fullan analyzes research pertaining to staff development as a strategy for implementing innovations, as an innovation in itself, and for institutional development. He concludes that the development of true human resource development systems in education depends on the redevelopment of the culture of the institution. He also asserts that the effects of implementing innovations short of genuine restructuring will be short-lived. He describes his and his colleagues' strategy for establishing a learning consortium devoted to long-term restructuring, but points out that the culture of the school has been resistant to change and that the research on how to modify it lies ahead of us.

This chapter focuses on three types of approaches designed to help teachers increase instructional skills: helping teachers obtain information about their behavior; changing the workplace in order to create a more freeing and stimulating environment; and training to help teachers acquire teaching strategies and use them effectively in the classroom. The question addressed is "What has been learned about how teachers learn?" The results are encouraging, especially about what can be expected if powerful staff development systems are put into place. However, this review also underscores the need for research on how to alter the culture of the school so that it will be more productive for teachers and students.

Hopkins examines the psychological states of teachers and the social climates of schools as contributors to the implementation of staff development programs. The dramatic influence of teachers' psychological states underlines the importance of motivation and the need to help people become fully functioning learners. The effects of social climate differences underscore the importance of leadership in developing positive environments for learning and schooling, and the urgent need for research on effective leadership development.

Part II
Changing Roles of the Shareholders
in North America

These four chapters forecast changes in the roles of the current shareholders in staff development. Each chapter calls for change—in the principalship, the structure of the school, relationships in district personnel, the organization of staff development, and in the university, its personnel, and their relationships to the schools.

   Leithwood has synthesized conceptions of levels of professional competence and psychological development theory into a model for guiding school administrators in their learning facilitator role. The resulting framework transforms the concept of instructional leadership from that of supervisor into that of a leader of learning who is guided by understandings about individual differences in development and how to arrange the environment to increase growth potential.

   Shanker describes a collegial workplace and a professionalization of teaching that generates levels and types of staff development far beyond most current practice. Some of the practices reported in this yearbook clearly have elements consistent with his vision. And although many authors argue persuasively for major changes in the culture of the schools and the organizational ethos of school districts, Shanker most sharply sees cultural change as a matter of moral urgency.

   Federally funded teacher centers had a short but energetic life. In this chapter, Yarger preserves the guiding concepts and sets forth the lessons learned from their achievements and limitations. He explains how teachers quickly learned to establish policies and manage economical, responsive organizations that served many of their colleagues. The experience testifies to the potential benefits were districts to apply the concept to portions of their staff development investment. Yarger also provides guidelines for making another generation of teacher centers more powerful than the first.

   Arends tackles one of the most vexing problems this yearbook attempts to address—connecting the university to the school. This thoughtful, realistic essay promises no easy routes but searches out avenues that can improve what nearly everyone agrees is a dreadful situation. The vast investment in education faculties—40,000 positions in the United States alone—is underutilized. The expansion of staff development is a opportunity we must seize to reconnect mutual ends and improve the quality of services.

Part III
Changing Roles of the Shareholders
in England, Wales, and Australia

These chapters are thorough analyses of the national programs in England and Wales and Australia. Written independently from the above chapters, they describe evolutions of systems and forecasts of changes that are strikingly parallel to those of North America.

> An interest in developing a vital workplace pervades Bolam's description. As in Canada and the United States, policymakers are trying to find avenues that will simultaneously lead to a better quality of education and professionalism in education personnel. The result is a blend of initiatives for curriculum change that attempts to increase the power of school faculties to improve the quality of education and the power of individuals to develop their own routes for development. Bolam's essay reflects frustration with the dilemmas created by schools that are organized to deliver educational services rather than to improve the content or quality of those services. Initiatives flounder because the necessary restructuring and reorientation of school culture has not yet taken place.

> Owen describes Australian efforts to build a more vital human resource development system. The attempt to strengthen curriculum implementation while increasing initiative from the schools reflects the need to balance the potential that comes from placing trust in faculties with the attempt to reduce isolation and localism.

Part IV
Opportunities to Learn: District Initiatives

Personnel research may not have discovered how to change the culture of the school, but some school districts are certainly making mighty efforts. By providing resources to individuals and schools, and by generating initiatives designed to affect the workplace, forward-looking districts are forecasting the next generation of staff development systems. In these five chapters, we visit two very large and three middle-sized school systems. All five are attempting to build environments that will radically change the growth potential of their teachers and administrators.

Bill Mell and Carol Mell

The Mells describe an initiative to develop collegial teams of teachers who share the study of teaching and curriculum. The teachers received extensive instruction in teaching strategies and shared the results of their practice. They enjoyed the activity, found it professionally profitable, and wished to continue and expand the enterprise. Why should maintenance and extension be difficult? The reasons have to do with the differences between an organizational ethos that sustains operations and one that supports what appears so simple on the surface—the establishment of the collegial study of teaching as a pervasive activity in the workplace.

Bruce Joyce and Carlene Murphy

Foreword

Yearbook editor Bruce Joyce has compiled a unique, research-based analysis of the field on which we depend in our efforts to improve education. The authors focus not on the content of staff development, but on its *structure and process*. What they are looking for is dramatic change—in staff development programs, in student achievement, and in the culture of the school—at all levels: district, building, individual, university. They see restructuring—integrating the change effort at all of the various levels—as a requirement, not an option. As restructuring continues to hold our attention and focus our school improvement efforts through the last decade of the 20th century, we have in the 1990 ASCD Yearbook a valuable resource for guiding our professional reflection, research, and daily practice.

During my year as ASCD President, when traveling in other parts of the world, I have been struck by the commonality of our efforts to bring to life the concept of the school as a place of continued learning for all who work there. The 1990 yearbook can have a powerful influence on this mutual goal and in the fulfillment of ASCD's mission: "To develop leadership for quality in education for all students." It can also be an impetus for more significant and less fragmented research efforts that will lead to designing responsive schools for a changing world.

PATRICIA C. CONRAN
ASCD President, 1989-90

Preface: Thoughts on Staff Development

Madeline Hunter

As a young psychologist, I left my position at the Children's Hospital, and subsequently at Juvenile Hall, feeling that most of my work was "too little, too late"; I was trying to solve problems that could have been prevented. So I became a school psychologist to work at the preventive rather than the remedial end of students' academic, social, and emotional growth. Certainly many of their problems were home-based, but educators had little control of that environment. At school, we had considerable control over five or six hours, about a third of a student's waking day. Surely, there were things we could do that might ameliorate, if not change, any undesirable effects from the other two-thirds of that day. For a student who had poor breakfasts and dinners, wouldn't a nutritious lunch contribute a great deal to health? Wouldn't a "nutritious" five to six hours at school every day also make a valuable contribution to a student's emotional, social, physical, and academic well-being?

Convinced it would, I began to work with teachers on ways they could

Madeline Hunter is Adjunct Professor, University of California, Los Angeles.

help students learn social, emotional, physical, and academic skills. I was surprised to learn that while teachers had taken the prescribed educational psychology course, they learned only the history, big names, and experiments in psychology. Unfortunately, they had learned little that they could apply in their classrooms. If they had ever heard of "massing practice for fast learning" and "distributing practice for long retention," they had forgotten it. "Reinforcement" meant salivating dogs, pecking pigeons, M&Ms, or tokens. "Transfer" meant changing students or classrooms.

As a school psychologist, I began teaching research based on principles of learning: those cause-effect relationships between teaching and learning derived from physiological psychology, behavioral psychology, social psychology, and cognitive psychology—generalizations that seemed most useful in the classroom. Each branch of psychology has important principles to contribute to teaching and learning, and no one branch has answers for all classroom situations. I found most teachers hungry for this basic knowledge, which could be used with all content and with students of all ages, abilities, and socioeconomic and cultural levels.

Finally, 30 years later, education has reached the status of a real profession. We now have an identified core of research-based knowledge not possessed by those outside our profession. We "know some things to do" even if we cannot control such external factors as socioeconomic status, family or neighborhood situations, or previous learning history.

Also, we now realize that we are decision makers. All principles of learning and methodologies are subject to teacher judgment. There are no absolutes in teaching. The only thing an educator must always do is think, using research-validated principles, emerging data, and intuition. The only thing an educator must never do is cause a learner to lose dignity. This proscription is also research based: When a learner loses dignity, psychoneurology has established that neural energy is diverted into restoring that dignity, leaving little or no neural energy for learning.

A final criterion of a profession is that its practitioners never stop learning better ways of providing service for their clients. Continuous examination and modification of practice is essential to professional growth. This yearbook is directed to that criterion of increasing professional excellence in education. The authors, however, focus on the delivery system rather than the content of professional competence.

My work has been focused primarily on translating the content of research into effective clinical professional practices. I believe that the same principles that increase student learning are relevant to the ongoing professional education of adults. Consequently, the content and delivery of professional development have an integral relationship.

I also maintain that we cannot *directly* affect students' attitudes, psychological make-up, or generic abilities, but we can powerfully affect what happens to them in school and, as a result, how much they learn. This, in turn, will affect them psychologically and even, possibly, neurologically. In the same way, we cannot directly affect teachers' attitudes, learning styles, or psychological make-up. We can, however, powerfully influence and increase their professional skills, which can have a profound effect on their professional self-esteem and their eagerness to learn, as well as their general outlook on life.

I have several wishes for the outcomes of future staff development:

1. I would like to see the establishment of a long-overdue partnership between research and clinical practice. Research exists to widen the gap between emerging knowledge and practice in the field. Staff development exists to close the gap between the "pure" world of the research lab and the "contaminated" world of the classroom. Each is essential for the guidance and success of the other.

2. A critical core of knowledge and skills would be identified as necessary for certification of an educator. Specializations would be developed in addition to, not in lieu of, that basic core. It is as inexcusable that an education professor does not teach well as it is inexcusable that an administrator or teacher violates common educational principles established by research.

3. We would stop seeking one simple solution for working with the most complex structure in the known universe: the human brain. The silliness of arguing whether discovery learning is better than direct teaching, whether cooperative learning is better than concept attainment, whether "hands on" is better than observational learning, whether cognitive psychology is better than social or physiological psychology, is tantamount to arguing whether aspirin is better than penicillin. Each has its specific function in the educational pharmacy from which the professional determines the best prescription for *this* student in *this* situation at *this* time. Turf wars only dilute our effectiveness. It is important to education that we learn that, "Blowing out another man's candle does not make yours burn brighter." There is no *one* best way of teaching. There is no *one* best type of coaching. There is no *one* best way of learning.

A common example of this commitment to simplicity is the violation of my work by the current practice of considering only a few aspects of complex professional behaviors and making a check list of presence or absence of those behaviors. (I can show you my scars!) *There are no teacher or student behaviors that have to be in every lesson.* We are *never* looking for presence or absence of any one behavior, technique, or organizational scheme. We are, however, becoming sensitized to the appropriateness, artistry, and outcomes of what is occurring in the classroom. Doing what is appropriate for *this* client in *this* situation to achieve *this* outcome and doing it with artistry is the hallmark of a professional. This necessitates skill in selecting from a pharmacy of educational alternatives, not being committed to one "best way."

4. All educational personnel with a responsibility for improving the quality of teaching would be equipped, at the time of their certification (something not currently happening) with the skills of analyzing observed teaching performance and delivering growth-evoking feedback that has a measurable outcome in future performance.

Those responsible for staff development should demonstrate the ability to make appropriate decisions as well as the professional skills being taught. Currently, there is too much emulation (robotics) without understanding. As one author puts it, "You have to play the instrument before you join the orchestra, much less conduct it!"

5. The expectation for continuing professional growth would be ubiquitous to all educators regardless of their status. As a result, staff development funding would be a routine budget item for all school districts and universities. Inadequate teaching is more the result of inadequate training than the result of generic shortcomings of teachers or professors. Expectations for beginners would, of course, be different from those for more experienced practitioners. The holding of any status, however, would involve demonstration of certain basic knowledge and skills, regardless of the higher education institution or school district that accorded that status. This requirement in no way implies rigidity or constriction in how that knowledge or skills are acquired. Rather, it implies rigor in the preparation and ongoing growth of a present-day educator.

This yearbook has been written to move education in that direction.

Prologue

Bruce Joyce

The future culture of the school will be fashioned largely by how staff development systems evolve. How good schools will be as educational institutions—how humane and vital they will be as places to work—will be functions of the energy and quality of the investment in their personnel. Whether better-designed curriculums will be implemented, the promise of new technologies realized, or visions of a genuine teaching profession take form, all depend to a large extent on the strength of the growing staff development programs, and especially whether they become true human resource development systems.

Until as recently as 15 years ago, very few school districts acknowledged their responsibility for the academic, social, or clinical health of their personnel. Services provided to teachers and administrators were actually declining. Certification requirements and salary incentives brought teachers and administrators to universities for courses that represented the bulk of inservice education for most personnel. By the early 1970s neither

Bruce Joyce is Director, Booksend Laboratories, Eugene, Oregon.

incentive operated powerfully as the work force aged and "staff development units" earned in brief workshops could be applied for salary credits. Cost cutting by many districts reduced diminished curriculum departments that were, after the universities, the second most prominent source of staff development.

During the 1970s, national, regional, and local leadership gradually began to face up to the fact that their teachers were virtually unsupported in the sense of being provided with continuing education. In Schaefer's (1966) words, teachers had been treated as functionaries who had been "wound up like an old Victrola and were expected to play sweet music forever." Teaching was the only complex vocation whose personnel were not provided with time for collegial activity or rigorous and continuing study of their work. The consequences of the lack became more and more evident. Districts were confronted with the acknowledgment that many principals and supervisors were not active in instructional leadership and lamented that they had not been prepared to provide instructional support.

The experience of the previous decade indicated that few districts were able to conduct curricular changes or implement new educational technologies. Teachers' knowledge of subject matter and instructional procedures derived from their admittedly weak preservice education. District budgets contained little evidence of responsibility for the academic or clinical health of their personnel, and they were suffering the consequences. As fewer teachers needed courses for certification, the universities became less connected to the teaching profession and did not develop mechanisms for connecting themselves to schools and school districts. The recognition dawned that something had to be done.

The response has hardly been either radical or powerful, but it has brought about the gradual emergence of staff development, which we hope will turn out to be the infant form of proper and pervasive human resource development systems. Today we can say that staff development is a living component of the educational system in North America and abroad. It has grown unevenly, but is now established. The authors of the yearbook have attempted to describe it and establish a conceptual base to guide its further evolution.

Building on the meager investment in exhortative speeches at the beginning of school years and the much-maligned "superintendent's days" once or twice a year, national, state, and local initiatives began to expand services to teachers in small increments. The National Teacher Corps provided considerable impetus in the United States with its programs, which built team leader positions into schools, increased the regular study of teaching, brought university and district personnel together to engage simultaneously in school improvement and preservice teacher education, and established technical assistance networks to disseminate innovations and training to its personnel and provide opportunities for local developments to be shared. Many states generated large-scale staff development initiatives. California, for example, established regional centers, trained staff development personnel, and funded local school faculties, through its School Improvement Program, to generate plans for school development and improvement. Districts began to form staff development offices and staff them.

The recognition of deficiencies in instructional leadership led to the first North America-wide substantive movement, as Madeline Hunter's work on instruction and supervision was disseminated in an effort to increase administrative leadership in instruction and provide frameworks for the design of teaching. The movement provided direction for staff development personnel, who provided workshops for administrators and teachers. A cadre of identifiable staff development personnel began to emerge.

Other substance appeared and was adopted by the staff development offices. The study of the learning styles of students, cooperative learning procedures, the "thinking skills" movement, computers in education, and other content expanded the range of offerings. Staff development offices learned to survey the needs of their staffs and generate programs to address identified concerns. They learned also how to locate teachers who can offer service to colleagues.

The current programs provide service largely through three avenues that address individuals, schools, and district initiatives, respectively. In the first case, the education agency identifies courses and workshops and offers them to individuals who govern their own participation. In some cases, agencies have generated vast arrays of such offerings, and in some they are meager. In the second case, often known as "site-based" programs, the agency provides resources or programs to schools as entities. Schoolwide school improvement programs are of this sort. In the third, district initiatives for curricular or technological innovation are supported by workshops, courses, and consultation.

While the best developed programs balance their individual, school, and district initiatives, there is increasing recognition that all depend on the ethos of the profession and the culture of the school. Individually oriented programs touch only small percentages of staffs. Most teachers do not take advantage of them, even when they are based on careful needs assessments. Successful school-based staff development needs unusual faculty cohesion. Because most faculties are not collegial organizations, many teachers opt to "sit out" school improvement efforts, even when they can determine the focus and nature of the activities. Districts generally provide training too weak to make significant curricular or technological changes. As a result, the leaders of the field, while still supporting initiatives by individuals, schools, and agencies, are turning to a consideration of how to change the culture of the school in order to strengthen all three types of initiative.

Therefore, staff development is reaching a crossroads. It may evolve into a more extensive array of offerings that constitute little "colleges" within the education agencies. Or, it may become the force for changing the culture of the school and the ethos of the education profession.

The Design of the Yearbook

This yearbook is designed to explore the possibilities of the latter avenue—elaborating the proposition that staff development will become a human resource development system designed to change the nature of schooling, the status and level of its personnel, and their relations with one another. It deals with the structure of staff development rather than its content. Therefore, there are no chapters about many of the topics that make up its present substance, such as clinical supervision, adult learning, learning styles, teaching skills strategies, curricular and technological options, the nature of effective schools, or the curriculum areas.

Part I deals with the research base as it bears on the design of culture-oriented staff development programs. Part II deals with the evolving roles of the shareholders in staff development, from teachers and principals to the profession and universities. Part III describes current developments in Australia, England, and Wales. Part IV describes the shape of several school district programs. Each of the Part IV cases was selected because it is an effort to design a staff development program that can significantly affect the workplace itself as well as deliver services.

For those who believe that only a direct connection between staff development and student achievement will justify increased investment in human resource development, it has been well demonstrated for some time that innovations that pay off in student achievement can be implemented through well-designed programs. (How many does one have to see?) However, significant changes in education require much more energy and a much greater change in the workplace than was thought 20 years ago. Agency policymakers must recognize the need for such dramatic change if staff development is to evolve into the powerful force for improvement that education so badly needs. The real issue involved in determining the future is whether we can stand to face the possibility of more vital schools and a better profession and are willing to learn a little to create them.

PART I
Messages from the Knowledge Base

1

Staff Development, Innovation, and Institutional Development

Michael G. Fullan

I t has been well known for at least 15 years that staff development and successful innovation or improvement are intimately related. However, even in the narrow sense of successful implementation of a single innovation, people have underestimated what it takes to accomplish this close interrelationship more fundamentally. I argue later in this chapter that we must go beyond the narrow conception of staff development to consider how it relates to instructional development of schools.

Staff development is conceived broadly to include any activity or process intended to improve skills, attitudes, understandings, or performance in present or future roles (Little, Sparks, and Loucks-Horsley (in press).[1] Despite the fact that we know a great deal about what effective staff development looks like, it is still not well practised. There are at least two

---

[1]Thus the terms "staff development," "professional development," "inservice," and "assistance" are used interchangeably in this chapter.

Michael G. Fullan is Dean, Faculty of Education, University of Toronto, Canada.

major and often mutually reinforcing reasons for this. One is technical—it takes a great deal of wisdom, skill, and persistence to design and carry out successful staff development activities. The other is political. Staff development is a big business, as much related to power, bureaucratic positioning, and territoriality as it is to helping teachers and students (see Little in press, Paris 1989, and Pink 1989).

The problem of harnessing staff development is compounded by its increasingly sprawling prominence. On the one hand, it is correctly seen as the central strategy for improvement. On the other hand, it is frequently separated artificially from the institutional and personal contexts in which it operates.

The purpose of this chapter is to provide some clarity concerning the different ways in which staff development and innovation are related. Putting staff development in an innovation perspective should help us in sorting out where and how to put our energies into approaches that will have both specific and lasting effects. I examine three different innovation perspectives. The first is "staff development as a strategy for implementation," and the second is "staff development as an innovation" in its own right. "Staff development as institutional development" is the third and more fundamental perspective. I conclude by claiming that the first two perspectives are useful for certain limited purposes but that only the third approach promises to make continuous staff development and improvement a way of life in schools.

Staff Development as a Strategy for Implementation

In an earlier review, Pomfret and I established beyond doubt that staff development and effective implementation of innovations were strongly interrelated (Fullan and Pomfret 1977). The logic and evidence were fairly straightforward. Effective implementation consists of alterations in curriculum materials, practices and behavior, and beliefs and understandings by teachers vis-a-vis potentially worthwhile innovations (regardless of whether the innovations were locally or externally developed). Put more simply, successful change involves learning how to do something new. As such, the process of implementation is essentially a learning process. Thus, when it is linked to specific innovations, staff development and implementation go hand in hand.

At the time (1977), in gross terms we learned that staff development should be innovation-related, continuous during the course of implementation, and involve a variety of formal (e.g., workshops) and informal (e.g., teacher-exchange) components. We also confirmed that most innovation attempts did not incorporate these characteristics. There were two things we did not know. First, we needed to identify some of the subprocesses of staff development/implementation success experienced by teachers. Second, although we could demonstrate that staff development and classroom implementation were closely linked, there was little evidence that these in turn were related to student achievement.

Since the earlier review, we have obtained further confirmation and additional insights into the link between staff development and implementation. Huberman and Miles (1984) put the case best in their detailed examination of 12 case studies of innovation:

> Large-scale, change-bearing innovations lived or died by the amount and quality of assistance that their users received once the change process was under way. . . . The forms of assistance were various. The high-assistance sites set up external conferences, in-service training sessions, visits, committee structures, and team meetings. They also furnished a lot of ongoing assistance in the form of materials, peer consultation, access to external consultants, and rapid access to central office personnel. . . . Although strong assistance did not usually succeed in smoothing the way in early implementations, especially for the more demanding innovations, it paid handsome dividends later on by substantially increasing the levels of commitment and practice mastery (p. 273).

Huberman and Miles, along with others, also contributed new insights into the process of teacher learning, which included the universal presence of early implementation problems in all cases of success, the role of pressure and support, the way in which change in practice frequently preceded change in beliefs and understanding, and the time-line of two or more years of active assistance during implementation.

The link between staff development and school achievement was not systematically demonstrated until recently. Stallings (1989) provides a precise response to this question. In several settings using different designs, Stallings and her colleagues set out to improve teaching and student achievement relative to reading practices in secondary schools. Stallings identified research findings on effective reading practices (i.e., the innovation), as well as research on critical factors related to effective staff development. Relative to the latter, Stallings states that teachers are more likely to change their behavior and continue to use new ideas under the following conditions:

1. they become aware of a need for improvement through their analysis of their own observation profile;
2. they make a written commitment to try new ideas in their classroom the next day;

3. they modify the workshop ideas to work in their classroom and school;

4. they try the ideas and evaluate the effect;

5. they observe in each other's classrooms and analyze their own data;

6. they report their success or failure to their group;

7. they discuss problems and solutions regarding individual students and/or teaching subject matter;

8. they need a wide variety of approaches: modelling, simulations, observations, critiquing video tapes, presenting at professional meetings;

9. they learn in their own way continuity to set new goals for professional growth (Stallings 1989, pp. 3-4).

The cornerstones of the model, according to Stallings, are:

• Learn by doing—try, evaluate, modify, try again.
• Link prior knowledge to new information.
• Learn by reflecting and solving problems.
• Learn in a supportive environment—share problems and successes (p. 4).

Over the years, Stallings was able to compare the effects of three different training designs: The question was, what would the effect be on secondary students' reading scores. . .

1. If only reading teachers were trained and their students tested?

2. If all language arts teachers and reading teachers in a school were trained—hence reaching all students—and all students are tested?

3. If all teachers in a district were trained . . . over a three-year period, what would be the effect on the school district's level of reading at the end of ninth grade? (pp. 1-2).

Without going into all the details, the first design involved 47 teachers in seven districts, along with a control group. Teachers in the treatment group, compared with the control group, changed their behaviour in the classroom and their students gained six months in reading scores over the control group. In the second design, all teachers in two schools were trained and compared with a control group of two schools. The differential gain in reading scores was eight months. In the third study, all teachers in the district were provided with the training, with no control group. Each group of 9th grade students across three years of testing steadily improved their reading scores.

These impressive results demonstrate the power of a carefully designed staff development strategy for implementing single innovations.[2]

---

[2]In a later section, I indicate how limiting this strategy is in the long run, but it does produce short-term results.

Joyce et al. (1989), in their recent work in Richmond County, Georgia, provide further confirmation of the link between staff development, implementation, and student outcomes. After 18 months of intensive training and follow-up with teams of teachers focusing on models of teaching, Joyce and his colleagues were able to claim considerable (but variable) implementation in the classroom, which in turn was related to a dramatic impact on student achievement and student promotion rates.

It is worth emphasizing that both the Stallings and Joyce initiatives required considerable sophistication, effort, skill, and persistence to accomplish what they did. Most staff development activities do not measure up to these standards, as Pink's (1989) review of four change projects illustrates. He found 12 barriers to innovation effectiveness that were common to all four projects. Paraphrased, they are as follows:

1. An inadequate theory of implementation, including too little time for teachers to plan for and learn new skills and practices
2. District tendencies toward faddism and quick-fix solutions
3. Lack of sustained central office support and follow-through
4. Underfunding the project, or trying to do too much with too little support
5. Attempting to manage the projects from the central office instead of developing school leadership and capacity
6. Lack of technical assistance and other forms of intensive staff development
7. Lack of awareness of the limitations of teacher and school administrator knowledge about how to implement the project
8. The turnover of teachers in each school
9. Too many competing demands or overload
10. Failure to address the incompatibility between project requirements and existing organizational policies and structures
11. Failure to understand and take into account site-specific differences among schools
12. Failure to clarify and negotiate the role relationships and partnerships involving the district and the local university—who in each case had a role, albeit unclarified, in the project (Pink 1989, pp. 22-24).

In short, staff development, implementation of innovation, and student outcomes are closely interrelated, but because they require such a sophisticated, persistent effort to coordinate, they are unlikely to succeed in many situations. Any success that does occur is unlikely to be sustained beyond the tenure or energy of the main initiators of the project.

Staff Development as an Innovation

A second useful, but still limiting perspective is to consider major new staff development projects as innovations in their own right. In particular, new policies and structures that establish new roles, such as mentors, coaches, and the like, are and can be considered as innovations in the states and districts in which they are adopted. The question is whether our knowledge about the do's and don'ts of introducing curriculum innovations is applicable to introducing new mentoring and coaching practices. This section provides some support for the notion that the establishment of new staff development roles or projects would benefit from knowledge of implementation theory.

In a recent review, Judith Little (1989) has applied such a perspective to the evolution of the mentoring phenomenon.[3] As Little states: "those who would implement mentor roles are confronted with a two-part challenge: to introduce classroom teachers to a role with which they are unfamiliar; and to introduce the role itself to an institution and occupation in which it has few precedents" (pp. 7-8). In reviewing empirical studies, Little identified three implementation problems: the pace of implementation, lack of opportunity to carry out the role, and precedents that constrain mentors' performance.

It is well known that major policy initiatives are often introduced rapidly, with little thought or time given to consider implementation (Fullan 1982). Among other studies, Little cites California's Mentor Teacher program:

> California launched a precipitous schedule of implementation. . . . A schedule of implementation limited to the state's fiscal year propelled them toward quick decisions about the form it would assume. The result was a pervasive effort to bring the definition of the mentor role within the boundaries of familiar roles and functions. Based on nine case studies and a summary of 291 districts, Bird (1986) concludes that, "a good deal was lost, and little or nothing gained, by haste in implementing the mentor program" (Little 1989, pp. 9-10).

Rapid starts involving complex innovations often result in simplifying and reducing the intended scope of the change. Little notes Huberman and Miles' observation based on their 12 case studies of innovation:

---

[3]In the following paragraphs, I concentrate on the mentor rather than the mentor-inductee pair. For reviews involving the latter, see Huling-Austin (in press), and Kilcher (1989).

Smooth early use was a bad sign. Smoothly implementing sites seemed to get that way by reducing the initial scale of the project and by lowering the gradient of actual practice change. This "downsizing" got rid of most headaches during the initial implementation but also threw away most of the potential rewards; the project often turned into a modest, sometimes trivial enterprise (p. 273).

A second problematic area of implementation relates to selection criteria, preimplementation training for mentors, and support during implementation, which Little sums up under the general label of opportunity. She starts with selection criteria, indicating the importance of basing selection of mentors on their expertise and credibility—both as classroom teachers and as colleagues who had track records of working successfully with other teachers. Little also found that preimplementation training for mentors was variable, often focusing only on general process skills. Relative to post-selection support, Bird and Alspaugh (1986) found that 40 percent of districts participating in the first two years of California's mentor program allocated no resources to support mentors during implementation.

The lack of precedents for the mentor role, combined with the previous two factors, frequently resulted in the mentor role's being played out at the lower and safer limits of its potential. The ambiguity of the role often left mentors to "invent their roles as they went along" (Hart 1989 cited in Little 1989a). According to Little, this permissive stance tends to produce a low rate of direct teacher-to-teacher involvement of the very sort needed to make the role credible and effective. Little concludes that lack of precedence for these new roles is a major normative barrier to their implementation.

Coaching faces similar implementation problems, but not on the same scale because, unlike mentoring, coaching projects have tended to be less formal (e.g., not involving legislation or formal policy), more voluntary, and smaller in scale. Coaching projects, perhaps because of these characteristics, have proliferated at a rapid rate. Many so-called coaching projects, as we shall discuss in the next section, appear to be superficial. Even if we assume rigorous coaching designs, the innovation perspective is instructive.

We can take as an example, Joyce and Showers' (1989) work because it is more developed and available in the literature. According to Joyce and Showers, coaching programs represent powerful strategies for implementing instructional improvements that impact on student learning. In their work coaching is (a) attached to training, (b) continuous, (c) experimental in nature, and (d) separate from supervision and evaluation. It involves theory-demonstration-practice-feedback-and follow-through support.

The innovation perspective is revealing because it starts with the question "In what respects is coaching an innovation?" Joyce and Showers' work implies at least three types of innovations for school systems. First, it represents a change in the technology of training. Coaching leaders have to learn and carry out a sophisticated training program over a period of time. Second, it involves organizing study groups of teachers at the school level. This entails restructuring the workplace in a more collegial mode. Third, (and related but more fundamental than the previous point) coaching implicitly raises questions about the deeper collaborative work cultures of schools, and the role of teachers as professionals.

Joyce and Showers have effectively tackled the first problem. They are able to implement the training model with desired effects. They are in the midst of working on the second problem—organizing study groups in individual schools within a district (Joyce et al. 1989). The third problem—how to change the culture of the organization—remains unaddressed.

The implications of this analysis are quite profound. While most districts do not provide the training support, the problem is much deeper than that. Even if districts were to address the training and study group issues, coaching as an innovation would be short-lived. It would be just another ad hoc innovation that has a short half-life. The danger is that coaching, which has powerful potential, will be trivialized, because the organizational necessities and cultural change implied by coaching will be missed altogether, or addressed superficially.

At this time, we will not take up further the problem of achieving cultural changes in schools. The main point is that mentoring and coaching projects would benefit if guided by innovation models. Miles (1986), for example, identified 14 key success factors across the three well-known phases of change projects:

Initiation
• Linked to high profile need
• Clear model of implementation
• One or more strong advocates
• Active initiation

Implementation
• Coordination
• Shared control
• Pressure and support
• Ongoing technical assistance
• Early rewards for teachers

Institutionalization
• Embedding
• Links to instruction
• Widespread use
• Removal of competing priorities
• Continuing assistance

The factors and processes of implementation can be used to analyze staff development projects and to guide implementation planning and monitoring. Those involved in coaching projects would be well advised to approach their work with some model of change in mind, which would enable them to take into account organizational factors known to affect implementation success (Fullan 1982, 1987, Huberman and Miles 1984). Although this will not be sufficient to achieve cultural change at the school level, it would provide more effective beginnings toward that goal.

It should be obvious that I am not advocating that coaching or mentoring projects become innovations as ends in themselves. Many such projects, for example, do not appear to be focused or clear about their pedagogical and student learning objectives. Joyce and Showers (1988), contrary to popular belief, have never advocated coaching per se. Rather, "the major purpose of peer coaching programs is implementation of innovations to the extent that determination of effects on students is possible" (p. 83). In pursuing this goal, I have suggested that it is important to consider coaching and mentoring as innovation, which they are, provided that one does not stop there.

Although mentoring and coaching have great potential, as long as they are treated as innovations or projects or even as strategies, their impact will be superficial and short-term and will be confined to a few participants. It is the ultimate thesis of this chapter that our attention must shift explicitly to how staff development fits into long-term institutional purposes and development of schools.

Staff Development and Institutional Development

By institutional development, I mean changes in schools as institutions that increase their capacity and performance for continuous improvements. The domain is the culture of the school as a workplace (Little 1982, Rosenholtz 1989, Sarason 1982). I want to start by examining the relationship between the culture of the school and the two perspectives just considered. This will amount to a critique of the limitations of the two perspectives. Second, it will pave the way for describing what it means to focus directly and more systematically on institutional development. I will provide an example from my current work. Finally, three major implications for staff development will be outlined.

To start with the "strategy for implementation" perspective, teacher collegiality and other elements of collaborative work cultures are known to be related to the likelihood of implementation success (Fullan and Pomfret 1977, Little 1982). Thus, all other things being equal, schools characterized by norms of collegiality and experimentation are much more likely to implement innovations successfully. The first point to be made is that those using staff development for implementation should take into account the nature of teacher collegiality that exists in the schools with which they intend to work. For example, as impressive as Stallings' (1989) staff development design is, there is no mention of these school level variables, which must have had effects that remain unknown on implementation and institutionalization. In other words, staff developers must work with schools as organizations as much as they work with individuals or small groups of teachers.

The second point to be noted is that even when teacher collegiality is taken into account, it is usually treated as a contextual factor or as a "given"; that is, it is used to explain differences in implementation more or less along the lines that some schools happen to be more collegial than others.

Third, it can be argued, at least hypothetically, that solid staff development projects, like that of Stallings, in addition to having a positive impact on change in teacher practice and student achievement, can also have a spin-off or residual impact on increasing collegiality among teachers. Put another way, since good staff development practices always incorporate teacher-teacher sharing and interaction, they could, if successful, demonstrate the value of new norms of collegiality. At a minimum, it would seem that people using the staff development for implementation strategy should explicitly concentrate on the dual goals of implementing a project successfully and influencing the collegial climate of the school as an organization. This would be a useful contribution, but I am afraid that the culture of the school is much too strong to be influenced for any length of time (or at all in some cases) by single, passing projects—no matter how well designed.

The coaching and mentoring phenomenon is much more intriguing. On the surface, it looks like these strategies are indeed tantamount to attempting to change the collaborative culture of the school. In fact, they are not.

Coaching is particularly instructive for examining the underlying issues. There are at least three basic problems: (1) the relationship of coaching to the culture of the school; (2) the form and content of coaching; and (3) the need for a more objective and balanced appreciation of the complex relationship between autonomy and collaboration. In effect, these three problem areas amount to cautioning advocates of coaching and collaboration against assuming that working toward increased interaction among teachers is automatically a good thing.

Coaching and the Culture of the School

As we have seen, coaching, mentoring, and other similar arrangements usually involve pairs or small groups of teachers working together. As such they represent only a small subpart of the total culture of the school. Thus, whether or not a particular coaching project finds itself in an hospitable environment (i.e., a school in which a collegial climate predated the coaching initiative) is a very important variable. Seller and Hannay (1988) examined a well-designed coaching project in two high schools and found that the pre-existing climate of collegiality explained whether or not the project was successful. At a minimum, the advice to those advocating coaching is to take into account the total culture of the school before deciding to proceed. One can also infer that even good coaching programs do not alter the culture of the school. Although coaching can be intentionally designed as a strategy for increasing the collaborative work culture of the school, there is no evidence that this by itself will work. Normative cultures are not that easily influenced.

Form and Content

Little (1989b) has provided the clearest exposition of the importance of considering variations in the form and content of collegiality. Form involves the degree and type of collaborative relationship. She suggests that there are at least four types of relationships ranked along an independence-interdependence continuum: storytelling and scanning for ideas, aid and assistance, mutual sharing, and joint work. In Little's words:

> The move from conditions of complete independence to thorough-going interdependence entails changes in the frequency and intensity of teachers' interactions, the prospects for conflict, and probability of influence. That is, with each successive shift, the warrant for autonomy shifts from individual to collective judgment and preference (p. 5).

Little claims that the first three forms represent "weak ties" of collegiality. Little (1989a, 1989b) cites evidence that most coaching and mentoring projects are of this relatively superficial, safe, inconsequential variety, and hence have little impact on the culture of the school.

For Little, joint work involves:

> encounters among teachers that rest on shared responsibility for the work of teaching . . . collective conceptions of autonomy, support for teachers' initiative and leadership with regard to professional practice, and group affiliations grounded in professional work. Joint work is dependent on the structural organization of task, time, and other resources in ways not characteristic of other forms of collegiality (pp. 14-15).

Little does not assume that joint work is more appropriate, only that it is much more demanding psychologically and organizationally to bring about and is more consequential for better or for worse. Thus, the content, not just the form of collaboration, is also critical:

> The content of teachers' values and beliefs cannot be taken for granted in the study or pursuit of teachers' collegial norms of interaction and interpretation. Under some circumstances, greater contact among teachers can be expected to advance the prospects for students' success; in others, to promote increased teacher-to-teacher contact may be to intensify norms unfavourable to children (1989b, p. 22).

Further, Little asks:

> Bluntly put, do we have in teachers' collaborative work the creative development of well informed choices, or the mutual reinforcement of poorly informed habit? Does teachers' time together advance the understanding and imagination they bring to their work, or do teachers merely confirm one another in present practice? What subject philosophy and subject pedagogy do teachers reflect as they work together, how explicit and accessible is their knowledge to one another? Are there collaborations that in fact erode teachers' moral commitments and intellectual merit? (p. 22).

Autonomy and Collaboration

We cannot assume that autonomy is bad and collaboration is good. One person's isolation is another person's autonomy; one person's collaboration is another person's conspiracy. Flinders (1988) speaks to the former:

> The teachers I observed not only accepted their relative isolation but actively strove to maintain it. At those points in the day when teachers had the greatest discretion over their use of time (during lunch breaks and preparation time), they typically went out of their way to avoid contact with others. . . . Teachers used their classrooms as sanctuaries during breaks as well as before and after school, remaining alone in their rooms to prepare lessons instead of working in their department offices where collegial interaction would have been more available (p. 23).

Flinders claims that for many teachers isolation is a strategy for getting work done because "it protects time and energy required to meet immediate instructional demands" (p. 25). Flinders observes that most of us seek periods of independent work in order to meet obligations:

> It is not uncommon to respond to increased job demands by closing the office door, canceling luncheon appointments, and "hiding out" in whatever ways we can. We do not attribute our motives for such behaviour to naturally conservative personality traits or to malevolent or unprofessional regard for our colleagues. On the contrary, it is professional norms that dissuade us from sacrificing our commitments to job responsibilities even when such a sacrifice can be made in the name of collegiality (p. 25).

None of this is to gainsay that isolation can be a protection from scrutiny and a barrier to improvement, but it does say that we must put the question of autonomy and collaboration in a perspective conducive to assessing the conditions under which each might be appropriate.

Hargreaves (forthcoming) formulates a useful typology for considering school cultures. He suggests that there are four types: fragmented individualism, Balkanization, contrived collegiality, and collaborative cultures. The first two are well known. Fragmented individualism is the traditional form of teacher isolation so clearly depicted by Lortie (1975). Balkanization, often found in high schools, consists of subgroups and cliques operating as separate subentities, often in conflict with each other when major decisions have to be made.

> The designation contrived collegiality is new:
> [It] is characterized by a set of formal, specific bureaucratic procedures . . . It can be seen in initiatives such as peer coaching, mentor teaching, joint planning in specially provided rooms, formally scheduled meetings and clear job descriptions and training programs for those in consultative roles (p. 19).

Contrived collegiality can ignore the real culture of the school and lead to a proliferation of unwanted contacts among teachers that consume already scarce time with little to show for it (see also Hargreaves 1989).

Hargreaves and Dawe (1989) elaborate on the problem of contrived collegiality by claiming that many forms of coaching are too technical, narrow, and short-term in focus. Hargreaves and Dawe argue that the current move away from teacher isolationism is locked into a struggle involving two very different forms of collegiality:

> In the one, it is a tool of teacher empowerment and professional enhancement, bringing colleagues and their expertise together to generate critical

yet also practically-grounded reflection on what they do as a basis for wiser, more skilled action. In the other, the breakdown of teacher isolation is a mechanism designed to facilitate the smooth and uncritical adoption of preferred forms of action (new teaching styles) introduced and imposed by experts from elsewhere, in which teachers become technicians rather than professionals exercising discretionary judgment (p. 7).

True collaborative cultures, according to Hargreaves (in press), are deep, personal, and enduring. They are not "mounted just for specific projects or events. They are not strings of one-shot deals. Cultures of collaboration rather are, constitutive of, absolutely central to, teachers' daily work" (p. 14).

In short, collegially oriented staff development initiatives either fail to address the more basic question of school culture, or vastly underestimate what it takes to change them. There is also evidence that collaborative cultures, when they do occur, are achieved through the extraordinary efforts of individuals. Often, such efforts either cannot be sustained over time or are vulnerable to the inevitable departure of key individuals (Hargreaves 1989, Little 1989b). In other words, what is at stake are basic changes in the professional institution of schooling.

An Illustration

The main implication of this chapter is to refocus staff development so that it becomes part of an overall strategy for professional and institutional reform. We provide here one illustration taken from our current work in The Learning Consortium. Although we do not claim that it represents a full-blown example, it reflects movement toward the type of comprehensive conception and strategy required for substantial institutional development of schools. Space permits only a brief description of the framework (see Fullan, Rolheiser-Bennett, and Bennett 1989 for more information).

The Learning Consortium is a three-year partnership among four major school districts and two higher education institutions in the greater Toronto area. There are two overriding assumptions in the Consortium. One is to design and carry out a variety of activities that make the professional and staff development continuum a reality (from the Bachelor of Education through preservice, induction, and career-long developments). The second major assumption is that classroom and school improvement must be linked and integrated if serious improvements are to be achieved.

We will not describe the various activities here, but they involve Summer Institutes and follow-up, cadre staff development and support, leadership inservice, team development in schools, and the like. They focus

on instructional improvements like the use of cooperative learning strategies, as well as on school-wide changes involving greater collaboration.

Our goal is to understand and influence both classroom improvement
and school improvement through identifying and fostering systematic links
between the two. The framework for analysis and action we are developing
is contained in Figure 1.1 (p. 18).[4] For classroom improvement, we and
others have found that teachers must work simultaneously (but not necessarily at the same pace) on all four subcogs. For both teachers and
students, the combined capacity to manage the classroom, the continuous
acquisition of proven instructional strategies and skills, and the focus on
desired educational goals and content are essential.

The subcogs in the far right of Figure 1.1 relate to school improvement. There is considerable evidence, we think, that the more basic features of school improvement (as distinct from a list of effective schools
characteristics) are the following four. Schools improve when they have, or
come to have, (1) a shared purpose, (2) norms of collegiality, (3) norms of
continuous improvement, and (4) structures that represent the organizational conditions necessary for significant improvement (Little 1987, Rosenholtz 1989). Note that these are not individual characteristics. They
are discrete and measurable features of collectivities—in this case, people
in schools.

It is necessary to comment on the interrelationship of the school
improvements cogs. Shared purpose includes such things as vision, mission, goals, objectives, and unity of purpose. It refers to the shared sense
of purposeful direction of the school relative to major educational goals.
Shared purpose is of course not static, nor does it arise by itself. The
other three cogs in interaction constantly generate and (re)shape purpose.
Norms of collegiality refer to the extent to which mutual sharing, assistance, and joint work among teachers is valued and honored in the school.
As stated earlier, there is nothing particularly virtuous about collaboration
per se. It can serve to block change or put down students as well as to
elevate learning. Thus, collegiality must be linked to norms of continuous
improvement and experimentation in which teachers are constantly seeking
and assessing potentially better practices inside and outside their own
school (and contributing to other people's practice through dissemination).
And, as the framework depicts, commitment to improving student engagement and learning must be a pervasive value and concern.

---

[4]The following paragraphs are adapted from Fullan, Rolheiser-Bennett, and
Bennett (1989).

Figure 1.1
A Comprehensive Framework for Classroom and School Improvement

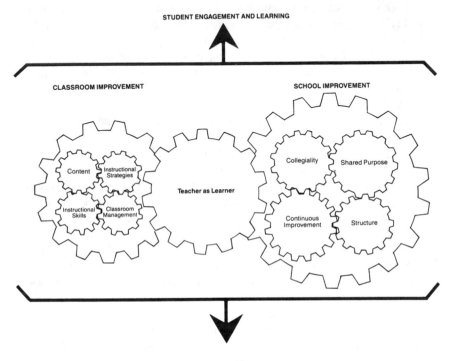

We use structure in the sociological sense to include organizational arrangements, roles, and formal policies that explicitly build in working conditions that, so to speak, support and press for movement in the other cogs. Time for joint planning, joint teaching arrangements, staff development policies, new roles such as mentors, and school improvement procedures are examples of structural change at the school level that is conducive to improvement.

The centerpiece, or bridge, linking and overlapping classroom and school improvement in Figure 1.1 is the teacher as learner. Figure 1.2 elaborates on this concept. There are two absolutely critical features of this component of the framework. First, the four aspects of teacher as learner—technical, reflective, inquiry, and collaborative—must be seen in combination. Each has its separate tradition of research and practice, and each has made important contributions in its own right. The mastery of

Figure 1.2

Teacher as Learner

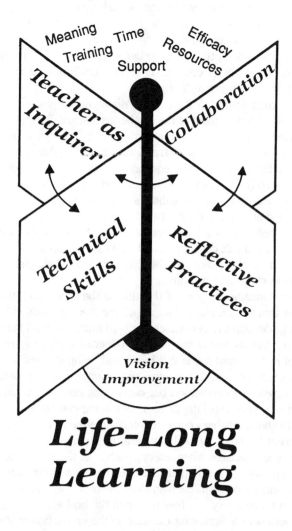

Life-Long Learning

From Fullan, Rolheiser-Bennett, and Bennett 1989

technical skills increases instructional certainty; reflective practice enhances clarity, meaning, and coherence; inquiry fosters investigation and
exploration; collaboration enables one to receive and give ideas and assistance.

Although many approaches address aspects of all four features of the
teacher as learner in one way or another, all models to this point have a
central tendency to stress only one or two of the four. Rarely (and we
would say never in a fundamental sense) have all four received intensive
attention in the same setting. It is easier said than done. The question is,
how can the strengths of each of these four traditions be integrated and
established in the teacher as learner.

The second critical feature is to distinguish between specific and
generic levels of development of the teacher as learner. By specific we mean
how particular improvements are experienced and designed. For example,
one can start with a technical instructional innovation, such as cooperative
learning, and find that it has consequences for all four aspects of the teacher
as learner (which is in fact how we started). Similarly, one could begin
with any of the other three subcogs—an action research project, for
example—and proceed to incorporate the development of technical instructional skills, reflective methods, and so forth. We do not know enough yet
about the very difficult conceptual and strategic questions of whether it is
better to start with a single teacher-learner dimension (and if so, which
one), or to work on all four equally.

A more fundamental point at this time is the recognition that teachers
(remember that we are still talking about the teacher as individual learner)
can come to develop the generic capacity to function on all four cylinders.
In this case, it is not just being good at cooperative learning but mastering
an array of instructional models; it is not just being involved in a reflective
practice project but being a reflective practitioner; it is not participating in
an action research investigation but conducting constant inquiry; it is not
being part of a peer coaching project, but being collaborative as a way of
working. In short, teachers come to internalize these ways of being to the
point where it becomes second nature to be a perpetual learner.

Now it is precisely when every teacher in the school develops this
"generic capacity" to learn that classroom improvement and school improvement entirely overlap. Such an ideal will never be achieved, of course,
but one can immediately see how powerful the bridge can become when a
school experiences a significant increase in the proportion of staff who are
learners as we have defined the term.

Two final aspects of the framework revolve around the singularly
important question of what drives the framework. It is, after all, not self-

generating. One of two key driving factors is the presence of student engagement and learning as a pervasive preoccupation. We propose that the impact on all students be front and centre for every cog and interrelationship among the cogs. Constant valuing and attention to student engagement and learning can be a powerful motivating force, if it is integrated with movement in the cogs. The second agent of change is leadership and mobilization. We explicitly rejected the idea that leadership be a particular component of the framework. Leadership can, does, and must come from a variety of different sources in different situations (and different sources in the same situation over time). Leadership for success variously comes from the principal, key teachers, the superintendent, parents, trustees, curriculum consultants, governments, universities, and so on. As the list reveals, the driving force for change can initially come from inside or outside the school and from a variety of different roles. Once the model is fully functioning, leadership does indeed come from multiple sources si multaneously.

The Learning Consortium has been operating for a little more than a year. It has been successful in mobilizing a great number of people to action which they and others agree has resulted in improvements in classrooms and schools. We do not think that The Learning Consortium, as much as it is becoming integrated into the lives of the institutions involved, will end up deeply affecting collaborative work cultures in the sense that Hargreaves and Little use the term. Nias' (1989) study illustrates how rich and complex collaborative cultures really are.

We do see very clearly, however, that the multilevel and multifaceted staff development activities that occur in all large school districts are, in the case of The Learning Consortium, being harnessed and interrelated in a more coherent and synergistic manner. There are still dilemmas between autonomy and collaboration, but staff development in these districts is becoming less fragmented and desultory, more purposeful, and more linked to classroom and school development as defined by teachers and principals.

Implications

Staff development will never have its intended impact as long as it is grafted onto schools in the form of discrete, unconnected projects. The closer one gets to the culture of schools and the professional lives of teachers, the more complex and daunting the reform agenda becomes. More powerful strategies are needed for more powerful changes. At least three strands of the problem require radical rethinking and integration, namely, the individual, the school, and the district.

First, those involved in staff development must think and act more holistically about the personal and professional lives of teachers as individuals. As we have seen, many staff development projects provide temporary resources and incentives for particular changes (e.g., Stallings 1989) but do not amount to much in the bigger scheme of teachers' lives (Smylie 1988). Huberman's (1989) research clearly shows the importance of recognizing career and life cycle experiences of teachers. What is at stake is the reconceptualization of the professional role of teachers (Fullan and Connelly 1989). Staff development in this view becomes the sum total of formal and informal learning experiences accumulated across one's career. The agenda then is to work continuously on the spirit and practice of lifelong learning for all teachers.

The second element involves working more organically with the school as an organization. This is turning out to be both complex and powerfully resistant to influence. It is not at all clear how autonomy and collaboration should be balanced. We do know, however, how powerful the school culture is. For example, despite massive effort and support over eighteen months, and despite some remarkable success in student achievement, Joyce et al. (1989) comment on the fragility of their accomplishments: "It depends on about forty teachers—only ten percent of the total" (p. 15).

We have seen that many of the reform efforts actually work at cross-purposes to intended directions by creating unnecessary status differences, role ambiguities, and superficial, inefficient relationships (Hargreaves and Dawe 1989, Little 1989a, and Smylie and Denny 1989).

There are endemic difficulties to establishing and maintaining collaborative work cultures. Nias (1989) found that teachers had great difficulty collaborating even when they wanted to work together. When collegiality is achieved, it is often short-lived because the social organization of the workplace is not conducive to maintaining collaboration in the long run (Hargreaves forthcoming, Little 1989b, Smylie 1989). Restructuring schools is complex and unclear (Elmore 1988a, 1988b) and will involve a long-term effort led by those within schools (Fullan 1989, Fullan and Hargreaves forthcoming). Finally, the centralization of policymaking and resources for staff development must be reconfigured. Little's (forthcoming) examination of district policy for staff development in California reveals the problem. Central office administrators and staff development specialists designed and delivered over two-thirds of the staff development experienced by teachers across 30 districts. "Leader time" was one of the highest cost items, more so than costs for time allocated to support learners (teacher participants). Many of the studies of mentoring reviewed by Little (1989a) also documented the centralization of staff development resources, which were devoted to supporting activities directed outside rather than inside schools. In the area of curriculum change, Paris (1989) chronicles the struggle between increased curriculum control at the district level and the uphill battle of one innovative school.

Neither centralization nor decentralization has worked in achieving educational reforms. The lines of development involving individuals, schools, and districts will require close collaboration between those inside and outside schools. Staff developers have a much bigger role to play in teacher development than hitherto realized.

References

Bird, T. (1986). "The Mentor's Dilemma." Unpublished paper. San Francisco: Far West Laboratory for Educational Research and Development.

Bird, T., and D. Alspaugh. (1986). *1985 Survey of District Coordinators for the California Mentor Teacher Program.* San Francisco: Far West Laboratory for Educational Research.

Elmore, R. (1988a). "Contested Terrain: The Next Generation of Educational Reform." Paper prepared for the Commission on Public School Administration and Leadership, Association of California School Administrators.

Elmore, R. (1986). "Models of Restructured Schools." Stanford, Calif.: Center for Policy Research in Education.

Flinders, D. (1988). "Teacher Isolation and the New Reform." *Journal of Curriculum and Supervision* 5, 4: 17-29.

Fullan, M. (1982). *The Meaning of Education Change.* New York: Teachers College Press.

Fullan, M. (1987). "Implementing Educational Change: What We Know." Paper prepared for The World Bank. Washington, D.C.

Fullan M. (1988). *What's Worth Fighting for in the Principalship?* Toronto: Ontario Public School Teachers Federation.

Fullan, M., and F.M. Connelly. (1989). *Teacher Education in Ontario.* Final report to the Teacher Education Review Committee: Ontario Ministry of Education, Toronto.

Fullan, M., and A. Hargreaves. (In press). *What's Worth Fighting for in the School.* Toronto: Ontario Public School Teachers Federation.

Fullan, M., and A. Pomfret. (1977). "Research on Curriculum and Instruction Implementation." *Review of Educational Research* 5, 47: 335-397.

Fullan, M., C. Rolheiser-Bennett, and B. Bennett. (1989). "Linking Classroom and School Improvement." Paper presented at the annual meeting of the American Education Research Association, San Francisco.

Hargreaves, A. (1989). "Teacher Development and Teachers' Work: Issues of Time and Control." Paper presented at the International Conference on Teacher Development in Toronto, Canada.

Hargreaves, A. (forthcoming). "Cultures of Teaching." In *Teachers' Lives New York,* edited by I. Goodson and S. Ball. Boston: Routledge & Kegen Paul.

Hargreaves, A., and R. Dawe. (1989). "Coaching as Unreflective Practice." Paper presented at the annual meeting of the American Educational Research Association, San Francisco.

Hart, A. (1989). "Role Politics and the Redesign of Teachers' Work." Unpublished manuscript. Salt Lake City: University of Utah.

Huberman, M. (1989). "Teacher Development and Instructional Mastery." Paper presented at the International Conference on Teaching Development in Toronto, Canada.

Huberman, M., and M. Miles. (1984). *Innovation Up Close*. New York: Plenum.

Huling-Austin, L. (forthcoming). "Teacher Induction Programs and Internships." In *Handbook of Research on Teacher Education* edited by Houston. New York: Macmillan Publishing and the Association of Teacher Educators.

Joyce, B., and B. Showers. (1988). *Student Achievement Through Staff Development*. New York: Longman.

Joyce, B., C. Murphy, B. Showers, and J. Murphy. (1989). "Reconstructing the Workplace: School Renewal as Cultural Change." Paper presented at the annual meeting of the American Educational Research Association, San Francisco.

Kilcher, A. (1989). "Mentoring Beginning Teachers: A Review of Theory and Practice." Paper prepared for The Learning Consortium in Toronto, Canada.

Little, J. (1982). "Norms of Collegiality and Experimentation: Workplace Conditions of School Success." *American Educational Research Journal* 5, 19: 325-340.

Little, J. (1989). "The 'Mentor' Phenomenon and the Social Organization of Teaching." *Review of Research in Education* 5, 16. Washington, D.C.: American Educational Research Association.

Little, J. (1986). "The Persistence of Privacy: Autonomy and Initiative in Teachers' Professional Relations." Paper presented at the American Educational Research Association.

Little, J. (In press). "District Policy Choices and Teachers' Professional Development Opportunities." *Educational Evaluation and Policy Analysis*.

Lortie, J. (1975). *Schoolteacher*. Chicago: University of Chicago Press.

Miles, M. (1986). "Research Findings on the Stages of School Improvement." Conference on Planned Change, The Ontario Institute for Studies in Education.

Nias, J. (1989). *Primary Teachers Talking: A Study of Teaching as Work*. London: Routledge & Kegen Paul.

Paris, C. (1989). "Contexts of Curriculum Change: Conflict and Consonance." Paper presented at the annual meeting of the American Educational Research Association, San Francisco.

Pink, W. (1989). "Effective Development for Urban School Improvement." Paper presented at the annual meeting of the American Educational Research Association, San Francisco.

Rosenholtz, S. (1989). *Teachers' Workplace*. New York: Longman

Sarason, S. (1982). *The Culture of the School and the Problem of Change*, 2nd edition. Boston: Allyn & Bacon.

Seller, W., and L. Hannay. (1988). "The Influence of School Climate on Peer Coaching." Paper presented at the annual meeting of the American Educational Research Association, New Orleans.

Smylie, M. (1988). "The Enhancement Function of Staff Development: Organizational and Psychological Antecedents to Individual Teacher Change." *American Educational Research Journal* 5, 25:1-30.

Smylie, M. (1989). "Teachers' Collegial Learning: Social and Psychological Dimensions of Helping Relationships." Paper presented at the annual meeting of the American Educational Research Association, San Francisco.

Smylie, M., and J. Denny. (1989). "Teacher Leadership: Tensions and Perspectives." Paper presented at the annual meeting of the American Educational Research Association, San Francisco.

Sparks, D., and S. Loucks-Horsley. (In press). "Models of Staff Development." In *Handbook of Research on Teacher Education.* New York: Macmillan Publishing and the Association of Teacher Educators.

2

The Self-Educating Teacher: Empowering Teachers Through Research

Bruce Joyce
with Barrie Bennett and Carol Rolheiser-Bennett

G etting control of research relevant to staff development policy requires a combination of speculative imagination and forbearance. It is easy to underplay the research base and fail to locate some of the solid material that has been accumulated. On the other hand, it is equally easy to make too much of some provocative but thin findings and imbue them with qualities of substance that are not yet warranted. For the practitioner of research, staff development is a field of great opportunity, crying out for good work. Its outlines are beginning to take shape, and some clear issues stand out to be studied. Yet it is only an infant, with the important work still to be done. Some of the most common practices and policies have hardly been studied at all. Some important areas have been opened up and promise to yield quickly to programs of research.

Bruce Joyce is Director, Booksend Laboratories, Eugene, Oregon. Barrie Bennett is a researcher and consultant for The Learning Consortium, Toronto, Canada. Carol Rolheiser-Bennett is Assistant Professor, University of Toronto.

This chapter contains a selective review. We have taken a number of topics that have received attention during the last few years, examined the available research, and asked of each the question, "What is being learned about teachers as learners?" Our concern here is to ferret out knowledge about professionals and what promises to enhance their power to educate themselves. Throughout the chapter, we attempt to identify policy-relevant propositions, the strength of the warrant for them, and needed programs of research. A serious limitation in the literature is that nearly all of it deals with staff development for teachers. *Very few investigations have occurred in which administrative or supervisory personnel were the students. The ambitious scholar has a wide-open field with respect to staff development for those populations.*

We have selected the following topics:

• Treatments designed to provide people with mirrors of behavior with the expectation that self knowledge will lead to change.

• Training designed to help teachers acquire specific teaching skills and strategies and learn to use them effectively.

• Treatments designed to change the workplace and, by building more positive social climates, to generate collective energy for learning.

These are the areas with the greatest concentrations of theories or investigations, and they are relevant to the design of practice. The important area of the culture of the school is not reviewed here except as it intersects with research on the workplace because it has been so thoroughly dealt with in Chapter 1.

Another critical and relevant area includes studies of individual differences in generic motivation—dispositions toward growth, particularly from the perspectives of self-concept, personality, and states of growth. This area is not treated here, except peripherally, because its most important recent study is the subject of Chapter 3. Part of the importance of that study, aside from its dramatic findings, is in the effect it should have in shifting attention from content-specific motivation toward general dispositions toward growth.

Much of the rhetorical literature of the staff development field has emphasized the effect of "buying in" toward the specific content of training. The proposition is frequently put forth that if teachers are attracted to, say, cooperative learning, prior to training, then they will participate enthusiastically, learn the content, and use it. The Evans/Hopkins study described in Chapter 3 suggests that general motivation to learn may be much more important than the attractiveness of the content of a particular offering. The findings are, for policy, congruent with an investigation reported by Crandall et al. (1982), which produced the thesis that commitment toward particular content follows, rather than precedes, competence (Miles and Huberman 1984). In other words, the initial appearance of commitment, being based on impressions or partial knowledge at best, may be fragile. Until participants achieved a fairly good degree of control over the content of the training, commitment remained insubstantial but rose as competence rose. High initial commitment, on the other hand, tends to decline unless competence is achieved. These findings are probably destined to generate some of the important operating principles of the field. It may be that helping persons develop competence and then judging the content will be a better course of action than trying to persuade people to "buy in" on the basis of superficial impressions. Or, perhaps, asking people to "buy in" to growth in general may be more productive than trying to generate motivation on an item-by-item basis. The conception of staff development programs may also affect the types of motivation to be emphasized. Where staff development is conceived as a collection of workshops, organizers may worry about whether people will be attracted to those courses. Where it is conceived as a human resource development system, generic motivation to exploit the possibilities in that system becomes of greater concern.

Mirrors for Behavior

One of the most common kinds of staff development takes the form of trying to provide practitioners with pictures of their behavior. The underlying idea is that if people can conceptualize their clinical performance, they will use the information to set goals for increasing their competence. The three versions that have been most used are instrument-driven feedback, nondirective clinical supervision, and structured clinical supervision.

Instrument-Driven Feedback

During the 1960s and early 1970s, highly structured instruments were popular. The title from this section is taken from a compilation of several dozen instruments (Simon and Boyer 1967) that was published at the height of their use. Either an observer would "code" classroom interactions, or the teachers would be taught how to record and code their own behavior. Sometimes the instruments contained behaviors believed to be desirable or undesirable, and attention was drawn to their frequency. Other instruments were neutral and were designed simply to provide a picture from which a teacher might move in any of a variety of directions. Much of the research was summarized in the Flanders (1970) volume, although there are other sources (including Joyce, Peck, and Brown 1981; Medley 1977). The key question was "Did the instrument-driven feedback result in changes in teacher behavior?" Taking the literature as a whole, the answer is "Not much."

In a few instances, behavior shifted toward the direction pointed out by the instruments (Good and Brophy 1974), and Flanders' (1970) "Inter-action Analysis" instrument pulled teaching styles somewhat away from extreme directive behavior. In nearly all studies, however, the shifts in behavior were negligible. In one study, teachers received structured feedback more than 20 times during one school year without substantial effect (Tinsman 1981). Yet in that same study, the teachers were very responsive to training designed to help them acquire teaching skills and strategies not in their "natural" repertoire. Although it seems to make good sense to provide teachers with mirrors for their professional behavior, the experience in most studies is that very few changes in behavior usually result. It is possible that changes requiring the addition of new repertoire will require more than information about present performance.

Nondirective Clinical Feedback

Cogan (1973) became the chief spokesman for organizing teachers into collegial teams and helping those teams study their teaching and set goals for experimenting with innovations that promised to increase their effectiveness. Unfortunately, this line of work was not accompanied by much formal research. It is not possible to say whether there was much effect or whether certain variations on the practice were more effective than others.

Structured Clinical Supervision

The most popular form of service to teachers has been the more structured forms of clinical feedback, generally versions of the conceptualization of teaching skills developed by Madeline Hunter (1980; see also Gentile 1988). It is arguable that its spread has actually sparked the development of the staff development field as a whole. In the most common application, teachers, supervisors, and administrators are provided with training to acquaint them with teaching skills based on research on effective teaching. Then supervisors and administrators are taught how to observe teaching, record teaching behavior, and report the results to teachers in conferences. In the last few years, some districts have been experimenting with teacher-provided feedback (sometimes called "peer coaching"). The community of practitioners of structured clinical supervision has produced little research. Therefore, it is difficult to estimate either the kinds or magnitude of changes it produces. Some reviewers (Slavin 1989) have complained that the method has not been proven to affect student learning, but a prior question involves whether it changes teacher behavior and how much, which was not clearly addressed by the most frequently cited study (Stallings 1985) and was minimal in Lloyd's (1971) investigation. In the Stallings study, changes in behavior were statistically significant, but the magnitude of change was not reported, including how close teachers were to the criterion before the intervention was undertaken.

Another important question involves how much "feedback" is necessary to bring about changes. This has not been addressed either. However, it stands to reason that where supervisors and principals are the chief agents of the feedback, then implementation of the clinical supervisory acts has to take place if changes are to occur. One recent study indicated that bringing about a sufficient density of supervisory sessions may present a problem in itself. In one statewide effort (Mandeville and Rivers 1989) where administrators and teachers had received fairly extensive workshops over a period of several years, it appeared that the average teacher was being visited by supervisory personnel about once a year, too infrequently for the method to have a reasonable chance to have an effect. To judge the method as ineffective in a situation where the training was not sufficient to achieve implementation would be careless indeed.

The Mandeville/Rivers study, which produced essentially the same findings as the California Staff Development Study (Joyce, Bush, and McKibbin 1982) has disturbing implications for the training of principals. Why it should be difficult to get principals to practice something so obviously related to their role is perplexing. In an era when we are preparing to ask principals to lead in the restructuring of the workplace and to understand and facilitate the complexities of growth by the individuals on their staffs (see Chapter 4), we have to worry about evidence that many principals do not provide clinical support for their teachers even after intensive training.

The entire field of clinical support of teachers, whether by peers, supervisors, or principals, badly needs study, particularly because it is by far the largest component of staff development in most districts, and its theoretical structure is attractive to district policy makers. To provide teachers with information about effective teaching behavior and with mirrors reflecting the extent to which their practice includes those behaviors appears eminently sensible. Not to study how to do it well, however, makes much less sense. It should not be difficult to locate some teachers who have not been exposed to the content and who do not manifest it in their normal classroom behavior, engineer a really solid treatment, and find out what it takes to make a difference. We believe it can and probably does in many districts, albeit undocumentedly, but we can scarcely believe that there is not better research in the area. The newer variations on the theme are on no better ground than the older ones. The persons currently disseminating the peer-oriented version are on very questionable ground until the important questions about the practice are studied.

Research on Training

Although research on training is generally designed to improve the effectiveness of the trainer and the training design, it generates information about how people learn and about their capacities for learning. In the late 1960s and early 1970s, Borg (1970) and his associates (Borg et al. 1970) developed a series of self-administering instructional systems at the Far West Laboratory for Educational Development designed to allow teachers to teach themselves teaching skills. Although they included manuals and other print materials, the distinguishing feature of the materials was the use of videotape to demonstrate teaching skills and to help teachers track their own progress. (Teachers would tape themselves and match their performance against the demonstrations.)

Borg's team successfully developed a number of these "minicourses," and they did work insofar as skill attainment was concerned. Having learned the skills, the teachers, however, varied considerably in their persistence in using them. Despite this, the great importance of the work was in the demonstration that teachers had great capacity for learning new skills and that the use of television both for modelling and enabling teachers to follow their progress could contribute to the process.

Joyce, Showers, and their colleagues extended the application of the theory-demonstration-practice-self-feedback paradigm to complex teaching strategies with success (Showers 1984) and attacked the problem of transfer to regular and appropriate use in the classroom. Baker and Showers (1984) first demonstrated that in-classroom "coaching" by expert trainers resulted in regular and persistent use. Later, they demonstrated that teams of teachers could provide much of the needed help by sharing plans and results and learning by observing one another until implementation was achieved.

At this point, the training research lines up with the organizational research, for organizing teachers into collegial study teams requires some of the cultural changes that lead to greater organizational cohesiveness and productivity. Showers and Black (1989) extended the idea, first by organizing a faculty into study groups to implement several models of teaching and then by using this organization to generate school improvement efforts that have affected the learning climate of the school.

The result of this line of research has been to extend the estimates of the learning capacity of teachers. It is clear that teachers can learn expanded repertoires of teaching strategies and use them regularly and strongly.

Joyce, Murphy, and Showers (1989) have recently reported a study that applies the results of the training research to the improvement of a school virtually filled with "at-risk" students. The entire faculty of the school was organized into study groups and provided with extensive training on the use of several models of teaching. The rate of promotion on merit in the school rose from 30 percent to 95 percent in a period of just two years. Judging from the results of the administration of standardized tests of achievement, it appears that the average student in the school increased in learning rate from about seven-tenths of the national average to a rate about equal to the national average. This study directly links the training research to general school improvement goals.

The same study also underlines the importance of the degree of skill achieved by the teachers and the effects of their teaching on student achievement. Hall and Loucks (1977) have stressed for several years the need to study the levels of use of innovations that result from training, focusing on the difference between "mechanical" use and deeper, more powerful skill and use.

In the study by Joyce, Showers, and others, where virtually all of the faculties of several schools achieved mechanical levels of skill, the achievement in the social studies of students of teachers who had reached the mechanical level only were compared with the achievement of students whose teachers had reached "executive" control of the models of teaching, using them more richly and appropriately. The results are equivalent to an effect size of 1.0 or more. The median student in the executive-control classes placed between the 85th and 90th percentile of the distributions in the mechanical-use classes. This finding suggests the probable extreme importance of training design, including the changes in the workplace that will permit "follow up" activities to be substantial enough to enable teachers to achieve a deep understanding of innovations and correspondingly high levels of skill in their use. We are optimistic that teachers can greatly expand their repertoires of teaching skills and that these can pay off for students, but the onus is on the designers of training to create environments where this will happen.

The Workplace as Teacher

That our social environments influence our behavior is hardly arguable, and it makes good sense to try to create productive environments for teachers. Studying how to build productive social systems in schools is quite another proposition. The research divides itself into studies of the productivity of schools having differences in organizational climate and studies about how to change them. The studies of productivity (see Little 1989, Rosenholtz 1989, and the discussions in Chapters 1 and 3) affirm the proposition that there are real differences in organizational climate and that these have significant effects on the behavior of teachers and the productivity of students.

Investigations designed to yield knowledge about how to build productive environments are rare, although there has been enough exploratory work to develop strategies that have a reasonable probability of success (see Chapter 1). The culture of most school faculties is highly individualistic; nearly all interaction is over day-to-day operations (Deal 1989, Lortie 1975, Little 1989, Rosenholtz 1989). Without collective action, schools have difficulty addressing problems that cannot be solved by individual action. Without a balance between operations and the study of teaching and curriculum, the school is liable to drift toward obsolescence and fail to adapt to the needs of the surrounding society. What we will term "collegial" social systems in schools generate greater productivity in school improvement efforts, resulting in significant differences for students in terms of opportunities to learn.

Reorienting school cultures toward collegial problem solving and study and incorporation of advances in research on curriculum and teaching has turned out to be difficult. The reason has not been an absence of models. The concept of collegiality has been very much alive throughout the 20th century in writing and leadership from Dewey (1916) through Judd (1934), Counts (1932), and Goodlad (1983). Robert Schaefer's marvelous 1967 essay, written at the height of the movements to improve the academic content of curriculum, involve students in driving inquiry, and develop collegial workplaces for teachers, synthesized those movements into a dynamic conception of the school as a workplace. Schaefer argued for schools that would not only involve students in academic inquiry but involve the teachers in the continuous study of teaching and learning. Experimentation with teaching would be a normal, shared activity as the teachers developed new procedures and instructional materials and tried them out. Bringing together, as it did, a concept of a community of collaborating teachers, a recognition that educational knowledge is emergent, a belief that the future science of education would be built around clinical inquiry, and a sense of an organization whose staff are truly empowered, the essay embodied a striking vision of professionalization.

The problem is less one of conception than one of implementation. The culture of the school has proved to be a very tough customer indeed. Proposals both for the "empowerment" of teachers and for an increase in the use of the knowledge base in education depend on the realization of a radically revised workplace with very different relationships among teachers and much greater attention to the application of professional knowledge than is the norm in educational settings today. Certainly the individualistic mode of operation mitigates against collective action. The experience of the National Teacher Corps (Blatt 1977), the California School Improvement Program (Berman and Gjelten 1983), and the Chapter One Programs (Berman and McLaughlin 1975) indicate that the provision of substantial resources succeeds in affecting the orientation toward change only where extraordinary leadership is present.

The report of the California School Improvement Program contains some arresting recommendations. The program provided substantial resources (from $50,000 to $100,000 per annum) to hundreds of high schools to organize themselves and engage in school improvement. There were virtually no restrictions on direction—the initiative was to fuel grass-roots perceptions of needs by providing discretionary resources for school improvement. After six years, the evaluation team recommended that the program be severely restructured or abandoned because very few faculties had been able to capitalize on the resources!

The organization development specialists have come to believe that cosmetic or minor organizational changes will have little effect. Those who would address the problem will have to involve themselves in the reorientation of deeply entrenched patterns (Schmuck, Runkel, Arends, and Arends 1981). Gardner (1978) and others see the problem as one of generating a moral force that gives the improvement of social conditions priority. Baldridge (1983) also stresses the importance of values as the core of the "culture" of the organization and the creation of a forceful ethos that increases the energy of the organization and the individuals who work in it.

The issues about initiatives to generate school cultures that support professionalization for teachers and those designed to improve the learning environment for children come together in these discussions of the workplace. Whether one enters the problem as one of increasing the opportunity for teachers to flourish in a dignified manner (Grant 1988)—as Shanker suggests in Chapter 5—or approaches it from the point of view of trying to create more powerful learning environments for students (Goodlad 1983), one ends up in the same theoretical space as Fullan (Chapter 1), which is somewhere close to the conception that Schaefer laid out. The Little and Rosenholtz studies support the inseparability of the concern with teachers and the concern with students, as does the Codianni and Wilbur (1983) review of school improvement programs. Showers' (1980) study demonstrated directly that teacher efficacy was related to the same dimensions of school environment that are emphasized by Little and Rosenholtz.

Given the contemporary concern with improving the productivity of schools for learners and creating improved workplaces for teachers, and the rather striking evidence that differences in the culture of schools, in fact, do affect student learning and teacher productivity and well being, it seems curious that we lack research on how to bring about changes in those cultures. The irony may be that to persuade a school district to permit the necessary experimentation would itself require a change in the culture of the district. Certainly the magnitude of progress made in Pittsburgh (Chapter 10) provides some evidence about what can happen when a superintendent approaches the problem as one of changing the cultural fabric of the district itself. Here we have another marvelous opportunity for extremely important research. Some recent work indicates that aspects of the workplace can be changed quite quickly, at least on a temporary basis, which should encourage research on how to change the organizational context and the effects of doing so.

Some Other Topics

We conducted searches for research on a number of topics that are sometimes discussed as if there were a research base, but turned out to be barren or nearly so. This is odd because they were all identified as important policy issues that badly needed research 15 years ago (Joyce, Howey, and Yarger 1975; Nicholson and Joyce 1975). These topics include voluntarism, governance, site, trainer credibility, and timing.

The widespread assumption that voluntarism increases both motivation and the likelihood to use the content of training has not been tested by its chief advocates. If it turns out that psychological states greatly determine who will volunteer and who within that group will follow up on their training, the whole issue may have to be rethought from a different perspective. The "commitment follows competence" thesis should also affect thinking on the issue. Also, as previous reviews have indicated

(Joyce, Showers, and Bennett 1987), poor training will not sustain enthusiasm among volunteers, just as good training will not overcome hostility at being forced to a training setting at gunpoint.

Governance options appear promising for approaching the problems of organizing initiatives for volunteers, school faculties, and the district staff, but the research on governance remains almost nonexistent, despite the fine examples of governance and planning practice that appear in this yearbook and elsewhere. That teachers can govern staff development centers is clear (Chapter 6); moreover, they have the same problems of selecting relevant content and attracting clientele to volunteer programs as do central office personnel. Research to lay a basis for engineering better governance procedures and developing collegial policy-making systems should make its way into the "urgent" file of some community of researchers, but it has not done so thus far.

Discussions about whether "on site" locations for workshops are more effective than workshops held in conference settings are probably going to be moot in the long run, for some highly effective programs have been run in all manner of settings. It may be as simple as who will travel for what. If you are marketing something that is inherently unpopular, it may be well to go door to door and be very nice. People will travel for good programs, however, and there are certainly times when they will choose to leave the school for training.

Another commonly discussed issue is whether role designation brings credibility (the familiar notion that teachers prefer learning from other teachers). Another unstudied question, it is probably another issue that evaporates in the air of sensible planning. Competence of the individual will probably override role. Members of all types of formal role groups have been good and poor trainers.

The importance of clear research on these topics can be seen in one type of decision where they all have relevance. In recent years, some school districts have decentralized their staff development budgets in the belief that on-site, site-governed training by role-relevant trainers is most effective. Some of the most dramatic effects from staff development programs have been achieved when research personnel and university professors have been the agents of training. Solutions to the problem of creating effective programs may not be as simple as providing on-site training by teachers on topics selected by teachers. Districts that are "decentralizing" their staff development budgets might take heed of one dimension of the California Staff Development Study (Joyce, Bush, and McKibbin 1983) or the Berman/Gjelten (1983) study, both of which focused on sites that were provided resources for school improvement and staff development. Many school faculties were simply not cohesive enough to generate truly collaborative efforts over significant missions.

Underanalyzed Sources of Information

Not all research pertinent to staff development is labeled "staff development research." All the areas in education that rely on staff development or training are potential sources of information. For example, implementations in curriculum (see Chapter 1) and educational technology have much to offer. The implementation of teaching strategies requires training. Therefore, those who engage in research on instruction have to engage in staff development activities, providing another area of potential.

The general area of "cooperative learning" is an illustration both of the problems and prospects that lie in store for those who would mine the study of instruction as a source. Cooperative learning is promising because it is an area of much recent research activity; and the research has produced rather convincing evidence that various forms of cooperative activity increase student learning in the academic, social, and personal domains (Johnson and Johnson 1981, Sharan 1980, Slavin 1983, Rolheiser-Bennett 1987).

Successful staff development obviously had to occur before the research could have been conducted and certainly could have produced such consistently positive results. Unfortunately, few of the reports contain information about the training, leaving us frustrated. An exception is Sharan and his associates (Sharan and Shachar 1988), who conduct their research on group investigation, one of the most complex of all models of teaching. Fortunately, they describe their training in some detail, and they study the classroom use of group investigation and report their results in terms of the degrees of executive control their teachers reach. The result is an almost exact replication of the findings from the set of investigations conducted by Showers, Joyce, and their colleagues over a variety of other models of teaching. Both groups use versions of the theory-demonstration-practice paradigm, with approximately equivalent results. Both have turned to collegial study groups and coaching to bring about classroom practice and transfer. Both found that teachers reaching only the more mechanical levels of control generate modest student learning effects that are far exceeded by the students of teachers who have mastered the model.

We can hope that research personnel who rely on training will increasingly report how they achieved implementation of their treatments and how differences in implementation affect results.

* * *

We have only just begun to learn how we learn, but the early results are promising. It is becoming clear that teachers have tremendous learning capacity that has been largely untapped. We are in much the same position as the U.S. space exploration program; that is, current knowledge is underused, and the need to generate more knowledge is urgent. There is enough sound technology that careful engineering from existing knowledge alone could carry us a long way toward the design of powerful, responsive programs that can enable teachers to expand their competence enormously. The clear areas where more knowledge is needed should be an impetus to design research that will lay the basis for program designs infinitely stronger—and more responsive—than we can now imagine.

References

Baker, R., and B. Showers. (1984). "The Effects of a Coaching Strategy on Teachers' Transfer of Training to Classroom Practice: A Six-month Follow-up Study." Paper presented at the annual meeting of the American Educational Research Association in New Orleans.

Baldridge, V., and T. Deal, eds. (1983). *The Dynamics of Organizational Change in Education*. Boston: Addison-Wesley.

Bennett, B. (1987). "The Effectiveness of Staff Development Training Practices: A Meta-Analysis." Ph.D. thesis, University of Oregon.

Berman, P., and T. Gjelten. (1983). *Improving School Improvement*. Berkeley, Calif.: Berman, Weiler Associates.

Berman, P., and M. McLaughlin. (1975). *Federal Programs Supporting Educational Change, Vol. IV: The Findings in Review*. Santa Monica, Calif.: The Rand Corporation.

Black, J. (1989). "Building the School as a Center of Inquiry: A Whole-school Approach Oriented Around Models of Teaching." Ph.D. thesis, Nova University, 1989.

Blatt, B., ed. (1980). *Providing Leadership for Staff Development*. Syracuse, N.Y.: National Council for the States in Inservice Education.

Borg, W.R., M. Kelley, P. Langer, and M. Gall. (1970). *The Minicourse*. Beverly Hills, Calif.: Collier-Macmillan.

Center for Research on Elementary and Middle Schools. (February 1989). *Success for All*. CREMS.

Codianni, A.V., and G. Wilbur. (1983). *More Effective School from Research to Practice*. New York: Columbia University Teachers College. ERIC Clearinghouse on Urban Education. ED 236-299.

Cogan, M. (1973). *Clinical Supervision*. Boston: Houghton-Mifflin.

Counts, G. (1932). *Dare the School Build a New Social Order?* New York: John Day.

Crandall, D. et al. (1982). *People, Policies, and Practices: Examining the Chain of School Improvement*. Vols. I-X. Andover, Mass.: The Network, Inc.

Dewey, J. (1916). *Democracy in Education*. New York: Macmillan, Inc.

Flanders, N. (1970). *Analyzing Teacher Behavior*. Reading, Mass.: Addison-Wesley.

Gardner, J. (1978). *Excellence and Education*. New York: Harper & Row.

Gentile, J. R. (1988). *Instructional Improvement: Summary and Analysis of Madeline Hunter's Essential Elements of Instruction & Supervision*. Oxford, Ohio: National Staff Development Council.

Good, T., and G. Brophy. (1974). "An Empirical Investigation: Changing Teacher and Student Behavior." *Journal of Educational Psychology* 66: 399-405.

Goodlad, J. (1983). *A Place Called School*. New York: McGraw-Hill.

Grant, G. (1988). *The World We Created at Hamilton High*. Cambridge: Harvard University Press.

Hall, G., and S. Loucks. (1977). "A Developmental Model for Determining Whether the Treatment Is Actually Implemented." *American Educational Research Journal* 14, 3: 263-276.

Holloway, S.D. (1988). "Concepts of Ability and Effort in Japan and the United States." *Review of Educational Research* 58, 3: 327-345.

Hunter, M. (1980). "Six Types of Supervisory Conferences." *Educational Leadership* 37: 408-412.

Johnson, D., and R. Johnson. (1981). "Effects of Cooperative and Individualistic Learning Experiences on Inter-ethnic Interaction." *Journal of Educational Psychology* 73, 3: 444-449.

Joyce, B., R. Bush, and M. McKibbin. (1982). "The California Staff Development Study." *The January 1982 Report*. Palo Alto, Calif.: Booksend Laboratories.

Joyce, B., K. Howey, and S. Yarger. (1975). *Issues to Face*. Syracuse, N.Y.: National Dissemination Center, Syracuse University.

Joyce, B., C. Brown, and L. Peck. (1981). *Flexibility in Teaching*. New York: Longman, Inc.

Joyce, B., B. Showers, C. Murphy, and J. Murphy. (1989). Reconstructing the Workplace: School Renewal as Cultural Change." *Educational Leadership* (in press).

Judd, H. (1934). *Education and Social Progress*. New York: Harcourt.

Little, J. (1989). "The Persistance of Privacy: Autonomy and Initiative in Teachers' Professional Relations." Paper presented at the annual meeting of the American Educational Research Association in San Francisco.

Lortie, D. (1975). *Schoolteacher*. Chicago: The University of Chicago Press.

Mandeville, G. K., and J.L. Rivers. (1989). "Effects of South Carolina's Hunter-based PET program." *Educational Leadership* 46, 4: 63-66.

Medley, D. (1977). *Teacher Competence and Teacher Effectiveness*. Washington, D.C.: American Association of Colleges of Teacher Education.

Miles, M., and M. Huberman. (1984). *Innovation Up Close*. New York: Praeger.

Nicholson, A. M., B. Joyce, D. Parker, and Waterman (1976). *The Literature on Inservice Teacher Education. ISTE Report III*. Syracuse, N.Y.: The National Dissemination Center, Syracuse University.

Rolheiser-Bennett, C. (1987). "Four Models of Teaching: A Meta-Analysis of Student Outcomes." Ph.D. thesis, University of Oregon.

Rosenholtz, S.J. (1989). *Teachers' Workplace: The Social Organization of Schools*. White Plains, N.Y.: Longman.

Schaefer, R. (1967). *The School as a Center of Inquiry*. New York: Harper & Row.

Schmuck, R., P. Runkel, R. Arends, and J. Arends. (1977). *The Second Handbook of Organizational Development in Schools*. Palo Alto, Calif.: Mayfield Press.

Sharan, S. (1980). "Cooperative Learning in Small Groups: Recent Methods and Effects on Achievement, Attitudes, and Ethnic Relations. *Review of Educational Research* 50, 2: 241-271.

Sharan, S., and A. Shaulov. (1989). "Cooperative Learning, Motivation to Learn and Academic Achievement." In *Cooperative Learning: Theory and Research.* Edited by S. Sharan. New York: Praeger Publishing Co.

Showers, B. (1980). "Self-efficacy as a Predictor of Teacher Participation in School Decision-making." Ph.D. thesis, Stanford University.

Showers, B. (1984). *Peer Coaching: A Strategy for Facilitating Transfer of Training.* Eugene, Ore.: Center for Educational Policy and Management.

Showers, B. (March 1989). "Implementation: Research-based Training and Teaching Strategies and their Effects on the Workplace and Instruction." Paper presented at the annual meeting of the American Educational Research Association in San Francisco.

Showers, B., B. Joyce, and B. Bennett. (1987). "Synthesis of Research on Staff Development: A Framework for Future Study and a State-of-the-art Analysis." *Educational Leadership* 45, 3: 77-87.

Simon, A., and E.G. Boyer. (1967). *Mirrors for Behavior: An Anthology of Classroom Observation Instruments.* Philadelphia: Research for Better Schools, Inc.

Slavin, R. (1983). *Cooperative Learning.* New York: Longman, Inc.

Slavin, R. (1989). "PET and the Pendulum: Faddism in Education and How to Stop it." *Phi Delta Kappan* 70, 10: 752-758.

Stallings, J. (1985). "A Study of Implementation of Madeline Hunter's Model and its Effects on Students." *Journal of Educational Research* 78: 325-337.

Stevenson, H.W., S. Lee,and J.W. Stigler. (1986). "Mathematics Achievement of Chinese, Japanese, and American Children." *Science* 231: 693-699.

Tinsman, S. (1981). "The Effects of Instructional Flexibility Training on Teaching Styles and Controlled Repertoire." In *Flexibility in Teaching*, edited by B. Joyce, C. Brown, and L. Peck. New York: Longman.

3

Integrating Staff Development and School Improvement: A Study of Teacher Personality and School Climate

David Hopkins

S ome years ago, Michael McKibbin and Bruce Joyce published two papers entitled "Psychological States and Staff Development" (1980) and "Teacher Growth States and School Environments" (1982). In thcse papers, they reported high correlations between a teacher's psychological state, as operationally defined by Maslow's (1962) hierarchy of needs, and the teacher's participation in and use of training. Among the 21 teachers involved, they found that mean implementation scores rose with the ratings of psychological state; those teachers with a

Author's note: I am grateful to Marilyn Evans for allowing me to draw on her work (Evans 1986) and our co-authored article in the *British Educational Research Journal* (Evans and Hopkins 1988) for this article. More details of the study will be found in these two sources. I am also grateful to Judy Grafton, Pat Holborn, Bruce Joyce, Peter Norman, and Ivy Pye for comments on an earlier draft, and to Devi Pabla and Eileen Mallory for typing.

David Hopkins is Tutor in Curriculum Studies, Cambridge Institute of Education, Cambridge, England.

psychological state rating of between 3+ and 5 made use of their training at a rate two and a half to three times greater than teachers who had a psychological state rating mean of 1.7 (1980). McKibbin and Joyce (1980) concluded:

> The general milieu of the school and the social movements of the times interact powerfully with the personalities of the teachers to create personal orientations which greatly influence how teachers view the world (and them-selves in it), and those views largely control what the individual can see as possibilities for personal and professional growth and the kind of options to which they can relate (p. 254).

These ideas and findings resonated with my own experience. As someone whose work involved both teacher development and school improvement, I felt, however, that sustained improvements in the quality of education would likely remain a utopian dream until the debate was reconceptualized and recentered on the dynamics and functioning of the school system at two levels—the structural and the psychological. As part of this recentering, more research studies were and are needed to link knowledge about school climate, as well as the psychological state of the individual teacher, to the process of using educational ideas at the school level.

The bulk of this chapter describes a research study that attempted to do this by extending the work of McKibbin and Joyce and introducing school climate as an additional variable in the research design. In brief, our results implied that variance in curriculum utilization could be ac-counted for by the prevailing school climate and the nature of the individual teacher. We found that teachers operating at a higher psychological level and in a more open, democratic school climate used the greatest number of educational ideas.

The subtext of this chapter is that the research on teacher develop-ment and school improvement has to be much more sophisticated to be of much value to students, teachers, or schools. In particular, we need to know much more about the process involved in both teacher development and school improvement, and about how the two interact. Another problem with most research and development work in these two areas is that it is particular rather than general. This results in detailed studies of discrete issues rather than broader synthetic inquiries.

In the following section, a brief overview is given of the main trends within the areas of teacher development and school improvement, and an argument is made for research designs that integrate both teacher and school development. In the main section, our research study on teacher personality and school climate is described. Finally, some observations are made about the implications of such research in teacher development and school improvement that is broadly synthetic rather than narrowly particular.

Teacher Development and School Improvement

The past decade has brought enormous progress in our understanding of both teacher development and school improvement. As compared with 10 years ago, we now know much more about the conditions under which teachers develop to the benefit of themselves and their pupils, the characteristics of effective schools, and, to some extent, the processes that lead to school improvement. The contentious debate of the '70s, over whether teachers and schools make a difference, is now passé. The fact has been proven and the debate has now been relegated to a footnote in the history of educational development.

Another indication of this progress is the extent to which research knowledge has become conventional wisdom and is implicit in policy formation at different levels of the educational system. Although the too-rapid assimilation of such knowledge into educational policy may be a double-edged sword, the debate is at least increasingly focusing on real(istic) issues. This self-congratulatory tone will not last much longer because, despite the progress, much remains to be done.

The main problem is the need to integrate teacher and school development. A considerable fragmentation of approach still exists within these two areas. For example, at least six areas of focus coexist under the general heading of teacher development (e.g., effective teaching, teacher as researcher, models of teaching, staff development, teacher's work, and teacher's personality); and four areas exist in the area of school improvement (e.g., school improvement, effective schools, case studies of change, and the dissemination of improvement ideas and practices). Because this tradition of investigation into discrete areas is so deeply established and represents the way knowledge has developed in these areas over the past ten years, it is instructive to briefly review some of them here.

The search for the defining characteristics of effective teaching, for example, has been a quest that has preoccupied researchers, mainly, though not exclusively, within North America, for the past two decades. This research has been characterized by a process-product design and has resulted in the identification of a number of concepts related to the organising, pacing, and management of instruction. The most recent "state of the art" is found in the *Third Handbook of Research on Teaching* (Wittrock

1986), where the chapter by Jere Brophy and Thomas Good (1986) provides the most comprehensive summary statement of the genre.

A contrasting approach is taken by Lawrence Stenhouse (1975, 1983) and Donald Schon (1983) in their respective images of the "teacher as researcher" and the "reflective practitioner." These characterizations reflect a view of teachers who, through a process of research and reflection, develop professional autonomy and transcend the "recipes" that sometimes emerge from the effective teaching research. As Stenhouse wrote (in Rudduck and Hopkins 1985, p. 104), "ideas and people are not of much real use until they are digested to the point where they are subject to the teachers' own judgment." He continues to argue that educational ideas need to be expressed in curricular terms because only in curriculum form can they be tested by teachers. Students consequently benefit from curriculum, not so much because they change day-to-day instruction, but because they improve teachers.

An example of such specifications is provided by Bruce Joyce and Marsha Weil (1986) in *Models of Teaching*. Their premise is that student achievement is enhanced through the teacher's use of appropriate and specific models of teaching. Since no single teaching strategy can accomplish every purpose, the wise teacher will master a sufficient repertoire of strategies to deal with the specific kinds of teaching problems he or she faces. This desiderata, although appealing, is difficult to achieve because the acquisition of new teaching styles requires sustained practice and feedback.

Inservice teacher education designs have, for too long, been unable to meet these challenges of skill acquisition and transfer. A fourth area of focus has therefore been training designs for effective staff development. Joyce and Showers' (1980) seminal paper on inservice teacher training, with its description of the five training components of lecture, modelling, practice, feedback, and coaching, has found widespread practical and empirical support. A comprehensive statement of their work, which links it to both school improvement and pupil progress, is found in their *Student Achievement Through Staff Development* (Joyce and Showers 1988).

A similar division of labour is evident in the area of school improvement. In this chapter, I adopt a broader than usual view of school improvement, and regard it as the search for practices, processes, and characteristics that define effective schools. School improvement is concerned, therefore, with defining the internal conditions of schools that predispose them to high student achievement (broadly defined), and defining the process whereby this infrastructure is established.

This challenge was taken seriously in many western countries during the mid-'80s, and it found its focus in the OECD International School Improvement Project (ISIP). This project produced a wide literature, of which the overviews by Van Velzen and his colleagues (1985; *Making School Improvement Work*) and Hopkins (1987; *Improving the Quality of Schooling*) are the most accessible. The project produced a large amount of case study data on and techniques for particular school improvement strategies. Of special interest was ISIP's work on School Based Review (Bollen and Hopkins 1987, Hopkins 1988), School Leader Development (Stego et. al. 1987), and External Support (Loucks-Horsley and Crandall 1986).

The other major area of focus has been the identification of the characteristics of the effective school. *Fifteen Thousand Hours,* the original study by Michael Rutter et al. (1979), was conducted in London and supported the contention that schools do make a difference. This study was soon complemented by a wide literature on both sides of the Atlantic. The work of Reynolds (1985) and Mortimore and his colleagues (1988) in the United Kingdom and Purkey and Smith (1983) and Clark et al. (1984) in the United States, for example is particularly noteworthy and illustrative. This approach to school improvement follows a "process-product" design similar to the research on teaching effects and has resulted in a list of effectiveness characteristics (e.g., safe and orderly school climate, high expectations of student achievement, curriculum-focused leadership, frequent evaluation of pupil progress, collaboration among staff, clear objectives, and a consensus on goals). From a school improvement perspective, the most exciting aspect of this research is that these characteristics are related to the school's social system and are not dependent on external factors; as such, they are amenable to change by the action of the school staff involved.

These two broad areas of work have been complemented by a small number of thoughtful and well-designed multisite school improvement case studies that provide a deeper understanding of the dynamics of change. The case studies conducted by Huberman and Miles for the large-scale DESSI project and described and analyzed in detail in their *Innovation Up Close* (1984) provide an excellent example of a "grounded theory" approach to school improvement (for a brief overview of the DESSI Study, see Loucks-Horsley 1983). Also of note are the various reviews of the school improvement, educational change literature, of which the work of Michael Fullan (1982, 1985) is exemplary.

Taken together, this body of work tells us a great deal about aspects of teacher development and school improvement. Although there have been attempts to review the whole area, for example, Wideen and Andrews' (1987) *Staff Development for School Improvement,* the field as a whole remains fragmented, and this fragmentation results in serious limitations. Besides concerns about inadequate research designs and conceptualisation, which present "objective dangers" to most empirical work, two other drawbacks are evident from this review. The first is that the discreteness of these various research activities inhibits the linking of theory and practice because the real world is not reflected in their research designs. The second concern is that such a fragmented view of the educational world leads to a reductionistic and impoverished view of both teacher development and school improvement.

This, of course, is not an original observation. Well-known figures associated with each of these two broad areas of inquiry have recently made similar comments. In a thoughtful review of "change processes in secondary schools," Fullan (1988) argues for, among other things, research that examines the long-term development of school organization factors, including the development of teachers and their interaction with the micro-processes of change. In a recent keynote address to the International Congress on Effective Schools, Thomas Good (1989) argued not only for more practitioner research on teaching effects but also for the linking of this integration to school effects characteristics.

This is easier said than done, as the work of Jaap Scheerens (1989) illustrates. He argues for a more comprehensive model of school effectiveness that is systems oriented, embodies a multilevel framework, and contains substantive findings from different types of educational effectiveness research. He consequently developed the model seen in Figure 3.1. Although this model is confined to the outcomes of "process-product" research, it is at least a serious attempt to link teacher and school development within a consistent empirical framework.

When, however, he begins to operationalise his model, he finds a very weak empirical base (see Figure 3.2, p. 48). So, even working within the traditional empirical-analytic paradigm, where much of the research has been conducted, Scheerens' task is not easy.

Fullan and his colleagues (1989) have developed a similar model (Figure 1.1, p.18), but one that has evolved from a school improvement perspective. Central to their approach is the concept of teacher as learner. It is this central focus that provides the links between classroom and school improvement. Although they report a promising initial response to their approach through their work with the Learning Consortium, empirical support for their model still has to be established, as they readily admit.

Although these two approaches are at an early stage of development, they provide examples of the type of work needed if we are to transcend the boundaries between teacher and school development and if researchers

Figure 3.1
Integrated Model of School Effectiveness
(from Scheerens 1989)

Context
• achievement stimulants from higher
  administration levels
• development of educational consumerism
• "co-variables" like school size, student-body
  composition, school category, urban/rural

Inputs
• teacher experience
• per-pupil expenditure
• parent support

Process
school level
• degree of achievement oriented
  policy
• educational leadership
• consensus, cooperative
  planning of teachers
• quality of school curricula in
  terms of content covered and
  formal structure
• orderly atmosphere

classroom level
• time-on-task (including
  homework)
• structured teaching
• opportunity to learn
• high expectations of pupils'
  progress
• degree of evaluation and
  monitoring of pupils' progress
• reinforcement

Outputs
student
achievement,
adjusted for:
• previous
  achievement
• intelligence
• SES

want to make their work less fragmented and reductionistic and to more realistically inform practice. In the following section, a more detailed example is given of another attempt to link teacher development and school improvement.

Teacher Personality and School Climate

Although the research study reported here attempted to link teacher development and school improvement, this is not to claim that the research

Figure 3.2
Degree of Empirical Support for Associated Educational Process Variables with Achievement
(Scheerens 1989)

characteristic	strong empirical basis	moderate empirical basis	an, as yet, weak empirical basis	mostly conjecture
Environmental incentives				x
Consumerism/parent involvement		x		
Teacher experience		x		
Per-pupil expenditure		x		
Achievement oriented policy, high expectations		x		
Educational leadership			x	
Consensus, cooperative planning				x
Quality of curricula			x	
Evaluative potential			x	
Orderly climate			x	
Structured teaching	x			
Time on task	x			
Opportunity to learn		x		
Reinforcement	x			

is exemplary or has met the problems outlined previously. It is simply an example of an inquiry that, because it did cross traditional research boundaries, enabled us to ask (as I have in the final section) more realistic questions about teacher development and school improvement.

Methodology

In essence, the design extended the research of McKibbin and Joyce described earlier by introducing school climate as an additional variable and by taking a sample of 30 teachers from 6 primary schools. The study was conducted in South Wales by Marilyn Evans and myself, and it focused on the use the teachers made in their classrooms of the ideas introduced during an exemplary inservice aesthetics course organised by the local education authority. The study investigated three main areas: school climate, the psychological state of the individual teachers, and levels of use regarding the individual teacher's use of educational ideas.

The particular course selected for the study extended over a calendar year, involved full- and part-time participation, and placed an emphasis on educational ideas, principles, and skills that could be used back on the job. The participants explored the meaning of these ideas and discussed their application for the work setting. On completion of the course, the teacher went back to his or her respective school to implement these ideas and to pass them on to the rest of the staff. The research was primarily concerned with the way in which these ideas became an accepted and understood component of the educational practice of these teachers. Thus, the study sought to answer the two fundamental questions about why some schools and why some teachers as individuals are more receptive than others to educational ideas.

On the learners' return to their respective schools, a five-month interim period was allowed for the spread of ideas from the course. This initial period, when teachers are struggling to become familiar with the nature and requirements of the ideas, developing instructional strategies, and learning and unlearning specific roles, is a time of high anxiety and uncertainty. We did not wish to heighten this sense of insecurity by beginning research work too early. Nor did we wish to risk appraising a nonevent by gathering data on teachers who, in the first flush of enthusiasm following the course, would not, for varying reasons (including school climate), sustain the innovation. Thus formal research work did not begin until five months after the end of the course and was conducted over a six-month period.

The research study used three main data-collecting techniques—interviews, questionnaires, and participant observation. This was to collect information on the three substantive areas of inquiry—school climate, psychological state of the teacher, and the level of use of educational ideas. The relationship between the particular data-collecting approach and the area of enquiry is represented in Figure 3.3. A full description of these six cells and information concerning data analysis is found in Evans (1986).

Results

The main research findings are presented in three ways, using a combination of statistical analysis and descriptive accounts. Presented first is an example of the series of profiles we developed, related to the three areas of inquiry for each of the six primary schools included in the study. Next, a brief summary is made of each of these areas of inquiry. These summaries are designed both to clarify the individual teacher's position in relation to the overall pattern of findings and to prepare the way for the task of pulling these identified strands of inquiry together. The synthesis

Figure 3.3
Data-Collecting Techniques Used to Investigate
School Climate, Psychological State of the Teacher, and
the Teacher's Use of Educational Ideas

	A	B	C
	The climate of the school	The psychological state of the individual teacher	The individual teachers utilisation of the ideas presented
Interviews	'Focused' interview, e.g. Miles' (1975) dimensions of organisational health	'Focused' interview, e.g. McKibbin & Joyce (1980)	Levels of Use interview, e.g. Loucks *et al.* (1976)
Questionnaire	Based on the work of Halpin & Croft (1963) and Fox & Schmuck *et al.* (1975)	Gregorc-style (1982) delineator. Telford's (1970) attitude and belief scale. Georgiades' (1967) attitudes towards change	—
Participant observation	—	—	To validate data obtained from level of use interviews. To provide implementation score (e.g. McKibbin & Joyce 1980)

of research findings is then presented in tabulated form. And, finally, attention is directed to some of the issues that can be drawn from this synthesis.

School Profiles. Space precludes reproduction of the six individual school profiles, but an example of a school profile depicting our approach to data reduction and display is found in Figure 3.4 on pages 52-53.

Summary of Findings Concerned with School Climate. School climate scores ranged from a low of 85.6 to a high of 116.3. Teachers in School A, operating in a climate rating of 116.3, were imbued with a spirit of collaboration, communication, and collegiality and felt their work to be fully appreciated. These characteristics were not evident in School F (85.6), where teachers generally felt isolated and were operating in a "closed" situation. The mean climate score was 97.2, a finding that is indicative of the fact that most of the schools in this study can be regarded as leaning towards a more democratic form of school management. While such a climate was perceived as being fairly open to innovation, actual use was hampered by the lack of an effective communication system and by teacher isolation and classroom autonomy.

Summary of Findings Concerned with the Psychological State of the Individual Teacher. *The Gregorc-Style Delineator* (Gregorc 1982). Forty-seven percent of this sample were found to be concrete-sequential in their mode of perception. While 23 percent were found to be abstract-random, a further 17 percent were abstract-sequential. The remaining 13 percent were concrete-random. Thus the dominant mode of perception of most of the teachers in this study was concrete-sequential. Gregorc (1982) describes the real world for these individuals as being the concrete physical. Their thinking processes are instinctive, deliberate, and methodical, and they use prescribed formulas in dealing with the world. These individuals, he claims, can be adverse to change and find it difficult to break with a habit or existing pattern of operation. Change, therefore, needs to come in slow, deliberate steps. These individuals need to be able to predict events and, if possible, play a role in the development and outcome of ideas.

Telford's (1970) Attitude and Belief Scale. The mean score of the results of this questionnaire was 181, indicating that most teachers in this study had a "fairly progressive" classroom orientation. These teachers were sympathetic to the developmental needs of the individual child. Although they did not believe that teaching should be dominated by subject areas, neither did they subscribe to the belief that children should decide their own activities or learn solely by self-discovery methods. In fact, they kept a fairly tight control on all curriculum activities. Discipline was seen as an essential component of good classroom practice, but a classroom atmosphere of cooperation was preferred to one of competition.

Georgiades' (1967) Attitude Towards Change Questionnaire. The mean score of 25 on this questionnaire indicated that most teachers in this study were not "consciously" adverse to change. There is a link here to Gregorc's (1982) description of the concrete-sequential individual who experiences difficulty in coping with change, not so much because of her attitude, but because of the difficulty of breaking an established pattern of operation.

Figure 3.4
Profile of School A Depicting School Climate, Psychological State of the Teacher, and the Teacher's Use of Educational Ideas

School climate		The psychological state			
			Rating		
Rating	Descriptive analysis	Gregorc (1982)	Telford (1970)	Georgiades (1967)	Maslow (1962)
116.3	1. *Goal focus.* The development of literacy and numeracy within a conducive atmosphere.	Teacher 1. AR	213	30	4
	2. *Communication adequacy.* Ease of communication attributed to smallness of staff group. Formal mechanics of communication in evidence. Staff meetings held on a regular basis. External support welcome. Parental involvement actively encouraged.				
	3. *Optimal power utilisation.* A collegial form of school management.	Teacher 2. CS	208	28	4
	4. *Resource utilisation.* (a) Effective use of scale post holders as curriculum leaders. INSET was greatly valued as an educational tool. (b) Small school capitation allowance proved a limiting factor, but staff worked together in an attempt to maximise resource utilisation.	Teacher 3. CS	179	15	3+
	5. *Cohesiveness.* The staff were perceived to be functioning as a 'whole' as regards curriculum matters.				
	6. *Morale.* The atmosphere was indicative of a feeling of well being and satisfaction.				
	7. *Innovativeness.* Innovative and realistic. Time, discussion and the provision of resources viewed as essential components.				
	8. *Autonomy.* Staff free to explore various educational ideas within their own classrooms.				
	9. *Adaption.* Staff flexible in approach, and able to adapt to new demands.				
	10. *Problem solving.* Staff functioned as a group in formulating school policies.				

of the individual teacher	The individual teacher's use of educational ideas		
	Rating		
Descriptive analysis	LoU	Imp. score	Descriptive analysis
Very confident: assured of own worth and value. A definite orientation toward achievement: constantly striving for perfection. This Abstract-random's approach to change is subject to the intensity of her interest. Capable of learning in a holistic manner, and has strong recollection ability.	IVA	83	Sound knowledge of aesthetic philosophy. Actively seeking out new ideas and collaborating with experts. Planning occurred at routine level. Assessment at mechanical level. Classroom performance at routine level. No difficulties reported in use. Overall use assessed at routine level.
Shows interest in growth and new experience: seeking further achievement. Stresses personal worth, while maintaining a sense of belonging to the group. Once an idea proves viable to this concrete-sequential individual he strives for perfection. Change must be structured and sequential.	III	61	Mechanical knowledge base. Actively involved in organised workshops. Seeking out further information. Planning and performance at mechanical level. No continuity or sequence established. Assessing remained at level of orientation. Overall use assessed at mechanical level.
An orientation toward belonging: striving to increase personal competence. This concrete-sequential individual required time to adapt to new situations. Change must come in slow, deliberate and incremental steps. Faith placed in specialists to explain phenomena which are not personally verifiable.	III	40	Knowledge base at level of preparation. Actively involved in organised workshops. Planning and assessing remained at low level. Performance at mechanical level: lack of confidence shown in offering child appropriate guidance. Overall use assessed at mechanical level.

Focused Interviews. Data were obtained from a series of focused interviews, in an attempt to analyse the psychological states of the teachers involved in this study (McKibbin and Joyce 1980). Fifty-four percent of the teachers in this study were identified as being, in Maslow's terms, at the level of belonging and security (Level 3). Twenty percent of the sample were identified as being at the level of self-acceptance (Level 5) or as having a definite orientation toward achievement (Level 4). A further 26 percent were found to be operating at the level of psychological safety (Level 2) or found to be oriented toward the satisfaction of basic needs (Level 1). It can, therefore, be reasonably assumed that the majority of teachers in this study were relatively happy in their work. Interest was shown in the ideas being introduced, but difficulty was experienced in breaking routine and ritualised classroom practice to allow for full use of ideas.

Summary of Findings Concerned with the Individual Teacher's Use of Educational Ideas. *Levels of Use* (Loucks et al. 1976; Hall et al. 1975; Hall and Loucks 1977). Forty-seven percent of the sample of teachers were found to be using ideas at the mechanical level (i.e., using the innovation in a poorly coordinated manner and making user-oriented changes.) Only 3 percent had reached the level of refinement, while 20 percent were identified at the routine level of use. Twenty-four percent were found to be at the level of preparation while 3 percent were at the level of orientation. The remaining 3 percent were identified as being at the level of non-use.

Implementation Scores. Scores can be seen to range from a low of 6 to a high of 98. The mean implementation score for all teachers involved in the study was 46. This finding appears to be in line with the identified mechanical level of use. The majority of teachers may thus be said to be trying out ideas more on the basis of emulation than on the grounds of understanding. It appears that techniques introduced in the course were being tried out with little regard to the importance of establishing continuity and sequence; in fact, confusion concerning appropriate teachers' strategies and behaviour was noted.

Summary of Research Findings

Most of the teachers in this study work in a climate where there is a discernible move towards a more democratic form of school management but where, as yet, no effective means of collegiality, collaboration, and communication has been established. These teachers are fairly progressive in classroom orientation and are not consciously adverse to change. However, being naturally sequential and structured in their thinking, they find it extremely difficult to break their existing pattern of behaviour. They prefer change to come in slow, deliberate, incremental steps; a statement given substance by these individuals' concrete-sequential mode of thought. Most of the teachers are reasonably content in their job, operate in a state of relative psychological security, and believe that they are accepted and respected at the current level of their job performance. The combination of these factors appears to make for mechanical use of the ideas being introduced; that is, the innovation appears to be used in a poorly coordinated manner and with little understanding of the epistemological and pedagogical implications of these ideas.

In sum, the following formula emerges:

Climate Rating + Psychological State = LoU = Implementation Score
   97.2   3*   III   46

*NB This score compiled from Gregorc (1982) (concrete-sequential); Telford (1970) (fairly progressive); and Georgiades (1967) (not consciously adverse to change); and data from McKibbin & Joyce's (1980) "focused" interviews. LoU is level of understanding.

These findings, thus summarised, serve to put into perspective the individual teacher's working conditions, his psychological state, and his use of educational ideas.

Synthesis of Research Findings

In order to synthesise the research findings, the individual teacher scores were grouped according to the analysis of their psychological states (e.g., Group 1, Maslow Rating 5, 4; Group 2, Maslow Rating 3+; Group 3, Maslow Rating 3; Group 4, Maslow Rating 2+, 2, 1). In line with these ratings, the individual teacher scores related to school climate, implementation score, and levels of use were added in three additional columns. Operating within this framework of the four identified groups of teachers, a mean score was calculated for each of these categories. The result of this synthesis is presented in Figure 3.5.

Figure 3.5, in summarising the findings of this study, points to the existence of a positive relationship among school climate, the nature of the individual teacher, and the use of educational ideas. The actual process of use (as evidenced in implementation scores and identified levels of use) was found to be considerably affected by the climate in which the teacher was operating.

With direct reference to Figure 3.5, it can be seen that all of the Group 4 teachers, operating at a low psychological level and in a "closed"

Figure 3.5
Synthesis of Main Research Findings Depicting Psychological State, Climate, Implementation Score, and Levels of Use

School	Teacher	Psychological state rating	Mean score	Climate	Mean score
Group 1					
E	1	5		97.6	
D	1	5		93.4	
A	1	4		116.3	
A	2	4	4.3	116.3	105.1
B	3	4		103.7	
B	4	4		103.7	
Group 2					
F	1	3+		85.6	
F	2	3+		85.6	
D	5	3+		93.4	
C	1	3+		87.0	
E	2	3+	3.5	97.6	96.6
B	2	3+		103.7	
B	5	3+		103.7	
A	3	3+		116.3	
Group 3					
D	2	3		93.4	
C	2	3		87.0	
F	4	3		85.6	
E	3	3		97.6	
E	4	3	3.0	97.6	95.7
E	5	3		97.6	
B	1	3		103.7	
B	7	3		103.7	
Group 4					
D	4	2+		93.4	
B	6	2		103.7	
D	3	2		93.4	
F	3	2		85.6	
F	6	2	2.0	85.6	91.4
E	6	2		97.6	
C	3	2		87.0	
F	5	1		85.6	

Implementation score	Mean score	Levels of use	Mean score
79		IVA	
82		IVA	
83		IVA	
61	71.8	III	IVA
83		IVA	
43		III	
78		IVA	
43		III	
35		III	
82		IVA	
63	50.7	III	III
34		III	
31		III	
40		III	
38		III	
41		III	
37		III	
98		IVB	
49	44.7	III	III
46		III	
27		III	
22		III	
23		II	
19		I	
23		II	
24		II	
16	18.1	II	II
16		II	
23		II	
6		0	

school climate, were low implementers of the educational ideas presented and were identified as being at the level of preparation. In contrast, Group 1 teachers, operating at a high psychological level and in an "open" school climate, were seen to implement ideas at a rate four times greater than Group 4 teachers, and were identified as being at the routine level of use. In effect, the main findings of this study serve to indicate that the more open and democratic the school climate, and the more self-actualising the members of the teaching staff, the more positive will be their effect on the process of use.

Discussion

For clarity, each of the factors related to use (i.e., psychological state and climate) are discussed in separate sections. Although the results from this study point to a stronger effect for the teachers' psychological state than the climate of the school, in practice these factors are inseparable— it is the total effect on the process of use that is important. In short, a positive climate evolved by positive people equals effective use.

The Psychological State of the Individual Teacher in Relation to the Use of Educational Ideas. A major conclusion of the study was that the more self-actualising the teacher, the greater the use of educational ideas. We have already seen that Group 1 teachers operating at a high psychological level of self-actualisation use educational ideas at a rate four times greater than the Group 4 teachers, who were operating at the low level of psychological safety. What this means to each of the four identified groups of teachers is now briefly discussed.

First, the mean implementation score of Group 1 teachers, at psychological levels 4 and 5, was a high 71.8, and overall use was at the routine level. Those teachers were perceived to be striving to achieve their inherent potential. They were happy in their work, tolerant, and supportive of their professional colleagues. Not trapped by their own self-concept, they displayed the qualities of self-understanding and self-acceptance. They did not feel unduly pressured by the expectations of external forces. In their minds, autonomy and creativity was equated. Opportunity for professional growth was seen as a basic requisite, and the importance of attendance at inservice courses was stressed. Their energy was oriented toward growth, rather than seeking possible impediments to it. The introduction of these new ideas was perceived as a challenge, and they strove to achieve certain goals they identified as being worthwhile.

The mean implementation score of Group 2 teachers, at psychological level 3+, was significantly lower, 50.7, and overall level of use was assessed at the mechanical level. These teachers were open and active in their acceptance of the ideas being introduced, but were more prone to the pressures of conformity than Group 1. In some cases, they were identified as being held back from a state of self-actualisation by the organisational climate. The case of teacher C1 illustrates this position. He took great interest in staff development programmes and was open and progressive in his orientation. Yet, the environment in which he was placed was too restrictive. He felt at odds with the educational philosophy of the head and found her behaviour too dogmatic. This teacher would have thrived in the stimulating environment of School A.

Group 3 teachers, at psychological level 3, mean implementation score 44.7, were also assessed at the mechanical level of use. These teachers were relatively happy in their work. They felt a sense of belonging to the staff group as a whole or had established themselves as a member of a particular reference group. Difficulty, however, was experienced in breaking routine and ritualised classroom practice to allow for the introduction of these ideas. Such a finding led Joyce et al. (1983) to label this group "passive consumers."

The orientation of Group 4 teachers, at psychological levels 2 and 1, was quite different. That the introduction of educational ideas was viewed as a threat is mirrored in their low implementation score, 18.1, and their being assessed at the level of preparation. At this level, there was a clear "motivation maintenance conflict" (Maslow 1962). The behaviour of these individuals was incompatible with that required for satisfying higher level needs. Such conflict resulted in their feeling isolated, ambivalent about their work, inconsistent in their patterns, depressed from time to time, and confused about their own confidence.

In sum, the motivational level of Group 1 teachers allowed them to generate considerable energy for themselves. Group 2 teachers became easily involved in the activities, while Group 3 teachers needed stimulating into activity. Group 4 teachers were not only difficult to involve, but they also consumed energy by weakening organisational spirit.

School Climate in Relation to the Use of Educational Ideas. The conclusion that the process of use is considerably facilitated by an open, democratic school climate is based on evidence contained in Figures 3.5 and 3.6. In Figure 3.5, the average implementation score for Group 1 teachers, operating in a mean climate rating of 105.1, was 4 times greater than the average implementation score for Group 4 teachers, who worked in a mean climate rating of 91.4.

In Figure 3.6, the individual school's climate score is ranked and compared with the average implementation score for its teachers. The comparison suggests a positive link between climate and implementation

Figure 3.6
Comparison of Individual Schools' Climate Scores with the Average Implementation Score for Teachers Involved in the Inservice Course (rankings for both scores in parentheses)

School	Climate Score	Average Implementation Score for Teachers involved in Inservice course
A	116.3 (1)	61.3 (1)
B	103.7 (2)	37.0 (5)
E	97.6 (3)	58.5 (2)
D	93.4 (4)	40.2 (4)
C	87.0 (5)	48.7 (3)
F	85.6 (6)	34.0 (6)

(with the exception of School B, which had a comparatively low average implementation score for its climate rating, and School C, where the implementation score was comparatively high). The explanation for School B is found in the pressure applied by a new and "forward-looking" head teacher on an established and conservative staff to provide a "good account" of the school to the researcher. The implementation score for School C was inflated by the individual score of teacher C1, whose case we have already considered.

This analysis supports the conclusion that the school's climate, as well as a teacher's psychological state, influences the process of use. Other data collected for the study suggest that two facets of the school's organisation seemed to make the difference: the role of the head of the school and a consensus (or not) on goals.

The role of the head is crucial. Heads in the schools studied tended to project themselves as highly democratic leaders, whereas staff in most of the schools felt their power to be limited in the formation of school policy. In all schools, the heads identified their role as one of enabling the teachers to take the lead in the introduction of the ideas involved and of supporting them throughout the process of use. In reality, only the heads of Schools A, B, and E were perceived as providing such support, insofar as they became actively involved in innovation and sought to foster a spirit of experimentation. In School C, the head was dogmatic in behaviour and reluctant to hand over authority. In Schools D and F, heads tended to adopt a low profile. In general, there is a need for positive endorsement on the part of the head; passive support does not facilitate use or help teachers to achieve their goals. In this study, the support members of staff perceived as being given to them by the head had a significant effect on the innovativeness of the school system.

It is now well established that effective schools purposefully link goals, curriculum, and evaluation. Few teachers in this sample, outside of School A, acknowledged any commitment to professional norms or goals. Teachers were still carrying out their roles in highly personal ways that were not congruent with a school's stated objectives. Not only do goals differ through varying perceptions of pupils' needs or differing educational philosophies, but the position is also made more complex by goals' being stated at a fairly high level of abstraction.

The process of achieving goals is far from understood, but it would seem obvious that a common culture for teaching can only emerge from an open debate about ends and means. Only Schools A and B had developed formal procedures to facilitate communication. In these two schools, staff were used to working together in groups to examine aspects of the curriculum. The teachers worked in climates where critical and constructive scrutiny of each others' practices and ideas were the norm. Heads often took classes to allow the teachers to work beside each other. In the remaining schools, opportunities for such discussion were limited. While many teachers spoke of the introduction of the ideas as having brought them into more contact with colleagues and having increased their responsiveness to schoolwide considerations, they simply lacked the necessary skills to work collaboratively.

In light of all the data, it seems that the following factors related to school climate had a beneficial effect on the process of use:

1. The self-determination of the organisation provides it with capacity to deal with its environment.

2. Heads who are perceived as supportive figures are actively involved in the use process.

3. A high degree of internal communication provides the opportunities for staff to engage in frequent discussions about an innovation (thus increasing the possibility of its successful implementation).

4. Time and opportunity are provided for observation of others and for reflection of classroom practice.

5. Staff collaboration is a continuous process. In schools where a full contribution is expected from everyone, teachers find themselves developing policies and bearing some responsibility for their implementation.

To summarize, this small-scale study has suggested that differences in implementation scores and levels of use may be explained not only on the basis of the teacher's individual interpretation and personal preference, but also on the basis of organisational climate. The use of educational ideas is an expression of the "self" and the "environment." The combination of these factors presents the individual with a mixture of opportunities and difficulties in varying proportions. The perfect combination would seem to lie in an open, democratic climate evolved by self-actualising people.

Toward the Integration of Teacher Development and School Improvement

The argument in the first part of the chapter was that more research is needed that links together the various elements in the teacher development/school improvement research tradition and uses an eclectic methodology. In particular, we need studies that are theory driven, build on wholistic designs, conscientiously search for empirical and practitioner support, and are modified in the light of that experience. In continuing to argue for increasing catholicism in substance and method, three implications for teacher development and school improvement that arise out of the research study just described are now considered.

Specific and General Motivation

As has already been suggested, the difference in implementation scores noted in the study was due to the specific motivation of the individual teacher and the general motivation provided by the school climate. This finding extends the work of researchers (such as Guskey 1986) who argue that teacher commitment follows the achieving of competence. The issue is more complex than that. Change in teacher behaviour is the result of a dialectic between specific and general motivation, between individual motivation and school climate. In the terms of our study, teachers at the level of self-actualisation are stimulated by energising schools, and in turn, add to the stimulation already present. However, a teacher at the level of psychological safety would be terribly threatened by such an energising environment. At the other extreme, a self-actualising individual who runs into a relatively dormant environment is likely to feel frustrated but would still maintain a sense of control over that environment.

Obviously, the organisational climate must strive to accommodate teachers of differing psychological states, while seeking to pull individuals up to higher psychological levels. The reinforcement of such internal factors as self-knowledge and self-determination are important in motivating teachers to expend more effort and make better use of their abilities. Such reinforcement is more likely to occur in a climate that supports self-actualisation than in a climate dominated by a survival orientation.

School Improvement and Effectiveness

Research into the areas of school effectiveness and school improvement are becoming increasingly convergent and more sophisticated and specific in identifying the characteristics of schools that lend themselves to the successful use of educational ideas (Hopkins 1990). These characteristics, however, cannot be imposed on the school by edict; they have to be evolved by the school itself. As the findings of this study indicate, if progress is to be made beyond the mechanical level of use, the concern must be with the creation of a school that acts as a place where teachers as well as students learn. The characteristics of the effective school provide indications of the type of environments required. The problem is how to get there. What strategies can be used to provide support for teachers in professional development, as well as in changing the school ethos?

Our current work on School Development Plans (Hargreaves et al. 1989) and Teacher Appraisal (Bollington et al. 1990) in England and Wales may provide one answer. We have found that setting tangible, concrete, and achievable targets for schools and teachers, in the context of action plans that detail timelines and resources, can have a dramatic effect on the climate of the school and the lives of teachers. An atmosphere of collaboration is engendered by work on the priority areas identified in the plan; an emerging critical climate develops with the classroom observation phase of teacher appraisal; and a sense of efficacy grows among individual teachers as the resolution of individual targets provides a direction for and results in professional growth. Although this is not the case in every school we have visited, the pattern is sufficiently well established to suggest that the combination of these strategies can powerfully affect school climate and teacher efficacy in quite short spaces of time.

Implementation and Staff Development

The majority of teachers in this study were at the mechanical level of uses. Borrowing Bussis et al.'s (1976) terminology, teachers were operating at the "surface level," that is, they were emulating techniques and skills without understanding the principles and rationale of the change. Most of the changes we saw were only modifications of practice—the majority of staff were not teaching in a way that was dictated by the methodological structure of the ideas presented on the inservice course.

Only 20 percent of the teachers in this sample were seen to possess an adequate grasp of the details of the curriculum innovation. To progress to further levels of use, teachers must be familiar with the subject both in terms of its propositional content and its methodological structure. Lack of such knowledge can account for the phenomenon of teachers' claiming to use the practice, but, in reality, turning out not to be using it in any recognisable form. Thus, for genuine change to occur, teachers need support in the actual process of use.

There are obvious implications here for implementation and staff development. Implementation planning needs to focus on knowledge and skill acquisition over time, and the consequent staff development programs must be sophisticated enough and sufficiently well resourced to promote and support these changes. In the light of this study, the current policy of devolving responsibility and resources for staff development to the school level presents both opportunities and pitfalls. On the one hand, schools obviously have more flexibility to tailor their staff development programs in support of specific, agreed-on innovations. On the other hand, in schools with poor climates, the possibilities for successful innovation are limited unless the school climate itself becomes the object of the staff development programme. This is difficult for a school to achieve by itself. Substantial external support is consequently needed, not only to support teachers in the acquisition of new knowledge and practices, but also in the effort to transform the culture of the school.

* * *

Strategies for powerful change are required that restructure and integrate teacher development and school improvement (Fullan 1988). Educational ideas must be differentially introduced into schools on the foundation of clarity of the concepts being used, an understanding of the processes involved, and an understanding of the school climate and psychological state of the individual teacher. Successful use also requires teachers to relate their educational aims to a particular curriculum innovation and to carry out a detailed and systematic analysis of their inservice needs. This proposal fits well with our current research and development work on school development plans and teacher appraisal. Development planning at the school and workgroup levels and target setting for individual teachers allow for both this differentiation and for the focus of the change to be tailored to school and individual teacher need.

As we move into the '90s, we need to build on what we have learned in the previous decade and to become bolder and more eclectic in our research designs and developmental strategies. We cannot afford to tinker with individual variables or with isolated approaches. The game is too serious for that. We now know a great deal about the conditions that make for high student achievement and what a school is like that is dedicated to the learning of both students and teachers. We need to use this knowledge creatively, sensitively, and humanely to create the vision we now know is possible.

References

Bollen, R., and D. Hopkins. (1987). *School Based Review: Towards a Praxis*. Leuven, Belgium: ACCO.

Bollington R., D. Hopkins, and M. West. (1990). *Teacher Appraisal for Professional Development*. London: Cassells.

Brophy, J., and T. Good. (1986). "Teacher Behavior and Student Achievement." In *Handbook of Research on Teaching*, edited by M. Wittrock. New York: MacMillan.

Bussis, A., E. Chittenden, and M. Amarel. (1976). *Beyond Surface Curriculum*. Boulder, Colo.: Westview Press.

Clark, D.L., L.S. Lotto, and T.A. Astuto. (1984). "Elementary Schools and School Improvement: A Comparative Analysis of Two Lines of Inquiry." *Educational Administration Quarterly* 20, 3: 41-68.

Evans, M. (1986). "An Investigation into Those Factors Affecting the Use of Educational Ideas Following an Inservice Course." M.Ed. thesis, University of Wales.

Evans, M., and D. Hopkins. (1988). "School Climate and the Psychological State of the Individual Teacher as Factors Affecting the use of Educational Ideas Following an Inservice Course." *British Educational Research Journal* 14, 3: 211-230.

Fox, R., and R. Schmuck. (1975). *Diagnosing Professional Climates of Schools*. Fairfax, Va.: Learning Resources Corp.

Fullan, M. (1982). *The Meaning of Educational Change*. Toronto: OISE Press.

Fullan, M. (1985). "Change Processes and Strategies at the Local Level." *Elementary School Journal* 85: 391-421.

Fullan, M. (1988). "Change Processes in Secondary Schools: Towards a More Fundamental Agenda." Faculty of Education, University of Toronto.

Fullan, M., R. Bennett, and C. Rolheiser-Bennett. (April 1989). "Linking Classroom and School Improvement" Invited Address, annual meeting of the American Educational Research Association, San Francisco.

Georgiades, N.J. (1967). "A Study of Attitudes of Teachers to Educational Innovation." M. Phil. dissertation, University of London.

Good, T. (January 1989). "Using Classroom and School Research to Professionalize Teaching." Keynote Address, International Congress for Effective Schools, in Rotterdam.

Gregorc, A.F. (1982). *An Adult's Guide to Style*. Maynard, Mass.: Gabriel Systems Inc.

Guskey, T. (1986). "Staff Development and the Process of Teacher Change." *Educational Researcher* 15, 5: 5-12.

Hall, G.E., S.F. Loucks, W.L. Rutherford, and B.W. Newlove. (1975). "Levels of use of the innovation: a Framework for Analysing Innovation Adaption." *Journal of Teacher Education* 26: 52-56.

Hall, G.E., and S.F. Loucks. (1977). "A Developmental Model for Determining Whether the Treatment is Actually Implemented." *American Research Journal* 14: 236-276.

Halpin, A.W., and D.B. Croft. (1963). *The Organizational Climate of Schools Chicago.* Midwest Administration Center: University of Chicago.

Hargreaves, D., D. Hopkins, M. Leask, J. Connelly, and P. Robinson. (1989). *Planning for School Development.* London: DES, HMSO.

Hopkins, D. (1987). *Improving the Quality of Schooling.* Lewes, East Sussex: Falmer Press.

Hopkins, D. (1988). *Doing School Based Review.* Leuven, Belgium: ACCO.

Hopkins, D. (1990) "The International School Improvement Project and Effective Schooling: Towards a Synthesis." *School Organisation* 10, 1: in press.

Huberman, M, and M. Miles. (1984). *Innovation Up Close.* New York: Plenum Press.

Joyce, B., and B. Showers. (1980). "Improving Inservice Training; the Messages of Research." *Educational Leadership* 37, 5: 379-385.

Joyce, B., and M. McKibbin. (1982). "Teacher Growth States and School Environments." *Educational Leadership* 40, 2: 36-41.

Joyce, B., R.H. Hersh, and M. McKibbin. (1983). *The Structure of School Improvement.* New York: Longman.

Joyce, B., and M. Weil. (1986). *Models of Teaching,* 3rd ed. Englewood Cliffs, N.J.: Prentice Hall.

Joyce, B., and B. Showers. (1988). *Student Achievement Through Staff Development.* New York: Longman.

Loucks, S.F., B.V. Newlove, and G.E. Hall. (1976). *Measuring Levels of Use of the Innovation: A Manual for Trainers, Interviewers, and Raters.* Austin: Research and Development Center for Teacher Education, University of Texas.

Loucks, S., ed. (1983). "Ensuring Success." *Educational Leadership* 41, 3.

Loucks-Horsley S., and D. Crandall. (1986). *The External Support System Profile.* Leuven, Belgium: ACCO.

Maslow, A.H. (1962). *Towards a Psychology of Being.* New York: Van Nostrand.

McKibbin, M., and B. Joyce. (1980). "Psychological States and Staff Development. Teacher Development, Personal and Professional Growth." *Theory into Practice* 19: 248-255.

Miles, M.B. (1975). "Planned Change and Organizational Health." In *Managing Change in Educational Organizations,* edited by J.V. Baldridge and T. Deal. Berkeley: McCutchan.

Mortimore, P., P. Sammons, L. Stoll, D. Lewis, and R. Ecob. (1988). *School Matters: The Junior Years.* London: Open Books.

Purkey, S.C., and M.S. Smith. (1982). "Too Soon to Cheer? Synthesis of Research on Effective Schools." *Educational Leadership* 40, 3: 64-69.

Reynolds, D. (1985). *Studying School Effectiveness.* Lewes, East Sussex: Falmer Press.

Rudduck, J., and D. Hopkins. (1985). *Research as a Basis for Teaching.* London: Heinemann.

Rutter, M., B. Maughan, P. Mortimore, J. Ouston, and A. Smith. (1979). *Fifteen Thousand Hours: Secondary Schools and Their Effects on Children.* Cambridge, Mass.: Harvard University Press.

Scheerens, J. (1989). "Process Indicators of School Functioning." Department of Education, University of Twente, Netherlands (mimeo).

Schon, D. (1983). *The Reflective Practitioner.* San Francisco: Jossey-Bass.

Stego, E., K. Gielen, R. Glatter, and S. Hord. (n.d.). *The Role of School Leaders in School Improvement.* Leuven, Belgium: ACCO.

Stenhouse, L. (1975). *An Introduction to Curriculum Research and Development.* London: Heinemann.

Stenhouse, L. (1983). *Authority, Emancipation and Education.* London: Heinemann.

Telford, D. (1970). "Some Progressive and Traditional Ideas in Junior School Education: An Investigation into the Relationship Between the Attitudes and Practices of Junior School Teachers." M.Ed. thesis, University of Newcastle upon Tyne, 1970.

Van Velzen, W., M. Miles, M. Ekholm, U. Hameyer, and B. Robin. (1985). *Making School Improvement Work.* Leuven, Belgium: ACCO.

Wideen, M., and I. Andrews. (1987). *Staff Development for School Improvement.* Lewes, East Sussex: Falmer Press.

Wittrock, M. (1986). *Handbook of Research on Teaching,* 3rd ed. New York: MacMillan.

PART II
Changing Roles of the Shareholders in North America

4

The Principal's Role in Teacher Development

Kenneth A. Leithwood

A leader's vision is "the grain of sand in the oyster, not the pearl"
(Murphy 1988, p. 650)

rincipals vary widely in how they conceive of their role. These variations are evident in the four different focuses identified in research on principals' styles or patterns of practice (Blumberg and Greenfield 1980, Hall et al. 1984, Leithwood and Montgomery 1986, Salley et al. 1978): an administration or plant manager focus; an interpersonal relations or climate focus; a program focus; and a student development focus. The first two patterns function primarily to maintain the school and appear to capture the practices of the majority of principals, at present (e.g., Morris et al. 1982, Trider and Leithwood 1988). The latter two patterns are less common and appear to be relatively effective in improving the school's contribution to student outcomes valued in most North American schools. These two patterns also correspond to what is usually meant by the term "instructional leadership."

Kenneth A. Leithwood is Professor and Head, Centre for Principal Development, The Ontario Institute for Studies in Education, Ontario, Canada.

Between 1975 and 1988, at least 65 original empirical studies in the English language have provided evidence for the claim that instructional leadership is an achievable expectation for principals (Leithwood 1988). These studies, as a whole, also provide detailed descriptions of what such leadership looks like in practice. Despite such evidence, some principals (and researchers; e.g., Gersten et al. 1982, Rallis and Highsmith 1986) continue to dispute the viability of an instructional leadership role for the principal, including teacher development, which is arguably the most central function of instructional leadership. Even principals who acknowledge their responsibility to foster teacher development often claim that it is not a function they feel capable of performing well.

To a significant degree, these feelings of inadequacy have two roots: an unclear image of what teacher development looks like, and uncertainty about just how a principal might help foster such development, given the usual job demands. This chapter attempts to shed light on each of these matters. The first section draws on evidence from three distinct areas of research to build a multidimensional description of teacher development. This description is offered to principals as an aid in reflecting upon, and possibly making more explicit and robust, their own views of such development. The second section of the chapter provides guidelines that principals may find useful in shaping their efforts to help teachers develop.

Dimensions and Stages of Teacher Development

Figure 4.1 summarizes three dimensions of teacher development that principals can influence: development of professional expertise, psychological development, and career cycle development. Each of these dimensions reflects quite different lines of inquiry about teacher development.

Development of Professional Expertise

The dimension of teacher development with the most obvious consequences for classroom, school, and district improvement is identified in Figure 4.1 as "Development of Professional Expertise." It is through such expertise that teachers contribute directly to the growth of students (amount learned, range of outcomes achieved, and ranges of students who benefit from instruction). Six stages of development are included in this dimension. Stages 1 through 4 are concerned with teachers' classroom responsibilities; Stages 5 and 6 explicitly address the out-of-classroom and out-of-school roles of the "mature" teacher. Each of the stages beyond the first includes expertise acquired in previous stages. Furthermore, it seems likely that the seeds of expertise in higher stages will begin to develop

Figure 4.1: Interrelated Dimensions of Teacher Development

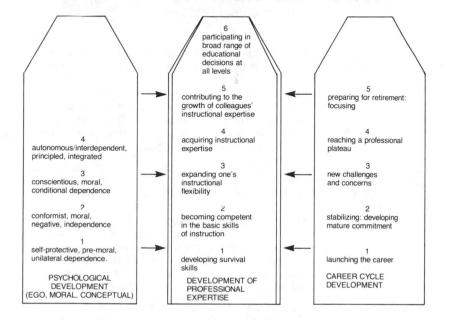

quite early, given appropriate, formative experiences. Hence, this conception of growth does not imply restricting teacher experiences only to those that will prepare them for their next stage of development. Some preparation for stage 6 practices might well begin during a teacher's initial entry into the role.

Figure 4.2 illustrates, in more detail, aspects of professional expertise likely to be a part of each of the six stages. While others might describe the aspect of expertise in each of these stages differently, there is at least good warrant for the substance of Figure 4.2. Stages 1 to 4 are based on an image of effective classroom instruction as requiring a large repertoire of instructional techniques; such a repertoire is reflected, for example, in Joyce and Weil's (1986) 23 models of teaching, organized into four "families" or categories. Expertise, in these terms, increases as teachers acquire greater skill in the application of a given teaching model and as an increasing number of such models are mastered. Teaching, however, involves more than the unthinking application of such models, although "automaticity" is an important characteristic of expertise in most areas of human endeavour.

Figure 4.2
Development of Competence in the "Technology" of
Educational Practice

1. Developing Survival Skills	• Partially developed classroom management skills; • Knowledge about and limited skill in use of several teaching models; • No conscious reflection on choice of model; • Student assessment is primarily summative and carried out, using limited techniques, in response to external demands (e.g., reporting to parents); may be poor link between the focus of assessment and instructional goal.
2. Becoming Competent In The Basic Skills of Instruction	• Well-developed classroom management skills; • Well-developed skill in use of several teaching models; • Habitual application through trial and error, of certain teaching models for particular parts of curriculum; • Student assessment begins to reflect formative purposes, although techniques are not well suited to such purposes; focus of assessment linked to instructional goals easiest to measure.
3. Expanding One's Instructional Flexibility	• Automatized classroom management skills; • Growing awareness of need for and existence of other teaching models and initial efforts to expand repertoire and experiment with application of new models; • Choice of teaching model from expanded repertoire influenced most by interest in providing variety to maintain student interest; • Student assessment carried out for both formative and summative purposes; repertoire of techniques is beginning to match purposes; focus of assessment covers significant range of instructional goals.

Along with Joyce and Weil (1986), Darling-Hammond et al. (1983), Bach-arach et al. (1987), Shavelson (1973; 1976), and others point out that deciding which model or technique to apply in a particular situation is central to instructional expertise. As teachers develop, their choice of models is based on increasingly defensible criteria (e.g., instructional ob-jectives vs. need for variety) and diagnosis of the instructional needs of students.

4. Acquiring Instructional Expertise	• Classroom management integrated with program; little attention required to classroom management as an independent issue; • Skill in application of a broad repertoire of teaching models; • Instructional goals, student learning styles, content to be covered, as well as the maintenance of student interests used as criteria for choice of teaching model; • Student assessment is carried out for both formative and summative purposes, using a wide array of techniques; program decisions are informed by assessment, and the focus of assessment is directly linked to the full array of instructional goals.
5. Contributing To The Growth of Colleagues' Instructional Expertise	• Has high levels of expertise in classroom instructional performance; • Reflective about own competence and choices and the fundamental beliefs and values on which they are based; • Able to assist other teachers in acquiring instructional expertise through either planned learning experiences, such as mentoring, or more formal experiences, such as inservice education and coaching programs.
6. Participating in a Broad Array of Educational Decisions at all Levels of the Education System	• Is committed to the goal of school improvement; • Accepts responsibility for fostering that goal through any legitimate opportunity; • Able to exercise leadership, both formal and informal, with groups of adults inside and outside the school; • Has a broad framework from which to understand the relationships among decisions at many different levels in the education system; • Is well informed about policies at many different levels in the education system.

While the notion of teacher-as-decision-maker appropriately recognizes the contingent nature of the classroom tasks routinely faced by teachers, it is not sufficiently comprehensive to encompass the unanticipated, nonroutine, "swampy" problems encountered in the classroom from time to time. Schon (1983) depicts the way in which experienced professionals in many domains think about and eventually resolve such problems. This involves a process of reflecting in action as well as a process of reflecting on action in which the unique attributes of the setting are carefully weighed and the professional's repertoire is adapted in response to such uniqueness.

Stages 5 and 6 acknowledge the roles of teachers in school improvement and educational decisions beyond the classroom and school. While such roles are by no means new, they have received greater attention recently. Peer coaching (Brandt 1987, Garmston 1987) and mentoring (Gray and Gray 1985, Wagner 1985) strategies, for example, assume those aspects of expertise identified in Stage 5, as do many of the recent career ladder programs that place teachers in the role of evaluators (e.g., Peterson and Mitchell 1985). Stage 6 conceptualizes the mature teacher as one who plays a formal or informal leadership role, in a variety of contexts both inside and outside the classroom and school. Teachers, according to this view, share in the responsibility for most decisions that directly or indirectly touch on students' experiences. Such a view is consistent with recent proposals for reshaping teacher education (e.g., Fullan and Connelly 1987) and for "empowering" teachers (e.g., Maeroff 1988) in the process.

Psychological Development

As outlined in Figure 4.1, "Psychological Development" is a synthesis of three distinct and independently substantial strands of psychological stage theory: Loevinger's (1966) seven-stage theory of ego development, Kohlberg's (1970) six-stage theory of moral development, and Hunt and associates' (1966) four-stage theory of conceptual development. These three strands of psychological development are both conceptually and empirically related (Sullivan, McCullough, and Stager 1970). The synthesis provided by Figure 4.1 is for heuristic purposes. It is a rough approximation of how the three strands might intersect in real time.

Generally, ego development occurs as a person strives to master, integrate, and otherwise make sense of experience. Greater ego maturity is associated with a more complex and better differentiated understanding of one's self in relation to others. Moral development occurs as the basis on which one's views of rightness and goodness shift from a basis of personal preference toward a basis of universal ethical principles. Finally, conceptual development occurs as one moves toward greater differentiation and integration of concepts—the growth from concrete toward more abstract thought processes.

Viewing the three strands of psychological development together, as in Figure 4.1, provides descriptions of teachers in various stages of growth. A "Stage 1" teacher has an overly simplistic view of the world and a tendency to see choices as black or white. Such a teacher believes strongly in rules and roles, views authority as the highest good, and sees most questions as having one answer. Stage 1 teachers discourage divergent thinking and reward conformity and rote learning (Oja 1979). Their classrooms are highly teacher directed.

Stage 2 teachers (conformists) are especially susceptible to the expectations of others. Their wish is to be like their peers, and they may hold stereotyped, distrustful views of those "outside" their immediate group. The classrooms of conformist teachers are what we think of as "conventional." Rules are explicit, and students are expected to adhere to such rules without much regard for individual differences or contingencies that might justify exceptions to the rules.

At the third stage of psychological development (conscientious), teachers have become much more self-aware and have developed an appreciation for multiple possibilities in situations (e.g., multiple explanations for student behaviour). Rules are internalized and applied with an appreciation for the need for exceptions to the rules, given the circumstances. Teachers at this stage are future oriented and achievement oriented: Their classrooms are the product of rational planning and a concern for good interpersonal communication.

At the highest stages of psychological development, teachers are inner directed but appreciate the interdependent nature of relationships in a social setting such as a classroom. In addition, according to Oja and Pine (1981), these teachers have achieved more of a synthesis in their classrooms between an emphasis on achievement and an interpersonal orientation, and are not only able to view a situation from multiple perspectives but are also able to synthesize such perspectives. Teachers at the highest stage understand the reasons behind rules and so can be wiser in their application: They maintain a broad perspective and are able to cope with inner conflicts as well as conflicting needs and duties. The classrooms of these teachers are controlled in collaboration with students, and the emphasis is on meaningful learning, creativity, and flexibility. Being more cognitively complex themselves, teachers at this stage encourage more complex functioning in their students (Hunt 1966, Oja 1979).

Career Cycle Development

The dimension called "Career Cycle Development" in Figure 4.1 views teachers' careers from a life-cycle perspective. Five stages of development have been derived primarily from recent research by Huberman (1988) and Sikes, Measor, and Woods (1985): The latter work adopted Levinson et al.'s (1978) conceptualization of life development as a framework.

Huberman and Sikes et al. carried out their research with secondary school teachers in Switzerland and Great Britain, respectively. Nevertheless, their results appear to be sufficiently similar and consistent with other research (e.g., Ball and Goodson 1985) to warrant tentative generalization to other contexts and teaching assignments in the modified form described in Figure 4.1.

Our main interest in teachers' career cycle development is how it interacts with the development of professional expertise; more particularly, we want to know what career experiences, at each stage, seem likely to foster or detract from the development of professional expertise.

Stage 1, "Launching the Career," encompasses up to the first several years of the teacher's classroom responsibilities. Sikes et al. (1985) suggest that most teachers at this stage experience a "reality shock in coming to grips with problems of disciplining and motivating students"—as well as some degree of culture shock, the amount depending on the values and perspectives of staff in their school. Nevertheless, Huberman's (1988) data suggest that experiences at this stage are perceived by some teachers as "easy" and by others as "painful." Conditions giving rise to perceptions of easy beginnings include positive relationships with students, "manageable" students, a sense of instructional mastery, and initial enthusiasm. Painful beginnings are associated with role overload, anxiety, difficult pupils, heavy time investment, close monitoring, and feelings of isolation in the school. For those who experience such pain, there may be a protracted period of trial and error in an effort to cope with such problems.

"Stabilizing," the second career cycle stage, often coincides with receiving a permanent contract and making a deliberate commitment to the profession. This stage is characterized by feeling at ease in the classroom, mastery of a basic repertoire of instructional techniques, and being able to select appropriate methods and materials in light of student abilities and interests. Furthermore, at this stage, teachers act more independently, are less intimidated by supervisors, and feel reasonably well integrated into a group of peers. Some teachers at this stage begin to seek greater responsibility through promotion or participation in change efforts.

The stage following stabilization may take several forms. In the main, teachers at this stage tend to be between the ages of 30 and 40. As Sikes et al. (1985) point out, their experience is substantial by this point, as is their physical and intellectual energy. For some teachers, such energy is channelled into intense professional effort. Huberman's (1988) study identified a category of teachers at this stage who actively diversify their classroom methods, seek out novel practices, and often look outside their own classrooms for professional stimulation. Another group of teachers at this stage focused their efforts on seeking promotion to administrative roles or appointment to key district or statewide projects. Yet a third group of teachers, also identified by Sikes et al. (1985), reduced their professional commitments. Members of this group sometimes experienced difficult classes and achieved poor results with their students. Building an alternative career was an option pursued by many teachers in this group.

Sikes et al. (1985) estimate the fourth stage, "Reaching a Professional Plateau," to occur between the ages of approximately 40 and 50 to 55. This is a traumatic period for many teachers who, at this stage, are reappraising their successes in all facets of their lives. Their own sense of mortality is accentuated by continually being surrounded by young students and by having, as colleagues, young teachers who may be the same age as their own children. Responses to this stage appear to be of two sorts. One group of teachers stops striving for promotion and simply enjoys teaching. These teachers may become the backbone of the school, the guardians of its traditions. They may enjoy a renewed commitment to school improvement. A second group, however, stagnates. They may become bitter, cynical, and unlikely to be interested in further professional growth.

Depending to a large extent on which of these two responses is adopted at Stage 4, teachers in the final stage, "Preparing For Retirement," may behave in quite different ways. Huberman's (1988) study identified three different patterns of behaviour, each of which involved some type of contraction of professional activity and interest. One pattern of behaviour, "positive focusing," involved an interest in specializing in what one does best. Such specialization might target a grade level, a subject, or a group of students. Teachers adopting this pattern, as Sikes et al. (1985) also found, are concerned centrally with pupil learning, their most compatible peers, and an increasing pursuit of outside interests. A second pattern of behaviour, "defensive focusing," has similar features to the first; however, teachers exhibit a less optimistic and generous attitude toward their past experiences with change, their students, and their colleagues. Finally, Huberman (1988) labels a third pattern of practice "disenchantment." People adopting this pattern are bitter about past experiences with change and the administrators associated with them. They are tired and may become a source of frustration for younger staff.

Guidelines for Principals in Fostering Teacher Development

An explicit, defensible conception of teacher development provides a foundation upon which principals, acting as instructional leaders, can formulate their own approach to teacher development. In this section, four broad guidelines for building this approach are suggested. These guidelines stress the importance of attending to all three dimensions of teacher development and creating school cultures and structures hospitable to such development. Based on assumptions about teachers as adult learners actively involved in bringing meaning to their work, the guidelines stress the importance of understanding teachers' own views of their world. Finally, the guidelines argue that the most helpful teacher development strategies available to principals are to be found among their normal responses to their work environment.

Guideline 1: Treat the Teacher as a Whole Person.

As Figure 4.2 indicates, growth in professional expertise consists of teachers' expanding their instructional repertoires, responding more flexibly to classroom circumstances, and taking responsibility for the welfare and growth, not only of students, but of their professional colleagues. Although the acquisition of knowledge and skill concerning instruction, as well as other educational matters, is an obviously necessary condition for such growth, it is not sufficient. That is, the practice of instructional flexibility depends on at least being able to weigh a variety of alternatives. Many instructional strategies also require the teacher to relinquish exclusive control over classroom activities and to trust students to be task oriented on their own or in groups.

This suggests that a prerequisite to acquiring instructional expertise (Stage 4 of the professional expertise dimension) is growth to at least the middle stages of the psychological development dimension, as depicted in Figure 4.1. Similarly, practices associated with professional expertise at Stages 5 and 6 appear to depend on the ability to synthesize alternatives, mutuality in interpersonal relations, the ability to cope with conflicting needs and duties, and other attributes of functioning at the highest level of psychological development. Indeed, failure to attend to the interdependence of professional expertise and stages of psychological development offers an additional explanation for lack of application in the classroom of skills acquired through training. To this point, the most compelling explanation for this "transfer" problem has been limited to the unique and often overwhelming demands placed on teachers' application of newly acquired skills by their particular classroom contexts (Joyce and Showers 1980).

Typically, staff development efforts (whether by principals or others) do not acknowledge the interdependence of psychological and professional development. While this may be due to ignorance or oversight in some cases, it may also be due to the commonly held view that psychological development is completed by adulthood. That such a view is unwarranted is clear from evidence reported by Harvey (1970) that a large proportion of teachers in his sample were at the lowest level of conceptual development. Oja's (1981) review of similar evidence suggests that teachers typically stabilize in the middle stages of psychological development.

So far, our attention has been limited to the relationship between psychological development and the development of expertise. What of career cycle development? The development of professional expertise seems to have an important relationship with such development. There is, for example, an obvious link between the challenges facing a teacher in the first three stages of his or her career cycle and the expertise to be acquired in the first four stages of development of professional expertise. Indeed, interventions designed to promote the development of such professional expertise seem likely to ensure positive career cycle development.

Principals have an opportunity to prevent painful beginnings. They are preventable through such interventions as realistic classroom assignments in combination with ongoing assistance in the development of classroom management skills, provision of a supportive mentor close at hand, and the avoidance of heavy-handed supervision practices. On the other hand, failure to provide opportunities for the development of professional expertise may well lead to professional disaffection when teachers are seeking new challenges and have new concerns. Providing opportunities to master an expanded, flexible repertoire of instruction techniques seems an effective way of ensuring that teachers experience a sense of professional self-fulfillment during this third stage in their career cycle.

A direct relationship appears also to exist between the career cycle stage "Reaching a Professional Plateau" and Stages 5 and 6 in the development of professional expertise. A significant part of the explanation for teachers perceiving themselves to be at a plateau is the failure, in many schools and school systems, to permit teachers greater scope to know and relate to multiple classrooms—to see and work with other teachers and their classrooms. Such challenges respond to the teacher's readiness to accept more responsibility and allow the school and school system to benefit from their accumulated expertise. Teachers who have experienced such challenges seem likely to enter their final career cycle stage either still in an expansionary frame of mind or at least as "positive focusers," to use Huberman's (1988) term.

In brief, then, principals should be sensitive to all three development dimensions and seek to help teachers develop these dimensions in a parallel, interdependent fashion.

Guideline 2: Establish a School Culture Based on Norms of Technical Collaboration and Professional Inquiry.

The reason teachers often appear to stabilize in the middle stages of psychological development is inadequate stimulation, not an innate shortcoming (Sprinthall and Theis-Sprinthall 1983). Such is the case with professional expertise, as well. Evidence suggests that the typical school culture and its organizational structures may be responsible, in part, for stifling teacher development (for this discussion, "culture" includes the underlying assumption, norms, beliefs, and values that guide behaviour).

Typical school cultures are characterized by informal norms of autonomy and isolation for teachers (Lortie 1973), as well as entrenched routines and regularities (Leiberman and Miller 1986, Sarason 1971). Indeed, some aspects of these cultures have been dubbed sacred (Corbett, Fireston, and Rossman 1987) and, as a result, are highly resistant to change. Teachers' individual, personal beliefs about the needs of students are far stronger influences on their classroom practices than other potential influences—for example, the views of their peers or principals, or prescriptions contained in curriculum policies (Leithwood, Ross, and Montgomery 1982). Such autonomy and isolation limit the stimulation for further development to what is possible through private and unguided reflections on what one reads and experiences outside the classroom and one's own informal classroom experiments. It is unlikely that such stimulation will create the sort of dissonance or challenge to one's ways of thinking that appears necessary to foster movement from one stage of psychological development to another. Nor would such stimulation provide the conditions, outlined, for example, by Joyce and Showers (1980), for the successful application of new instructional skills to one's classroom. Little (1981, 1985), on the other hand, found that staff development efforts were most successful where a norm of collegiality and experimentation existed.

Principals' teacher development strategies seem most likely to be successful within a school culture in which teachers are encouraged to consciously reflect on their own practices (Oberg and Field 1986), to share ideas about their instruction, and to try out new techniques in the classroom. Principals need to develop norms of reflection through the substance of their own communication with teachers and the example of their own teaching. Principals also need to take specific actions to foster norms of collaboration. As Rosenholtz points out, "Norms of collaboration don't simply just happen. They do not spring spontaneously out of teachers' mutual respect and concern for each other (in press, p. 44)." Rosenholtz identifies four conditions that influence the extent to which teachers are likely to engage in technical collaboration: teachers' certainty about their own instructional competence, and hence, self-esteem; shared teaching goals; involvement in the school's technical decisions; and team teaching opportunities that create the need to plan and carry out instruction with colleagues.

This guideline suggests, in sum, that principals look below the surface features of their schools—at how teachers are treated and what beliefs, norms, and values they share—and redesign their schools as learning environments for teachers as well as for students.

Guideline 3: Carefully Diagnose the Starting Points for Teacher Development.

Teachers are not passive recipients of principals' strategies "to develop them." Adopting the view of contemporary cognitive psychology (e.g., Calfee 1981, Schuell 1986), particularly as it has been applied to research on teacher thinking (e.g., Clark and Peterson 1986), teachers actively strive to accomplish implicit or explicit goals they hold to be personally important in their work. For example, when teachers judge a new form of instruction introduced to them by their principal as potentially helpful in accomplishing such goals, they attempt to understand and assess that new form of instruction. The primary resources teachers use to develop such understanding are what they already know (as contained in their long-term memory). Understanding develops as matches are made between the new form of instruction and what they already know (e.g., "Oh! 'Direct Instruction' means the traditional instruction I was taught in teachers' college."); as existing knowledge structures are modified to accommodate novel aspects of the new form of instruction (e.g., "Ah! 'Cooperative Learning' just means grouping with different rules than I have used."); and as links are established among previously unconnected pieces of information in the teacher's memory (e.g., "I think 'mastery learning' is a combination of what I call behavioral objectives, criterion-referenced testing, and remedial teaching."). These brief examples make clear that successful development strategies build on a careful diagnosis of the relevant knowledge already possessed by teachers. Such strategies will assist teachers to identify relevant aspects of what they already know and to use that knowledge as an instrument for giving meaning to new practices they may wish to understand and use better.

The formal mechanism most obviously available to principals for carrying out this diagnosis is teacher evaluation. Virtually all principals spend considerable time doing it. Nevertheless, such evaluation as it is normally practised rarely results in useful diagnostic information and generally appears to have little influence on teacher development (Lawton et al. 1986).

Recent research has provided some useful clues for how principals can redesign their approaches to teacher evaluation so as to be a more effective "needs assessment front end" for teacher development (e.g., Stiggins and Duke 1988). For example, such evaluation needs to be based on criteria or goals that both principals and teachers agree are relevant to teacher development. Multiple forms of data should be collected as a more powerful means of accurately reflecting teachers' practices and needs. Regular observation of classroom practice with considerable time in the classroom is an important part of such data collection. The formality, frequency, and length of evaluation should be adapted to individual teachers' characteristics and needs. Rosenholtz (in press) found that teacher evaluation with features such as these was one of four organizational factors contributing directly to teacher learning opportunities in the school (the other factors were school goal setting, shared values, and collaboration).

In sum, this guideline reminds principals that development is an incremental process that builds on teachers' existing stock of attitudes, knowledge, and skill: They are at the same time the objects of and instruments for development.

Guideline 4: Recast Routine Administrative Activities Into Powerful Teacher Development Strategies.

Many principals remain skeptical about the contribution that they can make to teacher development because they believe that the strategies required would place unrealistic demands upon them. They believe that such strategies would include, for example, detailed planning of inservice programs, creation of large amounts of teacher release time for participation in such programs, and perhaps acting themselves as inservice instructors. It is not usually the lack of know-how that causes principals the most despair in the face of such strategies. Rather, it is the lack of congruence between the demands such formal strategies place on principals' work and the real demands of that work. The point of this guideline is to argue that such a view of teacher development strategies is essentially misguided. As Pfieffer suggests, "Teachers don't need superman—Clark Kent or Lois Lane will do just fine (1986). " Indeed, the more informal strategies available to principals in their normal responses to the demands of the job can be much more effective in fostering teacher development than such formal, hard-to-implement strategies. Effective principals have learned this lesson well.

What are the "real" demands faced by principals in their work? We know, for example, that principals' activities are typically characterized by brevity, fragmentation, and variety (Bradeson 1986, Davies 1987, Gally 1986, Martin and Willower 1981, Willower and Kmetz 1982). Rarely, it seems, do principals spend more than ten minutes at a time on a single task, and they make about 150 different decisions in the course of an average day. Communication of one sort or another is the primary goal of most principals' activities. Almost three-quarters of such activities are interpersonal and take place with only one other person; over half involve face-to-face contact. Principals' work environments also require high levels of spontaneity: The largest single expenditure of a principal's time is reported to be unanticipated meetings.

Although most principals experience the demands just described, recent research suggests at least one compelling source of difference in the responses of "highly effective" as compared with "typical" principals (Leithwood and Montgomery 1986). What is different is the amount of consistency that principals are able to bring to their activities and decisions. Typical or less effective principals approach them in a relatively piecemeal fashion: for example, decisions about budget, discipline, timetabling, re-porting, and staffing all may be based on different criteria. As a conse-quence, the over-all effects of these decisions may work at cross purposes.

In contrast, highly effective principals base their decisions and actions on a relatively consistent set of criteria. They "can articulate direct and remote links between their actions and the instructional system" (Bossert 1988). As a result, the effects of the many, seemingly trivial, unrelated, and often unanticipated decisions made by these principals eventually add up to something. Their impact accumulates in a way that consistently fosters school improvement. And what is the glue that holds together the myriad decisions of highly effective principals? It is the goals that they and their staff have developed for their schools and a sense of what their schools need to look like and to do in order to accomplish those goals. Such a clear, detailed vision (incorporating a conception of teacher development) and its systematic, daily use appear to be absent among less effective principals (Stevens 1986).

This opportunistic but clearly directed approach by highly effective principals to their work, as whole, manifests itself in the strategies they use for teacher development. Such principals do not attempt to deny the fragmented, interpersonal, and spontaneous demands of the job (as would be required by a formal, in-service training approach to teacher develop-ment). On the contrary, they adapt and build on strategies that are part of their normal responses to their work demands. McEvoy's (1987) results illustrate, more specifically, the types of subtle, sometimes opportunistic teacher development strategies used by effective principals. In this study, 12 elementary and intermediate principals were observed using six strategies: informing teachers of professional opportunities; disseminating professional and curriculum materials to teachers with personal follow-up and discussion; focusing teachers' attention, through meetings and informal contacts, on a specific theme in order to expand the concepts and practices teachers considered; soliciting teachers' opinions about their own classroom activities as well as school and classroom issues, thereby contributing to a sense of collegiality among staff; encouraging teachers' experimenting with innovative practices and supporting their efforts; and recognizing, sometimes publicly, the achievements of individual teachers.

Examples of other teacher development strategies used by effective principals are provided in Leithwood and Montgomery's literature reviews (1982, 1986). These strategies included working alongside individual teachers in their classes to resolve problems or implement changes, helping staff gain access to outside resources, and helping teachers arrange to observe other teachers in other schools. Even relatively "impersonal" strategies normally available to principals may be designed to foster teacher development. Hannay and Chism (1988), for example, found that teacher transfers could become an effective means for fostering such development when the transfer prompted teachers to reexamine their practices.

Wilson and Firestone (1987) refer to most of the strategies that have been mentioned as "linkage strategies" and show how principals' fostering of both bureaucratic and cultural linkages can lead to teacher development. Bureaucratic linkages (such as creating more free time for teachers) can affect how teachers interact with each other. Cultural linkages (such as introducing more consistency into school communications) work on the consciousness of teachers "by clarifying what they do and defining their commitment to the task."

Effective principals, in sum, use the energy and momentum created naturally by the demands of their work for purposes of teacher development. They have redefined the problem as the solution.

Conclusion

Gideonese has suggested that the teaching profession is "undergoing revolutionary transformation" (1988), although many of us are too close to see it. That transformation appears to begin from a perception of teaching as a routine job conducted with craftlike knowledge in isolation from other adults in a hierarchical status structure. The new perception of teaching views it as a nonroutine activity drawing on a reliable body of technical knowledge and conducted in collaboration with other professional colleagues. Awareness of this transformation has been fostered by recent effective schools research and proposals included among second-wave reforms in the United States (Bacharach 1988).

Nevertheless, we need to devote much more attention to how this newly perceived image of the teacher can be realized. This chapter has outlined plausible stages through which teachers are likely to grow as they acquire the attributes associated with a collaborative professional image of the role. Some general strategies principals might use in fostering such teacher growth also have been proposed. These principal strategies, however, only touch the surface of a problem that requires much further thought. The implications are clear for the role of the principal in creating an image of teaching as a collaborative professional enterprise. Only when we have clearly conceptualized, coherent images of both teacher and principal roles and how they develop will we realize the combined contribution toward student learning of those in both roles. Much of the knowledge required for this task is already in hand. Although more knowledge will be helpful, using what we already know constitutes a crucial and immediate challenge.

References

Bacharach, S.B. (1988). "Four Themes of Reform: An Editorial Essay." *Educational Administration Quarterly* 24, 4: 484-496.

Bacharach, S.B., S.C. Conley, and J.B. Shedd. (1987). "A Career Developmental Framework for Evaluating Teachers as Decision Makers." *Journal of Personnel Evaluation in Education* 1: 181-194.

Ball, S., and I. Goodson, eds. (1985). *Teachers' Lives and Careers*. Lewes, Sussex, England: Falmer Press.

Bossert, S.T. (1988). "School Effects." In *Handbook of Research on Educational Administration* edited by N. Boyan. New York: Longman.

Bradeson, P.V. (1986). "Principally Speaking: An Analysis of the Interpersonal Communications of School Principals." Paper presented at the annual meeting of the American Educational Research Association in San Francisco.

Brandt, R.S. (1987). "On Teachers Coaching Teachers: A Conversation with Bruce Joyce." *Educational Leadership* 44, 5: 12-17.

Calfee, R. (1981). "Cognitive Psychology and Educational Practice." *Review of Educational Research* 56, 4: 411-436.

Clark, C.M., and P.L. Peterson. (1986). "Teachers' Thought Processes." In *Handbook of Research on Teaching*, edited by M.C. Wittrock. New York: Macmillan Publishing Co.

Corbett, H.D., W.A. Fireston, and G.B. Rossman. (1987). "Resistance to Planned Change and the Sacred in School Cultures." *Educational Administration Quarterly* 33, 4: 36-59.

Darling-Hammond, L., A. E. Wise, and S.R. Pease. (1983). "Teacher Evaluation in the Organizational Context: A Review of the Literature." *Review of Educational Research* 53, 3: 285-328.

Davies, L. (1987). "The Role of the Primary Head." *Educational Management and Administration* 15: 43-47.

Fullan, M., and M. Connelly. (1987). *Teacher Education in Ontario: Current Practice and Options for the Future.* Toronto: Ontario Ministry of Education.

Gally, J. (1986). "The Structure of Administrative Behavior." Paper presented at the annual meeting of the American Educational Research Association in San Francisco.

Garmston, R. (1987). "How Administrators Support Peer Coaching." *Educational Leadership* 44, 5: 18-28.

Gersten, R., D. Carnine, and S.W. Green. (1982). "The Principal as Instructional Leader: A Second Look." *Educational Leadership* 40, 3: 47-50.

Gray, W.A., and M.M. Gray. (1985). "Synthesis of Research on Mentoring Teachers." *Educational Leadership* 43, 3: 37-43.

Hannay, L., and N. Chism. (1988). "The Potential of Teacher Transfer in Fostering Professional Development." *Journal of Curriculum and Supervision* 3, 2: 122-135.

Harvey, O.J. (Dec. 1970). "Belief and Behavior: Some Implications for Education." *The Science Teacher* 37: 10-14.

Huberman, M. (1988). "Teacher Careers and School Improvement." *Journal of Curriculum Studies* 20, 2: 119-132.

Hunt, D. (1966). "A Conceptual Systems Change Model and Its Application to Education." In *Experience, Structure and Adaptability*, edited by O.J. Harvey. New York: Springer-Verlag.

Joyce, B., and B. Showers. (1980). "Improving Inservice Training: The Message of Research." *Educational Leadership* 37: 379-385.

Joyce, B., and M. Weil. (1980). *Models of Teaching* (3rd ed.). Englewood-Cliffs, N.J.: Prentice-Hall.

Kohlberg, L. (1970). *Moral Development.* New York: Holt, Rinehart & Winston.

Lawton, S.B., E.S. Hickcox, K.A. Leithwood, and D.F. Musella. (1986) "Development and Use of Performance Appraisal of Certified Education Staff in Ontario School Board." Toronto: Ontario Ministry of Education.

Leiberman, A., and L. Miller. (1986). "School Improvement: Themes and Variations." In *Rethinking School Improvement*, edited by A Leiberman. New York: Teachers College Press.

Leithwood, K.A. (1988). *Description and Assessment of a Program for the Certification of Principals.* Toronto: Ontario Ministry of Education.

Leithwood, K.A., and D.J. Montgomery. (1982). "The Role of Elementary School Principals in Program Improvement." *Review of Educational Research* 52, 3: 309-339.

Leithwood, K.A., and D.J. Montgomery. (1986). *Improving Principal Effectiveness: The Principal Profile.* Toronto: OISE Press.

Leithwood, K.A., J. Ross, and D.J. Montgomery. (1982). "An Investigation of Teachers' Curriculum Decision Making." In *Studies in Curriculum Decision Making.* Toronto: OISE Press.

Levinson, D.J. et al. (1978). *The Seasons of a Man's Life.* New York: Knopf.

Little, J.W. (1982). "Norms of Collegiality and Experimentation: Workplace Conditions of School Success." *American Educational Research Journal* 19, 3: 325-340.

Little, J.W. (1985). "Teachers as Teacher Advisors: The Delicacy of Collegial Leadership." *Educational Lendership* 43, 3: 34-36.

Loevinger, J. (1966). "The Meaning and Measurement of Ego Development." *American Psychologist* 21: 195-206.

Maeroff G. I. (1988). "A Blueprint for Empowering Teachers." *Phi Delta Kappan* 69, 7: 472-477.

Martin, W.J., and D.J. Willower. (1981). "The Managerial Behavior of High School Principals." *Educational Administration Quarterly* 17, 1: 69-90.

McEvoy, B. (1987). "Everyday Acts: How Principals Influence Development of Their Staff." *Educational Leadership* 44, 5: 73-77.

Morris, V.C., R. Crowson, E. Horowitz, and C. Porter-Gehric. (1986). "The Urban Principal: Middle Manager in the Educational Bureaucracy." *Phi Delta Kappan* 63, 1): 689-692.

Murphy, J.T. (May 1988). "The Unheroic Side of Leadership: Notes from the Swamp." *Phi Delta Kappan*, 654-659.

Oberg, A., and R. Field. (1986). "Teacher Development Through Reflection on Practice." Paper based on presentations at the annual meeting of the American Educational Research Association in San Francisco.

Oja, S. (April 1979). "A Cognitive-Structural Approach to Adult Ego, Moral and Conceptual Development Through Inservice Education." A paper presented at the annual meeting of the American Educational Research Association.

Oja, S.N., and G.J. Pine. (1981). "Toward a Theory of Staff Development: Some Questions About Change." Paper presented at the annual meeting of the American Educational Research Association in Los Angeles.

Peterson, K.,and A. Mitchell. (1985). "Teacher Controlled Evaluation in a Career Ladder Program." *Educational Leadership* 43, 3: 44-49.

Pfieffer, R.S. (1986). "Enabling Teacher Effectiveness: Teachers' Perspectives on Instructional Management." Paper presenhd at the annual meeting of the American Educational Research Association in San Francisco.

Rallis, S.F., and M.C. Highsmith. (1986). "The Myth of the Great Principal: Questions of School Management and Instructional Leadership." *Phi Delta Kappan* 68, 4: 300-304.

Rosenholtz, S. (in press). *Teachers' Workplace*. White Plains, N.Y.: Longman.

Sallcy, C., R.B. McPherson, and M.E. Baehr. (1978). "What Principals Do: An Occupational Analysis." In *The Principal in Metropolitan Schools*, edited by D. Erickson and T. Reller. Berkeley: McCutchan Pub.

Sarason, E. (1971). *The Culture of the School and the Problem of Change*. Boston: Allyn & Bacon.

Schon, D.A. (1983). *The Reflective Practitioner*. New York: Basic Books.

Schuell, T.J. (1986). "Cognitive Conceptions of Learning." *Review of Educational Research* 56, 4: 411-436.

Shavelson, R.J. (1973). "What is the Basic Teaching Skill?" *Journal of Teacher Education* 14: 144-151.

Shavelson, R.J. (1976). "Teachers' Decision Making." In *The Psychology of Teaching Methods*, 75th Yearbook of the National Society for the Study of Education, edited by N.L. Gage. Chicago: University of Chicago Press.

Sikes, P.J., L. Measor, and P. Woods. (1985). *Teacher Careers: Crises and Continuities*. London: The Falmer Press.

Sprinthall, N.A., and L. Theis-Sprinthall. (1983). "The Teacher as an Adult Learner: A Cognitive Developmental View." In *Staff Development*, edited by G.A. Griffin. Chicago: The University of Chicago Press.

Stevens, W. (1986). "The Role of Vision in the Life of Elementary School Principals." Unpublished doctoral dissertation, University of Southern California.

Stiggins, R., and D. Duke. (1988). "The Case for Commitment of Teacher Growth." Albany: State University of New York Press.

Sullivan, E.V., G. McCullough, and M. Stager. (1970). "A Developmental Study of the Relationship Between Conceptual, Ego and Moral Development." *Child Development* 41: 399-41 1.

Trider, D., and K.A. Leithwood. (1988). "Exploring Influences on Principals' Behaviour." *Curriculum Inquiry* 18, 3: 289-312.

Wagner, L.A. (1985). "Ambiguities and Possibilities in California's Mentor Teacher Program." *Educational Leadership* 43, 3: 23-29.

Willower, D.J., and J.T. Kmetz. (1982). "The Managerial Behavior of Elementary School Principals." Paper presented at the annual meeting of the American Educational Research Association in New York.

Wilson, B., and W.A Firestone. (September 1987). "The Principal and Instruction: Combining Bureaucratic and Cultural Linkages." *Educational Leadership* 45, 1: 18-23.

5

Staff Development and the Restructured School

Albert Shanker

Every teacher in America's public schools has taken inservice courses, workshops, and training programs. But as universal as the practice has been, so is the disappointment among teachers and management as to the usefulness of most staff development experiences. Why such a dismal record? Given the amount of energy and time put into the enterprise, one would imagine greater success.

Answering this question requires more than a cost/benefits analysis. It may in part be attributable to the observation made by Phillip Schlechty that the staff development function has never been the primary function or even a priority goal for any of the institutions that have been the providers—not the districts and not the universities. In fact, staff development often is perceived as being in conflict with other priority goals of schools. For example, when children are dismissed at midday in order to permit classroom teachers to attend workshops or inservice programs, student

Albert Shanker is President, American Federation of Teachers, AFL-CIO, Washington, D.C.

learning and the custodial function are overtaken by staff development, resulting in a tension among competing goals. Beyond conflicting priorities and the question of appropriate providers, however, is the question of premises. To uncover the problem, we have to examine the premises underlying present staff development practices.

The first premise is that teaching knowledge exists primarily outside the teacher and outside the classroom. Accordingly, the function of staff development is, in part, to bring knowledge to the teacher. Operating on this "deficit" model, elaborate staff development programs have been designed to do something to teachers that will make them into better teachers.

The second premise too often underlying staff development programs is that the best way to teach people something is to tell them. The collective result has been thousands of hours spent in lectures and workshops being talked at by people, some of whom have little or no knowledge of life in classrooms.

A third premise upon which the staff development structure is built is that the more courses and workshops taken, the better the teacher is going to be. This is really analogous to the rationale underlying the whole course-credit system for students in high school. Originally, the offering of credits for courses may have been a legitimate way to ensure quality and substance. It has since become merely an accounting device in the crudest sense of the word. Too often, diplomas are earned on the basis of seat time and courses "taken" rather than on the basis of what has been learned.

The relationship between staff development and school structure is not coincidental. The model for staff development currently operating is, in fact, consistent with the traditional structure of schools and the premises that underlie them. Knowledge is received; one teaches by telling and learners learn by listening; productivity is measured by curriculum covered and courses taken.

Staff development, as we have known it, is a reflection of that traditional, bureaucratic, factory-like public school system. It is consistent with the role definition of the teacher whose job it is to get through the curriculum, cover the material, and demonstrate complete objectivity through standardized practice. It is a system built on the model of the individual, isolated classroom practitioner. It is a system designed to support that role. It not only perpetuates that structure, it is a component of it. If we restructure schools, what would happen to staff development?

Staff Development in the Restructured School: What Would It Look Like?

Restructured schools are founded on a different set of premises than are traditional schools. As centers of inquiry (Schaefer 1967), they are places where both teachers and students are the learners, and where learning is an active process that takes place in many different ways. Student success is the shared goal. Time, space, instruction, and people are organized to achieve that goal. Teaching in such a school requires not only skills and a sound knowledge base but also the capacity to make complex decisions, identify and solve problems, and relate theory, practice, and outcomes.

Further, it requires teachers and all school staff to know how to examine their practices, individually and collectively. Because practice is not standardized and the school organization is flexible, teachers have choices, and they must know what they are and how to make them. Teachers' roles are dramatically different in such a school. Staff development is different also. It is based on different premises regarding the nature, source, and locus of learning. The premises might include the following:

1. Teachers are viewed as an important source of knowledge that should inform what happens in schools.

2. Teachers' learning comes about through continuous inquiry into practice and interaction with colleagues, as well as through exposure to new research and ideas from the academic and broader communities.

3. The locus for staff development is in the school. This does not mean that workshops are held in the school at three o'clock. It means that the school is structured so that staff development is an ongoing, continuous, and integral part of the school's mission. Teachers' time is legitimately spent in the improvement of practice.

What might it look like? Let's imagine what might go on in a restructured elementary school in the year 1998.

A SCENARIO FOR THE FUTURE

Mary Jones is on the faculty at Shepherd Elementary School in a medium-sized urban district. She has been at the school for 8 years, although she has been in the district for 20. Student enrollment is currently 300 students, ages 5 through 11. Five years ago, students began entering kindergarten on their 5th birthday as a result of a primary group petition to the district office. Shepherd Elementary piloted this alternative kindergarten enrollment program for four years. Follow-up evaluations clearly indicated the benefits to the children. The Shepherd School faculty have documented the ways in which they have adapted their program to accommodate and take advantage of this change. It is now an option for all elementary schools in the district. In fact, last week, a team of three teachers from Park Elementary spent two mornings observing the ungraded primary students. They are considering having their school adopt this alternative enrollment pattern. They will be presenting the case for it in their school-based management team meeting very soon.

Ms. Jones teaches in the ungraded primary group, which serves children ages 5 through 7. There are three teams of two teachers each in the primary group. Each team is responsible for a group of 50 youngsters over the three-year period they are in the primary group. Ms. Jones' day is divided between classroom teaching responsibilities, individual tutorials with students in her team, and professional development time that is spent in a variety of different ways throughout the week.

Each week, Ms. Jones spends approximately 25 percent of her time work-ing with fellow teachers. Today she is "presenting." The primary diagnostics group is meeting, as they do every Wednesday morning, for the presentation and discussion of an individual student problem or some other pedagogical issue relevant to the group. Ms. Jones has carefully assembled a portfolio on Jimmy to illustrate the problem she has observed in his ability to deal with specific number concepts. She even has some videotape of Jimmy working in a small group that she managed to have filmed by the media coordinator. The children loved being able to see themselves on television, and the tapes allow Ms. Jones and the teachers to analyze individual and group behaviors in their faculty sessions. Ms. Jones will present the "case" as she has observed it. The other teachers in the group, who are both primary and intermediate teachers, will have a chance to ask questions and then make suggestions to Ms. Jones as to how she might vary the instructional program for Jimmy on the basis of their experience and what they know about similar situations. Because some of the other teachers in the group also have taught Jimmy, they can contribute their perspectives on him.

In this particular case, one of the teachers remembers recently reading an article in Educational Researcher that dealt with similar problems, but cannot remember the author or exact date. The teachers are meeting in the Teacher Resource Room, and one of them pulls up the education research data base on the computer. In less than one minute, she has identified the article and the teachers can either view it on the screen, or, if they choose, get a hard copy of the relevant research. While they are at it, one of the teachers suggests that there might be some other relevant literature and they decide to do a search later that day. It is quite possible that some of the articles will be right there amidst the professional literature kept in the stacks of the Resource Room. The professional library has been growing. Last year, the budget allowed for several new subscriptions and multiple copies of a few key publications that the faculty chose.

For now, they go on to the second presentation of the day—an instruc-tional management issue, that another of the teachers brings up. She is having difficulty organizing cooperative small groups in her language section. She thinks it is because she has a wider age range represented among the children this year than she has had in the past. The teachers who have been working with cooperative small groups the longest walk Ms. Smith through some of the *guidelines and ask questions to see if there are some things she might be overlooking. The discussion does not yield any answers that seem to be useful. Ms. Smith suggests that it might be a good idea if someone would volunteer to come and observe the children in her language section and watch her working with them in cooperative groups, to see if they could help analyze the problem. The 40-minute meeting closes with a reminder that applications for the school-based teacher development grants need to be submitted by next Friday. Teachers interested in doing observations in other schools, either in the district or elsewhere, related to a specific plan they have for their own practice, can apply for funds to cover travel costs and the costs of substitute teachers.*

When she returns to her classroom, Ms. Jones finds that five 11-year-olds have arrived to work with the small science groups. Cross-age tutoring has become a regular part of the instructional program at Shepherd Elementary School. The teachers have found that not only does it assist them in doing hands-on science instruction with the younger children but that the interaction between younger and older children benefits the older children as well. The tutoring program has become a vehicle for communication between the primary and intermediate teachers as they meet to discuss it and how the different participants are doing.

Ms. Jones has been looking forward to this science class. The children have been playing with balance toys of assorted kinds. Today is the day they will balance scales. In the past, she has given them a set of tasks to do with the scales and had them observe the findings. Today, she will try another strategy. She will distribute the materials and observe what they do with them. She is interested in the questions behind their actions. They will reveal to her what they have already observed in the "balance play." She has been documenting the discoveries made by two children who have been "working" together in the play corner, and those made by Kevin, who has played with the balance toys himself. She is interested in observing whatever differences there may be in rates of learning when students work in pairs. This will help her decide how to group the class in other activities. The objects they will have include some of different sizes and shapes but the same weights, and some of the same size but varying weights. Ms. Jones has the students grouped in clusters of five for this activity.

After the children have gone home for the day, Ms. Jones has coffee with some colleagues in the lounge and gets ready for a meeting of the school-based management/shared decision-making team on which she serves this year. The team will be meeting tomorrow, and Ms. Jones wants to talk to her colleagues about a proposal that will be discussed then. Faculty and parents have been concerned about the number of students who are slipping behind grade level in reading in the primary grades. Some of the faculty believe that more frequent assessment will catch problems before they grow too large to deal with in the regular instructional program. Introducing such a change will have to involve the teachers. It will require their time and their contribution to the development or identification of appropriate frequent assessment instruments that can be used. She uses this informal meeting to raise the question with some of her colleagues.

Returning to her desk in the office that she shares with two colleagues, Ms. Jones answers some phone calls. Two are from parents concerning their children's work, and one is from John Clark, a teacher in the middle school. Mr. Clark has called about arranging the next meeting of the professional study group to which Ms. Jones belongs. Some time ago it became typical for education professionals in the area in which Ms. Jones lives to participate in these informal groups. The purpose of the group is to keep current on professional literature and books that are of mutual interest to the members. The idea actually was suggested by Phil Harvey. His wife Betty, a psychiatric social worker, has long belonged to a professional study group, along with two psychiatrists, three psychologists, and two other social workers. Each member has a chance to select a reading for the group. It helps the members keep up with new developments in the field and provides an interesting professional dialogue. Informal study groups have been operating in the field of psychology for years; it is no surprise that educators have found it similarly valuable.

When she arrives home, Ms. Jones picks up the mail and turns immediately to the letters exchange page of the bi-monthly journal on teaching. She looks for her letter responding to another reader's inquiry regarding the benefits of teaching the same primary age children for two or three years—a practice that is increasingly being tried in America's elementary schools. These letters are really mini-articles, and the exchanges go on for months. Some of the responses have provided excellent suggestions and insights for Ms. Jones in her practice. She is pleased to see her letter is there.

There was a time, not so long ago, that Ms. Jones did none of these things outside her classroom teaching. She did, however, attend regularly scheduled district inservice programs. Content often reflected timely issues as well as ongoing needs and concerns of school people. There were courses on mastery learning, multicultural classrooms, effective management practices, computer literacy, and children's literature, just to name a few. For the most part, they were workshops and demonstrations directed by staff development personnel from downtown. Ms. Jones also earned the necessary 30 credits beyond her Master's Degree in early childhood education to qualify for the top of the district pay scale. While some of those courses she recalled as being interesting, there seemed to be a gap in her own developmental process. She had little opportunity to focus on her practice, or, together with her colleagues, on school issues and students' needs.

This vision of staff development is not as removed from reality as one might think. In fact, one can point to models today for each of the kinds of activities in which Ms. Jones is involved. They may be found either in schools or school districts, or as practices followed in other occupations. For example, there is a long tradition of exchange in medical journals among practitioners and medical researchers on subjects of interest in practice. These letters are considered to be a part of the literature of the profession and are indexed accordingly (i.e., they are included in data bases along with scholarly, academic research). Practitioner knowledge in education is accorded no such recognition. There are, however, some local publications in which practitioners write about their practice and share perspectives, for example *Reflections*, the Brookline, Massachusetts, Educational Journal. A recent issue carried 17 articles submitted by elementary and secondary school teachers and administrators that ranged from a discussion of a teacher appraisal system in Texas, to the differences between teaching sixth grade and first grade as experienced by a teacher who had made the change.

Similarly, the presentation of difficult, interesting, or challenging cases is common practice in teaching hospital settings and among psychologists and social workers. Although it does not happen much in schools, it is happening in the Prospect Archive and Center for Education and Research in North Bennington, Vermont. Prospect Center is an alternative school for children from kindergarten through ninth grade, as well as a teacher training institution and research center. Over the past 23 years, its staff have developed various documentary processes of which "Staff Review of a Child" is but one. Documentation and reflection may focus on individual students, pieces of their work, or on particular settings such as the playground, lunchroom, or classroom. Teachers learn how to observe, collect information, and keep records. The presentations bring practitioners together to focus on learning and teaching. Teachers use what they learn through these documentary processes to modify their classroom strategies and curriculum. Empirical knowledge becomes the basis for refining practice so that it meets individual needs. The teachers report that focusing on individuals helps them be more effective with groups as well (*Harvard Education Letter* 1988).

Finally, school-based management/shared decision-making teams are functioning in over 40 Dade County/Miami public schools, as well as in public schools in Rochester, New York; Hammond, Indiana; Pittsburgh, Pennsylvania, and other cities across the country. Other sites are developing such models of their own. Instructional programs, budgets, curriculum decisions, and school organization are all a part of the agenda for these groups as professional staff in school buildings become the locus for educational decision making.

Staff Development in Restructured Schools: Making It Happen

A redesign for staff development such as the one above would reflect the conceptions of knowledge, teaching, and learning that underlie the restructured school. It would have individual and school-level dimensions, with implications for district involvement. It would rely heavily on the profession for design and implementation.

The individual dimension might include some of the activities we have described in our scenario of the future. Personal involvement in study and reading groups, as well as journal activity in the form of submissions, letters, and inquiries, might all be a part of that development. Few of these traditions exist in teaching today. They are more characteristic among professionals who are educated for public practice. They have a common language to use and are comfortable with peer involvement. Therefore, it is not likely that these traditions will develop until the education and training of teachers changes dramatically.

The school-oriented dimension of staff development for the future is really at the heart of the matter. The continuous examination of practice is integral to the improvement of practice. School structures that support this are key. Collegial interaction among teachers that allows them to discuss, observe, analyze, and study problems together is necessary if teachers are to be able to generate the kind of practitioner-based knowledge needed for improvement of practice.

But this is not going to happen in the schools we have today. Building a staff development program, like scaffolding around the current structure, will not, by itself, change the structure. Even if it could, it would cost too much and require additional personnel we do not have and cannot expect to attract, given the demographics and competition from other sectors.

In order to support this kind of change, the very structure of schools will have to change. Student work and teacher work will be organized differently. Varied instructional strategies will be employed, including teaming, peer teaching, and the use of technology. Such change will probably necessitate the invention of a whole new institution, as well as a dramatic shift in policy.

Professional Practice Schools

The establishment of professional practice schools—exemplary schools dedicated to staff development and teacher education in a restructured setting—may be one way of getting schools to change.

Professional practice schools are the educational equivalent of teaching hospitals in medicine—the places that model both best practice and the institutional structures and characteristics that support professional practice. Not every school would be a professional practice school in that not every school would take on the responsibility of teacher education; but professional practice schools could be models of good practice for all schools. Although they do not yet exist, they are on the way, and they may provide solutions to some of the problems identified here. They would legitimatize the staff development function by identifying it clearly as a mission of the school and by providing structure and resources dedicated to its support. For example, a professional practice school would provide adequate time for teachers to meet for purposes of planning and discussing pedagogical questions, organization issues, individual and group learning problems, and so on. They would be designed on a school-based management/shared decision-making model, which would ensure professional involvement in educational decisions. Teachers would have access to current literature in education and related fields. Time would be structured to permit observation of peers. Teachers would legitimately spend time in research and peer assistance and the improvement of practice. Staff development in a professional practice school is really just a part of professional practice. It is, in part, what teachers do.

Once established, professional practice schools could have considerable impact on defining institutional standards for schools. They could be exemplars for school-based, integrated staff development.

Policy Implications

Numerous changes need to take place to support staff development for the restructured school. Some will occur at the district level, some at the school building level, and others in the universities and colleges that prepare teachers for their professional lives. These changes might include the following considerations:

1. If the locus of staff development needs to be centered more definitively in the school, then funding needs to move from the district level, where it is typically located, down to the school building level. There are some examples of this happening. The Philadelphia Writer's Project, a staff development program, is funded at the school building level, and it has resulted in teachers' budgeting observation time through the use of substitutes when they visit other schools. More opportunities to observe and get feedback from peers is certainly a part of the scheme for staff development for restructured schools. Pilot programs with school-based management and shared decision making in places like Dade County, Florida; Hammond, Indiana; and Rochester, New York, involve school-site budgeting for staff development activities. The establishment of professional practice schools will necessitate the rearrangement of funding for teacher education and staff development, as well.

2. If teachers are to be afforded the opportunities to meet, discuss, solve problems, and do research, then the school day will have to be structured to accommodate these activities. To the extent that these activities are viewed as integral to providing quality schooling, they will be supported. The key to this seems to be the recognition that the focus of

teacher collegiality is learning and teaching. The subjects of discussion, presentation, and observation are practice and student learning. The teacher team that comes together for the purpose of focusing on student needs in a primary group is performing a teacher role as surely as when they spend time with a group of children in direct instruction. This perhaps is the essence of the issue: the question of what is professional practice and what is staff development. Professional practice is teaching based on knowledge, inquiry, and reflection, involving complex decisions made in value-laden situations and in accordance with agreed-upon standards. Staff development is not something that is done to teachers; rather, it is what teachers do in order to enhance their professional practice.

3. If teachers are to assume these responsibilities in schools, they need support and incentives. The concept of teacher leaders, teacher experts, and mentor teachers represents recognition of the fact that knowledge resides in teachers, and that professional teaching is inherently a staged career.

4. If change takes place at the school building level, the roles played by district-level organizations will change. As decisions are moved down to the school building level, the district moves from being a top-down mandator or regulator to functioning in a responsive mode, helping school building faculties identify what they need and then helping them find ways to meet those needs. Districts will, for example, no longer offer or require specific districtwide inservice programs. Schools will have charge of their own budgets, including staff development budgets. This represents a major change in how districts are organized and will have important implications for the staffing of central offices.

Some management experts (Drucker 1988, Peters and Waterman 1982) suggest we will see a flattening of the organizational charts as industries and institutions become information-based organizations in which the generation of knowledge by specialists is acknowledged and supported. Major role changes for teachers will be accompanied by equally significant changes for management. In school systems we may well see movement take place from downtown offices into the schools that will allow schools to achieve some of their restructuring goals through the introduction of additional personnel.

5. If teaching is a staged career, then new teachers have different things to learn than seasoned teachers do. Furthermore, if some teachers develop to greater levels of expertise than do others, then those differences need to be acknowledged through different roles and responsibilities.

Some Lessons in Restructuring

How Do We Get There?

Some lessons can be learned from the experience of other organizations that have undergone such drastic changes in their goals and in their structures and culture. Terry Deal and others (1984) have identified a number of them. The first lesson we need to pay attention to is that nothing changes if the people in the organization do not change. We in education know that from our own past. What we have not learned, however, is that in order for people to change, it takes a significant investment in helping them to do so. This means commitment from the top (i.e., school board, teacher union, superintendent) to support change at the building level. It may be in the form of a trust agreement or contract language, but it must be loud and clear. It also means the creation of structures through which change can be explored and on which it can be supported. It can begin with study groups among faculties or across faculties in school districts. These groups can examine what they have been doing, look at themselves and their school, and ask what it is they want to be doing. This self-assessment and development of a shared vision is essential. Without this kind of process, one runs the risk of imposing structures and ideas on people who do not have a commitment to them. Without that commitment, they are unlikely to be able to sustain the effort needed to actually begin to make changes in their schools.

The second lesson we can learn in looking at change in industry is that a certain amount of chaos has to be tolerated when change is taking place. For example, the transition of AT&T, essentially a monopolistic bureaucracy, to a number of smaller, independent, competitive corporations was highly disruptive to all involved. People need to expect this, and they need to know also that they will make mistakes as they begin new activities and new ways of doing things. They need to feel comfortable taking risks. They need to know that making mistakes is okay. This means that school building staffs need to be supported in the decisions they make—even if they are not perfect. They need to learn and they will learn by doing.

People experienced in managing change have come to know that putting aside the old ways needs to be accompanied at times with ceremony and ritual. Even when the old ways are disdained, as were the time clocks in New York City schools, putting them in the past means letting go of the familiar, which is often difficult for people to do. It is especially so when they are not exactly sure of what the future looks like. This is the third lesson.

The fourth observation has to do with what people need in order to be able to function in new roles and new environments. Other organizations, attuned to these needs, invest heavily in education and training for restructuring. As new roles and responsibilities develop in the schools, teachers and administrators are learning that they need some different skills in these restructuring schools. For example, teachers who begin to function in decision-making teams need to develop their interactional skills and their decision-making skills; and they need access to a much broader range of information, research data, and technical assistance as they begin to work in areas formerly closed to them (i.e., curriculum planning, instructional program development, budgeting, and pupil progress management).

Will We Get There?

Perhaps the most important lesson for educators to heed is the one that suggests that if we ignore the signals we are getting that major change is needed, we are doomed to failure. The restructuring of American industry, driven by demographic, economic, and technological demands, offers a useful analogy.

Public schools today need to be competitive. They must compete for their fair share of the professional workforce, and they must compete by graduating students prepared to live in a complex and changing society— students who will be lifelong learners. The structures of our schools were not designed to accomplish these goals. American industry has learned that survival can mean restructuring. We need to pay attention to that lesson.

As schools restructure, guided by a shared vision of learning that is designed to help students be successful in a changing and competitive world, the definition of teachers' work will change as well. Staff development will become a part of teachers' work. It will take on a more complex meaning. It will be not only what teachers do to improve their practice, but also what teachers do in the course of their practice to enhance student success.

References

Deal, T.E., and A.A. Kennedy. (1984). *Corporate Cultures: The Rites and Rituals of Corporate Life.* Reading, Mass.: Addison-Wesley.

Drucker, P. (1988). "The Coming of the New Organization." *Harvard Business Review* 66, 1: 45-53.

Gage, N.L. (1984). "What Do We Know about Teacher Effectiveness?" *Phi Delta Kappan* 10: 87-93.

"Learning from Children: Teachers Do Research." (1988). *Harvard Educational Letter* 4, 4: 1-3.

Peters, T.F., and R.H. Waterman, Jr. (1982). *In Search of Excellence: Lessons from America's Best Run Companies.* New York: Harper & Row.

Shaefer, R.J. (1967). *The School as a Center of Inquiry.* New York: Harper & Row.

Sugarman, J., ed. (1988). *Reflections: The Brookline Educational Journal* 5, 1.

6

The Legacy of the Teacher Center

Sam J. Yarger

The federally sponsored Teacher Centers Program lasted for about 1,000 days. It was created in an effort to involve practicing elementary and secondary teachers directly in their own staff development. The program touched the professional lives of thousands of teachers in about 90 sites throughout the country.

Studying teacher centers in isolation would not help one understand this aspect of teacher education. Rather, one must develop a context, taking into account the fact that the politics of education were different in the late 1970s and early 1980s than they are today. Education was not in the public's eye. There was no talk of major reforms. It was, in fact, business as usual, just as it had been for the past 20 or 30 years. It is entirely possible that if the program were funded today, it would carried out under a very different set of circumstances. There would be many more critical observers and much more scrutiny.

Sam J. Yarger is Dean and Professor, School of Education, the University of Wisconsin-Milwaukee.

In order to provide a context for understanding teacher centers, this chapter first discusses policy boards, the centerpiece of the Teacher Centers Program. Next, program activities are presented as they emerged over the three-year life of the federal project. Finally, an attempt is made to delineate the meaning that one can take from studying this distinctive, federally funded program.

Policy Boards—The Centerpiece of the Teacher Centers Program

The teacher centers legislation (PL94-482) was signed into law in October 1976 by President Gerald Ford. The rules were developed during 1977, and the program was announced early in 1978. The proposals were submitted in the spring of 1978, and the first projects were funded late in that year.

One need only read the teacher center regulations to understand how important the policy board was in the Teacher Centers Program. In fact, the regulations make practically no mention of programs that would be emanating from individual projects. No attempt was made to influence the program's content, focus, or duration, or to specify who might serve as teacher center instructors. There was specification concerning who the teacher centers clients would be, but even this was vague. Only fleeting mention was made of evaluation. There was little in the regulations that suggested that the Teacher Centers Program would be held accountable based on the productivity of individual projects. In essence, evaluation and, to a lesser degree, documentation were viewed as good things that ought to happen; but they clearly were not required.

One might think that neglecting to mention program activities and paying only lip service to evaluation were serious shortcomings in the regulations. There was, however, a logic that made this understandable. It would make no sense to prescribe program content and then to create a policy board that was to oversee the development of individual teacher center projects. By the same token, the project was to be monitored and evaluated by the policy board itself. Policy boards clearly were the centerpiece of the program, empowered to develop and evaluate project activities.

The regulations were very specific concerning the governance structure that would supervise individual projects. Practicing elementary, secondary, and special education teachers were to constitute a majority of all policy board members. The manner in which the teachers were to be selected was also specified. They could be selected either by popular vote or by bargaining agent, if appropriate. Having teacher members of the policy board selected by administrative personnel was prohibited.

Teacher center policy boards had supervisory powers over the projects. This was clearly specified. Local school districts accepted grants under the conditions that the policy board would have the final say in the selection of staff as well as the allocation of funds—provided that these decisions were in accordance with local, state, and federal laws and regulations.

While this provision generated apprehension at the outset, there was a built-in check and balance (or a built-in conflict, depending on one's point of view). In most cases, the grants were awarded to individual school districts. The fear was that while policy boards were to have "supervisory responsibility," it would be easy for district administrators to exercise real control, because they had to authorize the expenditure of funds. This fear was never realized. In fact, once the teacher center projects were up and running, few problems were encountered in regard to control of the purse strings. In practice, the policy boards exercised a great deal of control over the resources, often delegating control to teacher center staff.

Description of Policy Boards[1]

Teacher center policy boards were rather large, usually consisting of 20 to 22 members: 13 or 14 members were classroom teachers, 4 or 5 were school administrators, and 1 or 2 were higher education members and often a member from outside the above-mentioned configuration. About 90 percent of the policy boards were chaired by classroom teachers. Most teacher center policy boards met at least monthly with less than 15 percent meeting more infrequently.

The meetings were usually held after school or in the evening, and they averaged about two and a half hours in length. The teacher members' attendance record was slightly better than other role groups, but the attendance record for all role groups was quite high.

Policy boards developed a surprising camaraderie considering the tension associated with their creation by federal regulation. Members took their work seriously, quickly formed alliances, and developed communication patterns that allowed them to function smoothly. There were few instances of dysfunctional teacher center policy boards. Even though

---

[1]For a more complete presentation of these and other data presented in this chapter, see Mertens and Yarger (1981).

teacher union hostility and bickering was occurring at the national level, local policy boards generally worked cooperatively and ignored external pressures that might have created project problems.

Policy Boards in Action

Policy boards were, for the most part, active groups. On the average, they made about five formal decisions per month. A "formal decision" is defined as action on a specific motion brought before the board for either approval or rejection. Other decisions that reflected the interests of the policy board and were influenced by it, were made in a more informal manner.

About 40 percent of the decisions made by policy boards were in the project management domain. These decisions, required to operate the project, typically involved such topics as the fund expenditure, personnel, equipment, materials, facilities, and coordination and communication with other agencies or institutions.

About a quarter of the decisions made by the policy board dealt with internal policy board matters and operations. These decisions might regard the time and location of meetings, the establishment of committees and subcommittees, or the approval of minutes and other internal reports.

About one-third of the policy board decisions actually dealt with the details of the programs for teacher center clients. These decisions related to the determination of program content, professional development resources, travel, needs assessment or evaluation, and other program-related logistics.

Another way of viewing these data suggests that if a teacher center policy board made 60 decisions per year, 24 of them would be in the area of project management, 16 would concern internal policy board operations, and 20 would relate to programs for clients. Of the 20 decisions made annually regarding programs for clients, about six would focus on the actual determination of program content.

As we will see in the next section of this chapter, these data can easily be misunderstood. Teacher center policy boards purposefully embraced the letter and the spirit of the regulations (i.e., the program should be responsive to the needs of teachers). Thus, it was not unusual to see the policy board reluctant to make substantive decisions. Rather, the teacher center staff was provided with a great deal of autonomy and freedom, with the explicit understanding that they would be responsive to teachers.

Further evidence of the ability of teacher center policy boards to work harmoniously can be noted in the types of decisions they made. Over 85 percent of their decisions approved something. This type of voting record does not suggest a contentious body. Rather, it suggested that people wanted to say yes, to relate well with their colleagues.

Concerning the limited number of decisions made by teacher center policy boards and the generally high level of affirmative decisions, it should be pointed out that not all decisions were of equal importance. Probably the most important decisions they made were in the hiring of the teacher center project director and other center staff. In addition to hiring personnel, the policy board provided a public, political support base for teacher center staff to move ahead with the programs that the teachers wanted. They were, in fact, very effective.

The Impact of Policy Boards

One way of addressing the question of policy board impact is to look at the characteristics of other federally sponsored inservice and staff development programs and to compare the characteristics of teacher centers with them. The Rand Change Agent Study (Berman and McLaughlin 1975) surveyed 293 federal projects (Title III, Vocational Education, Bilingual Education, and Right to Read) operating in school districts across the country and followed that up with in-depth field work at 30 of these projects. Mertens (1982) compared the results of that study with the study of federally funded teacher center projects (Mertens and Yarger 1981) and discovered a strong congruence in the findings relevant to inservice education.

Berman and McLaughlin developed 13 generalizations from the Rand study regarding successful change agent programs. Mertens, using data from teacher center projects, confirmed the congruence between teacher centers and these other projects on all 13 dimensions. These congruent characteristics included the following:

    1. Administrators and teachers make joint decisions about needs and project activities.

    2. Inservice activities are directed at teacher-identified needs to assure programming relevant to current classroom needs.

    3. Resources exist for timely response to teacher identified needs.

    4. Small-group programming is central to the inservice program.

    5. "Hands on/concrete" experiences for teachers are central to the inservice program.

    6. Local people, especially teachers, are used as a primary resource in facilitating inservice activities.

    7. Inservice activities are offered during the school day.

8. Resources are available to provide ongoing support for individual teacher needs.

9. Emphasis is on local materials development.

10. Resources such as release time and money are available for individual teacher use.

11. Participation in inservice is voluntary.

12. Opportunities exist for informal peer interaction.

13. The point of view that teachers are professionals pervades the school district.

A fair analysis of the contributions of teacher center policy boards might be that, although they worked well, they did not necessarily forge new inservice patterns. Rather, they functioned much like other federally funded programs, perhaps reflecting the state of the art between 1978 and 1982. Policy boards provided oversight for programs and supported a great deal of program activity. In sum, teacher center policy boards were consistent with the spirit of the times. They also reflected the influence of the teacher unions in the legislative and bureaucratic process. In that sense, they were crucial components of the teacher center projects.

The Programmatic Contribution of Teacher Centers

The typical teacher center was funded for between $100,000 and $200,000 per year. In order to ensure that as much money as possible would be used for programming for teachers, the typical center rarely had more than one or two staff members. Additionally, a small amount of money (usually less than $10,000) was set aside for consultants or for contracts with outside vendors. Teacher centers also made great use of volunteers, who were often teachers interested in helping their colleagues. The average teacher center served one school district, though a few represented consortiums of two or more districts. On the average, about a thousand teachers in the service area were eligible to take advantage of the teacher center.

The typical federally funded teacher center was housed in a school building. Although much programming occurred during the school day, the majority of it took place after school, in the evening, and on weekends. Teachers also made use of the teacher center for social and informal purposes. At the very least, a teacher could usually be assured of finding a cup of coffee, something interesting to read, a colleague to chat with, or a teacher center staff member willing to discuss a specific problem. This "hospitality characteristic" served to endear the teacher center to teachers, making the centers very popular.

Distinctive Features

Teacher centers provided a variety of group activities for their clients. Variously described as workshops, seminars, symposia, or courses, the average teacher center sponsored about 60 events per year, each serving about 25 teachers. While about two-thirds of these activities met only once, some lasted as long as a semester.

The traditional group activity was an important part of the federally sponsored Teacher Centers Program. These activities were highly focused, served specifically identified groups of teachers, were developed with a short turnaround time, and covered a short time span (typically no more than one day).

Although they were not distinctive, it is important to have some sense of the content of teacher center group activities. Over three-fourths of the group activities focused on the instruction of children. Teachers were interested in learning about pedagogical techniques, curriculum development, specific types of children who might be in their classroom, and the special needs that these children possess. Clearly, teachers were looking for ways to improve their instruction in the classroom.

A distinct contribution of teacher center group activities was the specificity of programming. One rarely saw workshops or courses with general titles, such as "Methods of Teaching Reading." More commonly seen were highly focused workshops such as "The Use of DISTAR with Disadvantaged Children in the Primary Grades." Teacher centers were able to focus programming so narrowly because center staff members were constantly involved in talking to their clients about program needs and in translating these needs into specific activities. Teacher centers pioneered the development of specific, tailored, focused group activities for teachers. The message that came through was that the more general, abstract workshops simply would not meet their needs.

Another distinctive contribution of teacher centers was their ability to respond quickly to the perceived needs of even small numbers of teachers. Whereas a school district or a university might require six to ten weeks— or even a semester—to organize a workshop, seminar, or course, teacher centers could do it quickly. It was not unusual to see a group activity provided within one to two weeks after the need was identified. The importance of a short turnaround time was highlighted by the emphasis that teacher center projects and policy boards placed on keeping bureaucratic constraint to a minimum.

A possibly unique contribution of teacher centers was the development of a variety of ways to serve teachers individually. Individual service to teachers was not happenstance; it was actually built into the projects and grew as the project developed. In fact, more teachers were served individually than were served in formal group activities. The typical teacher center project served slightly more than 1,700 teachers annually (or about 145 per month) in group activities and nearly 2,300 per year (or about 190 teachers per month) individually. This was notable when we consider that the typical teacher center had only one or two staff members.

Teacher centers devised several ways to serve teachers individually. Staff consulted with teachers in areas such as materials development, follow-up to teacher center activities, and curriculum development. Sometimes they performed demonstrations and videotaped teachers, with feedback sessions afterwards. In addition to direct consultative services, teacher centers also offered facilitative services. For instance, they developed ways of matching teachers with both materials and other teachers, and they provided a variety of hotlines for teacher use.

The centers also served teachers by providing a variety of resources. The developmental work to provide resources and keep them available consumed a great deal of time and energy on the part of teacher center staff. Material resources, such as a teacher center library, instructional aids, "make and take" supplies, and resource files, were readily available to teachers. Additionally, teachers found an abundance of equipment at teacher center project sites. Probably the most popular was the laminating machine. In addition to laminating machines, teachers also found copier and thermofax machines, button-makers, and a variety of hand tools for "make and take" projects. The traditional availability of these kinds of resources was rare, making them all the more "special" for teachers.

Teacher centers frequently provided substitutes so teachers could become involved in inservice activities during the school day. Additionally, incentive awards were made available for teachers, typically through a competitive process. Professional development funds were available to enhance teacher travel to professional meetings. Finally, some teacher center projects offered tuition assistance for teachers involved in university coursework.

Teacher centers mixed the ordinary with the distinctive as they played out their three-year life on the American educational scene. The activities emanating from teacher centers were usually designed to serve small numbers of teachers (up to 15) in highly specific content areas over a short period of time. More distinctly, teacher centers found innumerable ways to help individual teachers solve specific problems. Through a series of services and resources that were an integral part of the project, teacher centers forged a unique contribution to the field. This type of programming is practically nonexistent today.

Perhaps the most distinctive contribution is the cadre of staff development professionals that developed over the three-year life of the program. As a group they were clearly different, being dedicated almost completely to the betterment of teaching through sensitive support of their colleagues. Many from this cohort remain, in some way, committed to the type of work they performed so well in the teacher center projects. Others have moved on to leadership roles in a variety of educational settings.

The Importance of Teacher Centers

A legacy can be defined as something received from the past and passed on from one generation to the next. In order to understand the legacy of teacher centers, we must understand the conditions that existed when they were operating. In doing so, we can better understand why they functioned as they did, as well as why we must speak of their legacy, not their reemergence.

Relevant to the Late 1970s

The history of inservice education is not difficult to understand. Prior to the onset of the 1970s, there were essentially two forms of program delivery. School districts often had well-entrenched but minimal provisions for the delivery of inservice education. It was not unusual to have a "superintendent's day" when all the teachers would convene at a single building to listen to inspiring speeches. Progressive school districts might break that down and provide two half-day sessions (in some cases even two or three days). Regardless, the decisions concerning the content of the programs came from the administration, not from the teachers. The consultants and speakers were selected by administrators, and the teachers were expected to be motivated only. Rarely did these programs deal with real problems encountered by teachers in their professional lives.

The other form of inservice education was delivered by colleges and universities. Constrained by the need to generate student credit hours, the nearly exclusive form of delivery was the semester-long course. Typically, these courses were linked to either degree or state certification requirements. Teachers had minimal options. And although many of the courses may well have been high quality, they often lacked relevance and credibility in the eyes of the clients.

These traditional forms of inservice were, at best, tolerated by teachers. In most cases, they had little freedom to choose whether to attend or not. Either they were required to attend district programs or they needed credits for salary advancement, certification, or degrees from the university. Real evaluations of these forms of inservice took place in teachers' lounges. As one might suspect, not only did they not receive high marks, they were a constant source of frustration to teachers who were looking for practical help in dealing with real classroom problems.

The teacher center idea emerged in the early 1970s (Bailey 1971). The term originated in Great Britain and quickly gained popularity in the United States. In those early days, it was a concept in search of attributes. In fact, education professionals could do just about anything they wanted and describe what they were doing as part of their "teacher center." Various attempts were made to delineate the concept (see Schmieder and Yarger 1974, Yarger and Leonard 1974). Differential definitions were constructed and typologies became popular. The truth is that people still wanted to do a variety of different things and describe what they were doing as "teacher centering." The term "teacher center," in the early 1970s, referred to something good, albeit not very specific. In essence, it was a concept, with nearly universal acceptance, waiting to be defined.

The National Education Association (NEA) saw this lack of definition as an opportunity and seized it, forging yet another advantage in the ongoing internecine battle with the American Federation of Teachers (AFT). The support was strong, the lobbying intense. The teacher center legislation was introduced, passed, and signed into law. The NEA clearly prevailed in the teacher center battle. Once the legislation was in place, however, both teacher unions assumed an ownership stance. In essence, the teacher organizations scored a double victory. They were responding to the frustration about inservice education that teachers were exhibiting while making a political statement concerning the power of classroom teachers. The importance of the teacher centers legislation and resulting program was highlighted by the fact that since the demise of Teacher Corps, there had been no federal program specifically (categorically) targeted for teacher education. In this case, the program was targeted not only for teacher education, but exclusively for teachers.

The time was right in the 1970s for the emergence of teacher centers. Categorical funds were still available for education. Virtually no teacher education programs were being funded, and the teacher unions, particularly the NEA, were flexing their considerable muscles. Given the results-oriented, conservative, business-like approach to education that exists today, teacher centers would probably emerge quite differently, if they emerged at all.

Important Characteristics

Teacher centers made several very important contributions to the field of inservice education. While not necessarily unique, these contributions were brought together in a different form that accommodated teachers in new and successful ways. Chief among these contributions was the notion of "responsiveness." If any principle undergirded the development of the federally sponsored Teacher Centers Program, it was one related to the need for program activities to be responsive to teachers' self-determined needs.

An obvious offspring of this responsiveness was the teacher centers' ability to offer relevant, focused programming. If responsiveness to self-determined needs was important, relevance was a natural outgrowth. The ability to target and focus inservice programming for individual or small groups of teachers was one way that teacher centers met the prerequisite of responsiveness.

Teacher centers also made an art out of working with individual teachers and addressing their self-determined needs. Probably for the first time for many teachers, they could walk into the teacher center and meet someone who would listen to them, help them define their individual classroom problem, and then work with them until that problem had been addressed. No inservice program has been as successful in this endeavor either before or since teacher centers.

Teacher centers made staff development credible for many teachers. This occurred because teachers were the source of the needs to be addressed and were central to developing the programs that would address these needs. By involving teachers heavily in program development, teacher centers avoided the dilemma of understanding the need to be addressed but totally missing the mark in the development of a program.

Finally, teacher centers contributed a new breed of education professionals to the field. These professionals accept as a given that teachers define the need and suggest solutions, while their job is to translate that need and develop a program that is viewed by the client to be helpful. In teacher centers, the staff and the clients were typically seen as colleagues, rarely as expert and novice, and never as superior and subordinate. This new type of staff development professional brought to the inservice enterprise a different point of view, one that reflects a high degree of respect for the client.

Though not always recognized, the contributions made by teacher centers incorporate many of the characteristics that are still essential if one expects to develop a successful inservice program. Assuming that the teacher client is a mature adult professional, it is difficult to conceive of a program in which they are not involved, that is not responsive, that does not focus on their needs with a targeted program, and that does not result in highly credible staff development. In too many instances, those contributions are ignored today in both school district and university staff development efforts.

The Legacy

Thus far, this chapter has reported descriptive information concerning the federally funded teacher centers. Additionally, a minimal amount of interpretation has been provided. This section offers some commentary on the meaning of teacher centers.

Although there is no way it could have been known at the time, retrospective analysis has made it quite clear that teacher centers were, in many ways, the precursor to teacher empowerment, which has been central to the increasing movement toward the professionalization of teaching. This basic empowerment of teachers constitutes perhaps the most important teacher center legacy.

Teachers, many for the first time, discovered that in the teacher center they could not only admit their own professional development needs, but could speak quite candidly about them. Teacher centers provided an environment in which teachers could seriously address practical professional problems, rather than simply "exhibit deficiencies." This freedom to be open about one's professional needs constitutes the most fundamental basis for teacher empowerment. The classroom doors could now be open, and teachers could welcome their colleagues in an attempt to better understand their life's work as manifested in their own classroom activities.

While some might describe empowerment as enhanced collegiality, the fact of the matter is that empowerment comes from being able to relate with others like yourself, sharing a common language. Teachers who cannot talk to one another about their profession can never be empowered. An individual teacher cannot be empowered if, in fact, all teachers are not empowered.

The policy board was the formal structure for teacher empowerment. For the first time, the administrator had to work with teachers in a political structure in which teachers were the dominant force. At the onset, both teachers and administrators were wary and cynical; but before long they all learned that the process could be productive and cooperative. The policy board and the teacher centers project provided an opportunity and structure for them to work together on a long-term, ongoing basis. This interaction did much to wear down the resistance to the notion that teachers must, in fact, have an important voice. Teacher centers were an instrument of teacher empowerment.

Teacher empowerment is not yet universal; if it were, it would constitute only a first and very important step toward the professionalization of teaching. While this process unfolds, as it surely will, historians will hopefully note the brief but crucial contributions that teacher centers made to the process.

References

Bailey, S.K. (1971). "Teachers' Centers: A British First." *Phi Delta Kappan* 53, 3: 146-149.

Berman, P., and M. McLaughlin. (1975). *Federal Programs Supporting Educational Change: The Findings in Review*. Santa Monica: The Rand Corporation.

Mertens, S.K. (1982). "Beyond Pro Forma Teacher Education." *Nexus* 4, 2. Syracuse: Central New York Study Council, Syracuse University.

Mertens, S.K., and S.J. Yarger. (1981). *Teacher Centers in Action: A Comprehensive Study of Program Activities, Staff Services, Resources and Policy Board Operations in 37 Federally Funded Teacher Centers*. Syracuse: The Syracuse Area Teacher Center, Syracuse University.

Schmieder, A.A., and S.J. Yarger. (1974). "Teacher/Teaching Centering in America." *Journal of Teacher Education* 25, 1: 5-12.

Yarger, S.J., and A. Leonard. (1974). *A Descriptive and Analytical Study of the Teaching Center Movement in American Education*. Syracuse: School of Education, Syracuse University.

7

Connecting the University to the School

Richard I. Arends

A common theme found throughout this volume is that the field of staff development in schools is maturing from an uneven effort of courses and workshops to a more coordinated human resource system built to ensure the continuous growth of teachers and other educational personnel. This emerging system requires new structures and commitments from local educational agencies and the professional organizations of teachers. It requires the same commitments from faculties in institutions of higher education. Although universities,[1] through their schools of education, have been historically linked to the public schools, these linkages have been weak. Today's challenge for universities is to find

---

[1] I use the label "universities" to refer to the departments, schools, and colleges of education who have the primary responsibility for making these connections to professional in schools.

Richard I. Arends is Professor of Education, College of Education, University of Maryland, College Park.

new and different ways to connect with schools so that the resources of the university can be put to work in appropriate and beneficial ways. This challenge, however, cannot be met if universities focus on ways to strengthen involvement in staff development by itself; more substantial changes and reforms are required in the ways universities connect to schools for the initial preparation of teachers and for knowledge production and use.

The changes in schools and the teaching profession are important phenomena to consider as faculties in universities determine how they can best connect themselves to their professional fields for the purpose of contributing to human resource development. Take, for instance, the significant changes that have taken place since World War II in the teaching profession and in the ways local educational agencies have responded to a maturing profession. In 1940, less than 50 percent of the teachers in the United States held bachelor's degrees. By 1961, 85 percent held degrees. Currently, less than one-third of one percent are teaching without a bachelor's degree. In 1961, only 23 percent of the teaching force held master's degrees.

In 1986, for the first time, more than half of all teachers held master's degrees and almost 1 percent held doctorates (see National Education Association 1987).

Similarly, education attainment has increased for other educational personnel. In 1988, 67 percent of public school superintendents and 60 percent of public school principals had seven or more years of college, and it is not unusual for a large proportion of curriculum specialists and other leadership personnel in many larger school systems to hold doctorates (see Feistritzer 1988).

Prior to 1970, it was difficult to find a local educational agency that committed resources of any magnitude to teacher development. They relied upon the local college or university to accomplish this goal through summer school or evening courses. Today, an array of organizational units and roles exist to deliver educational opportunities for teachers and other school personnel. In larger school agencies, these roles and units are district based; for smaller systems they are found in intermediate service centers.

Significant changes have also occurred in other educational organizations and at the national level. Prior to 1960, no system existed to provide assistance to people in schools for keeping up with new ideas and the research on teaching and learning. Today, primarily through funding by the federal government begun in 1964, there is an extensive network of university-based research and development centers and regionally based educational development laboratories whose primary purpose is to expand the knowledge base on education and to turn new knowledge into useful curriculum materials and teaching strategies for teachers. Further, the ERIC Clearinghouses and the National Diffusion Network provide teachers with electronic and face-to-face access to an impressive collection of tested ideas and materials totally unavailable in earlier eras.

The teachers' professional organizations have recognized the growing sophistication of the profession and the emergent desire of their membership to have available training and development opportunities. Both the American Federation of Teachers (AFT) and the National Educational Association (NEA) have launched several major staff development and school improvement projects during the last decade. The AFT's Educational Research and Dissemination Project and the NEA's Mastery in Learning Project are two examples of this type of effort. Both projects, along with a number of others, have provided resources and training to promote teacher development and to encourage faculties to work toward restructuring and improving schools.

Finally, the role of staff developer has become formalized not only at the local level, but at the state and national levels as well. Role occupants have created their own professional organization, the Council of Staff Developers. This organization has a substantial membership of over 4,500, sponsors well-attended regional and national meetings, and publishes the widely respected *Journal of Staff Development.* Affiliate chapters of this national organization are starting to emerge in several states.

These historic shifts significantly affect the ways universities should and can connect to the teaching profession and the ways they can expect to do business with teachers in the future. They also affect traditional obligations and reciprocalities. For instance, the fact that large numbers of teachers have advanced degrees shapes the kind of learning experiences they will seek for themselves. Courses carrying credit are no longer the "coins of the realm" in the training and learning exchange.

The fact that many local school agencies have their own human resource development units and their own staff developers makes learning opportunities available locally that only the universities delivered in earlier eras. For instance, between 1971 and 1986, the percentage of teachers, nationwide, who reported participating in professional growth activities sponsored by their school system increased from 58 to 72 percent. Correspondingly, the percentage reporting attending college summer school decreased from 30 to 12 percent and those reporting taking a college course during the school year decreased from 40 to 21 percent (National Education Association 1987). Finally, the national network of research and consultative services allows locally based staff development personnel to look to a national cadre of researchers and consultants rather than rely on the local university. In sum, the local college and university is no longer the "only store in town" when teachers consider buying and participating in professional development.

If old ways of doing business are no longer appropriate, what obligations do universities have today in the field of training and development and what contributions should and can they make? Fortunately, new purposes and structures that define evolving university obligations and contributions are beginning to emerge that provide the basis for important work left to be done.

In the following pages, I provide examples of current efforts and describe ways universities can put their resources to work to improve teaching and schooling. I attempt to show how universities have obligations in three important domains: knowledge production and use; the initial preparation of the professionals who work in schools; and continuing education, including working toward school and systemwide change. I describe promising projects in each of these domains. In some instances, examples come from my own work and that of colleagues at the University of Maryland, where for the past several years, we have pursued an active agenda of initiating human resource development programs and conducting research on that work. In other instances, I rely on examples from other universities that have initiated similar programs and projects. Unless universities find ways to strengthen and to perform well in all three of these domains, their contributions in any single domain will remain disconnected and ineffective. I also argue in the concluding section of the chapter that a redirection and restructuring in the universities' schools of education are required if new commitments and connections to schools are to become widespread and if the university is to become a fully participating partner in a coordinated human resource system for education.

Connecting for Knowledge Production and Use

The cornerstone for all professional endeavor is, in one way or another, the technical knowledge that can be brought to bear on problem situations. An interesting and perplexing set of circumstances exists around the production of knowledge and its use to inform teaching and learning in the United States today. On the one hand, some significant progress has been made. In a relatively brief period of time, faculties in a few universities have made teaching and learning respectable subjects for serious inquiry, have developed an array of research methods for studying these complex phenomena, and have produced a rather extensive knowledge base on teaching and learning for the profession. The advances made in the research on teaching over the past 30 years are particularly striking. Compare, for example, the significant increase in size, the number of topics, and the maturity of the research reported in the three *Handbooks on Teaching*, the first published in 1963 and the latest in 1986. Most knowledgeable observers (Berliner 1987, Joyce and Showers 1988, Reynolds 1989) believe this knowledge base is sufficiently strong to provide guidelines for best practice and professional behavior.

On the other hand, the contributors to this knowledge base have been few compared to the total number of resources dedicated for that purpose in the more than 1,200 colleges and universities that have departments or schools of education. Noncontributors exist on two ends of a continuum. On the one end can be found a substantial proportion of the education professorate, particularly in major research universities, who have distanced themselves from the study of teaching and learning in favor of more general social science inquiry and who have abandoned processes and programs associated with the initial and continuing education of teachers. This phenomenon was described almost a decade ago by Great Britain's Harry Judge. It has been more recently studied and criticized by Geradine Clifford and John Guthrie in *Ed School* (1988). The problem with this type of inquiry is that, although it may expand our understanding in more general ways, it is deemed irrelevant by many beginning and experienced teachers. It has not been conceptualized from the practitioner's and user's frame of reference. Arthur Bolster made this point nicely in a piece he wrote in 1983 when responding to the question of why research has had so little influence on practice:

> The major reason, in my opinion, is that most such research, especially that emanating from top-ranked schools of education, construes teaching from a theoretical perspective that is incompatible with the perspective teachers must employ in thinking about their work. In other words, researchers and school teachers adopt radically different sets of assumptions about how to conceptualize the teaching process. As a result, the conclusions of much formal research on teaching appears irrelevant to classroom teachers—not necessarily wrong, just not very sensible or useful. If researchers are to generate knowledge that is likely to affect classroom practice, they must construe their inquiries in ways that are much more compatible with teachers' perspectives (p. 295).

On the other end of the continuum can be found another sizeable proportion of the professorate who are not connected to knowledge production and use. We have known about this situation for a long time. Conant (1963) described the low knowledge production of education faculty in his book on teacher education in the '60s. Joyce and his colleagues (1977), as well as Clark and Guba (1975), described this circumstance during the decade of the '70s. Clark (1978), for instance, reported that median level of institutional productivity as assessed by the measures they employed was "zero." This situation has not changed substantially. For the past four years, researchers sponsored by the American Association of Colleges for Teacher Education have been surveying annually a random sample of education faculty and students from the more than 700 institutions that belong to that organization. The sample has been stratified to include large research universities, regional universities, and liberal arts colleges. A survey of foundations' faculty found that well over half the faculty in smaller liberal arts institutions and in regional state universities have never written an article for publication. A similar survey of secondary methods instructors found that less than half had ever published; less than a third read journals such as the *American Education Research Journal* or the *Journal of Educational Research*, and only 12 percent belonged to the American Educational Research Association. A survey of students in these professors' classes found that just slightly more than one-third reported rarely, if ever, being asked to review research or engage in research activity as part of their course work (see AACTE 1987, 1988). What is significant about this set of circumstances is that a sizable proportion of teacher candidates is being prepared either in environments where faculty have purposefully distanced themselves from teacher education and its problems or in environments where the conduct of inquiry is weak or nonexistent.

It is important for faculties in university-based schools of education to continue efforts to extend the knowledge base on teaching and learning and to make this knowledge available to the human resource community and the teachers they serve. It is equally important to make this knowledge available to the larger teacher education community and to teacher candidates. The future of educational research will also depend more and more on the active involvement of practicing teachers, and their involvement will only be ensured if the research community can find ways to communicate honestly the "idea" of research (including its limitations) and find ways to create stronger linkages and collaboration with teachers for the purposes of conceptualizing and "doing" research.

The "idea" of research and its limitation have not been clearly communicated to teachers in the past. For example, we have not given adequate credit to practicing teachers whose "wisdom" of practice many times is ahead of theory. Take, for instance, the research on classroom management. Many researchers and educators would agree that today we have a fairly substantial knowledge base on classroom management, a topic of keen interest and importance to classroom teachers. The research community, however, has not invented these effective classroom management practices. The contributions of research have been to systematically observe experienced teachers, to tease out behaviors that make some of them more effective than others, and to label and codify this information. The wisdom of practicing teachers has made this whole line of inquiry possible.

The way teacher candidates and experienced teachers will start to value research and the way university researchers will start to understand teachers' perspectives is through joint involvement in the process of doing research. Researchers in the future will need to be perceived not only as persons who appear in schools to do their own research but also as persons who are there to engage in joint inquiry and to interact with experienced teachers for the purposes of improving teaching and schooling. Several groups of researchers around the country are currently experimenting with processes for including teachers in the conceptualization and the conduct of research. The work on coaching by Joyce and Showers (described earlier in this volume), the work of researchers at Michigan State University, and that of Marilyn Cochran-Smith and her colleagues at the University of Pennsylvania all include processes for involving teachers. These researchers have found procedures for engaging practicing teachers in helping define researchable questions, in joining in the conduct of research, and in communicating the results to their peers. David Hopkins (1985) of the United Kingdom has also found ways to engage teachers in their own research aimed at improving their own teaching and the processes of learning to teach.

Connecting for Initial Preparation of Professionals

The initial preparation of teachers and other school personnel is and will remain the arena in which universities can make their most important long-range contribution to human resource development. It is also the domain in which universities have the strongest obligation. Other organizations and structures simply do not exist to do this work. Unfortunately, this underlying purpose of the university's work has, at times, according to some observers, been badly ignored (see, for example, Clifford and Guthrie 1988, Joyce and Clift 1984, Judge 1982).

For whatever reasons, faculties have found other professional activities more engaging and rewarding. This neglect is one reason that connections to schools are so weak and why many of the training and development activities currently provided by local educational agencies have such a strong flavor of remediation. For instance, some of the most popular inservice workshops deal with effective teaching strategies, classroom management, or how to plan instruction that ensures student motivation and transfer. There is little reason to believe that locally based staff developers would allocate their scarce resources for this type of training if teachers had been prepared appropriately in the beginning. Is it not reasonable to expect beginning professionals to know how to teach concepts to enhance student thinking or how to use cooperative learning to promote social understanding? Is it not reasonable to expect simple skills such as checking for student understanding, modeling a particular idea or skill, or establishing rules and routines for building productive learning environments?

Recommendations by the Holmes Group, Tomorrow's Teachers (1986), and the Carnegie Forum's Teachers for the 21st Century (1986) make it clear that this neglect has not gone unnoticed and that many stakeholders expect reform. The kind of reforms currently being discussed, such as creating professionally oriented master's of teaching degrees with strong "learning how to learn" components, extending internships, and residencies in schools, will require clear statements and commitments by the university community, particularly faculties in schools of education. It will also require the creation and maintenance of more linkages to practitioners and their professional organizations everywhere.

The university's challenge in the next decade is to recognize that two basic settings are available for preservice teacher education—the college classroom and the field experience. Neither, working alone, however, is sufficient for the effective preparation of the beginning teacher. Research-based knowledge can be introduced in existing university classrooms relatively easily. However, the constraints of the typical university classroom limit the kind of training available to transfer this knowledge into actual practice in schools. Neither can we rely solely on the field experience to accomplish transfer. Recent research has shown that field experiences (as they exist in many places) do not help prospective teachers solidify their learning about research-based teaching practice, nor do they help them become more reflective and analytical about their work. For universities to prepare teachers who have a command of the knowledge base on teaching and a repertoire of teaching models and processes requires new structures and new roles.

Teacher Education Centers

A few universities, such as Syracuse University and the University of Maryland, have created and maintained teacher education centers to coordinate experiences for teacher candidates and to provide staff development to experienced teachers. One of the oldest and most established programs exists at the University of Maryland at College Park. In collaboration with surrounding local school agencies (Anne Arundel, Charles, Howard, Montgomery, and Prince George's County Schools), the University maintains seven such centers. The typical center is staffed by a coordinator, a secretary, and, in some instances, an assistant. The coordinator has a joint appointment between the university and the local school agency. Budgets for the centers and salaries for personnel are shared. A cluster of schools in a geographic area agree to become a part of center activities for a specified period of time (normally three to five years). Teachers in center schools agree to provide supervision of preservice students' practica and intern experiences.

In return for this assistance, teachers in center schools receive resources provided by the university for travel and materials to support their own staff development. Teachers in center schools also have access to special staff development activities coordinated and arranged by teacher center personnel. These activities consist of short workshops, special conferences, or courses for credit aimed at increasing the skills of individual teachers. Other activities are planned for whole faculties to assist them in a variety of schoolwide change and improvement initiatives. Some activities are taught or coordinated by center personnel, some by university faculty, and still others by special consultants brought to the school from outside the region with university resources. The personnel in the teacher education centers thus become an integral part of the staff development efforts of the local school agencies. This arrangement provides a tight connection for the initial preparation of teachers and for their ongoing professional development.

The Learning Consortium

Another interesting structure, initiated very recently, can be found at the University of Toronto in Canada and four partner school systems with whom relationships have been developed—Durrerin-Peel Roman Catholic Separate School Board, Durham Board of Education, Halton Board of Education, and North York Board of Education. Partners have agreed to establish a "Learning Consortium" for the purposes of creating innovative, field-based programs for teacher education and for developing collaborative staff development opportunities for experienced teachers and administrators (see Watson 1988). Although it is too soon to know the effects of this project, it is encouraging that consortium members are designing their activities on research and intend these to have an inquiry orientation. It is also encouraging to find an instance in which each partner school and the University of Toronto contribute equally the human and financial resources needed to support consortium activities.

Clinical Teachers

Other universities are experimenting with the role of clinical teacher. Although the clinical teacher concept has been around for a long time, it has seldom been realized. Examples from three universities show how the role is being conceptualized and used currently.

The University of Virginia seeks applications and nominations of teachers from the local schools to become clinical teachers. Successful applicants receive university appointments and a salary. In return, clinical teachers supervise the university's student teachers and pursue their own staff development by attending university-sponsored workshops. Through this resource exchange and appointment arrangement, the University of Virginia has developed a cadre of clinical teachers who are committed to helping beginners learn to teach and a network of practitioners who have high regard for their participation in a variety of special research and knowledge utilization projects.

A second approach to the role of clinical teachers is found in Maryland. The Clinical Classroom Project is carried out collaboratively by four institutions of higher education (University of Maryland, Coppin State College, Salisbury State University, and Towson State University), seven local educational agencies, and the Maryland State Department of Education. Faculty and teachers from these agencies have created and maintained a cadre of clinical classrooms in sixteen elementary schools, four middle schools, and five senior high schools. Unlike the Virginia approach where the focus is on the student teaching experience, clinical classrooms in Maryland have been designed to be used for early field experiences with preservice students and with beginning teachers. Each clinical classroom provides a setting for learning about and reflecting on five research-based teaching approaches: direct instruction, presentation using advance organizers, concept teaching, cooperative learning, and classroom management. Through training, clinical teachers understand the knowledge base behind these five approaches, can demonstrate each approach, and can hold special seminars. Clinical classrooms thus become special settings for focused observation, practice, and reflection by preservice and beginning teachers and have been designed to be used at various levels of difficulty. The process works as follows.

Pre-observation: Preservice students using the clinical classrooms as part of a college or university class are introduced first to the particular practice through campus instruction and through the use of specially prepared textual materials and videotapes that describe and demonstrate the practice. Specially designed observation templates, called theory-practice wheels, provide preservice teachers with a way to understand the approach and to focus observations when later visiting the clinical classroom. For beginning teachers, this initial instruction is obtained through special workshops conducted by staff development personnel or through independent reading.

Observation: The preservice or beginning teachers observe in the clinical classroom and use the theory-practice wheels introduced during the pre-observation period. Logistics and agreements have been worked out for how both preservice and beginning teachers arrange for using clinical classrooms.

Post-observation: Preservice or beginning teachers attend a seminar conducted by the clinical teacher and explore the practice observed and decisions the clinical teacher made as the lesson went along. Theory-practice wheels provide the focus for the seminar and for analysis and reflection. For preservice teachers, the college instructor follows up each observation with discussion and critique.

A more advanced level of use has been designed for beginning teachers who are already familiar with the research-based teaching approach but who want additional practice. Participants attend classes or workshops that concentrate specifically on one of the research-based strategies, gaining more in-depth understanding. The beginning teacher observes in the clinical classroom with new understandings. Logistics have been worked out for participants to micro-teach a lesson in teams with a small group of students from the clinical classroom and to coach one another. Afterwards, participants attend a seminar conducted by the clinical teacher, explore the teaching practice, and receive feedback on micro-teaching lessons. The "coaching pairs" reflect on the experience and give each other feedback using the coaching wheels.

A third approach of working with the role of clinical teacher can be found at the University of North Carolina. Here, experienced teachers borrowed from the participating local schools are given one-year appointments in the School of Education at the University. During this year, clinical teachers co-teach methods courses with faculty, help with supervision of teaching interns, and participate in research.

The clinical teachers' classrooms in all of these projects become settings for videotaping model lessons to be used in college classrooms.

Clinical teachers have increasingly become actively involved in on-campus instruction via video demonstrations and team teaching. They have also become able and willing collaborators in research on the processes associated with learning to teach, as well as critical linkpins between the university and local classrooms.

To create and maintain the types of structures represented in teacher centers and learning consortiums or the types of roles represented in clinical teachers obviously takes resource commitments on the part of the university. Each center, for instance, is a highly complex organization jointly governed by the university and the local education agency. Clinical roles similarly cut across organizational boundaries. Keeping this type of activity going requires personnel in both the university and the local education agencies who can commit time and energy to these tasks. Directing centers or consortia and coordinating cadres of clinicians also require a person who can span the boundaries of two very different organizations and maintain affiliation and influence in each. It is not a role that can be managed as a part of a load of either a faculty member from the university or a teacher from the local school. The structures of the teacher education center and learning consortium and the role of clinical teacher do, however, link the university and the field more tightly and allow better development of both preservice and experienced teachers.

Connecting for Development of Experienced Teachers and Schools

In an earlier chapter, Joyce and Showers describe a human resource system for experienced teachers with three major purposes: (1) enhancement of individual clinical skills and academic knowledge, (2) the study of school improvement, and (3) districtwide initiatives to improve the educational program. The university can connect with local agencies and help with all three purposes, but this collaboration will require a different set of relationships than those required for conducting research or providing initial professional training. In the latter, the university has the major responsibility for setting the agenda, connecting faculty to school, and seeking the help of experienced teachers to make their efforts successful. When the focus of the work turns to experienced teachers, however, universities must now look to staff development personnel in schools to establish the agenda and take the leadership role. The appropriate role for university faculty becomes one of helping and supporting, instead of directing or leading. This role shift is new for many faculty, and many find it difficult. Several model projects point the way for how this type of helping and supportive relationship may work in the future.

Helping Enhance Individual Clinical Skills and Knowledge.

Obviously, the university makes a major contribution to the enhancement of individual teacher's clinical skills and academic knowledge through its advanced degree programs. Currently, teachers in large numbers pursue university degrees to improve their own teaching knowledge and skills and to enhance their careers. University programs exist that help experienced teachers become special educators, reading specialists, school counselors, administrators, or curriculum specialists. The university is willing to devote resources for these programs because they are in the mainstream of what universities do best. To maximize the university's contribution in the future, however, will require stronger linkages to the profession, mainly through greater input from practitioners in the field to ensure that courses and experiences required in degree programs match practitioner needs. Several examples show how current cooperative degree programs have been worked out.

Cooperative Master's Program. At the University of Maryland, we have introduced an interesting twist in the traditional master's degree in collaboration with the Howard County Public Schools. The university offers a master's degree for elementary teachers who are interested primarily in enhancing their own clinical skills, but provides specific courses within the framework of Howard County's school improvement initiatives. Teachers enroll as a cohort and are required to complete 36 semester hours of course work. Eighteen hours of this work is offered in Howard County, the content of which is cooperatively determined by university faculty and Howard Country staff development personnel. Obviously, this aspect of the work is tailored to local school initiatives and priorities. The remaining 18 hours is taken by teachers on the University of Maryland Campus who select courses or experiences most likely to enhance individual goals and career aspirations. Besides allowing teachers to pursue their own individual goals, this simple idea allows the university to maintain a measure of autonomy over its degree programs, yet serves some of the system needs of the local schools.

The Oberlin Teacher Academy. For several years, Oberlin College in Ohio has made its resources available to high school teachers and administrators in the Cleveland area. Stallings (1989) reports that the Teacher Academy "offers summer institutes and week-end workshops in such areas as English, biology, chemistry, computer science, French, mathematics, Soviet and American relations, and Japanese history and culture." Oberlin

129

College credit is awarded for summer seminars and week-long workshops. Teachers who participate in Academy programs over an extended period of time and perform at a consistently high level of excellence are given the title "Fellow of the Oberlin Teachers Academy." A high level of excellence includes a significant project that makes a contribution to the field of pedagogy or curriculum. Several hundred teachers have participated in Academy activities to date. According to Stallings (1989), who has studied the project, several have been awarded fellow status.

The Ohio State University Teacher Induction Program. Anderson and his colleagues (1988) report how faculty at the Ohio State University have initiated a third type of program aimed at helping teachers enhance their individual clinical skills. Working with beginning teachers and a group of mentor teachers, the Ohio State University and the Columbus Public Schools provide a variety of assistance and support. In a year-long series of eight three-hour meetings held monthly, beginning teachers are provided staff development in several areas of prime concern, including classroom discipline, management, and organization. Special sessions are also held to help mentor teachers focus on their role. Both mentor and beginning teachers are introduced to activities and tools aimed at helping them reflect on their teaching experiences. A teacher leader cadre has also been trained in leadership skills to support the mentors and the beginning teachers. In addition, three-credit graduate courses are available with the following titles: Issues and Concerns of Beginning Teachers, Leadership Strategies for Mentor Teachers, and Issues and Processes for Development of Programs for Beginning Teachers.

Programs for Specialists in Staff Development. A final connection universities can make to enhance individual teacher growth is by providing programs for the preparation of teachers who aspire to district-based staff development positions. A recent survey (Bahn 1988) identified 12 institutions of higher education in the United States that have developed doctoral programs in staff development. Mostly developed during the past decade, they include such large institutions as UCLA, the University of Minnesota, the University of Maryland, and the Ohio State University. An analysis of these programs shows that the curriculum draws upon multiple perspectives, with a core of studies emphasizing adult development, the study and analysis of teaching, models and processes of staff development, and school change. What is interesting about these programs is that they all appear to have practitioner advisory boards; and, compared with more traditional doctoral programs in education, specialist programs seem to leave more room for individually tailored experiences, including extended practica and intern opportunities.

Supporting Faculty Study of School Improvement

The issues associated with the university's role in supporting faculty study of school improvement become more complex, and appropriate connections become more difficult as contrasted to efforts to enhance individual growth. This purpose does not readily translate into courses for credits or even workshops in the traditional sense of the term. Neither does it depend on volunteerism on the part of the school faculties involved. To help support faculty in school improvement efforts successfully, requires rearranging the traditional ways in which resources have been allocated and exchanged. It also requires the participation by university faculty who are knowledgeable about processes of school improvement and change. Two efforts, one using people, the other machines, point the way to how universities in the future can contribute and connect for this purpose.

Cadres of Organizational Specialists. In the early 1970s, Richard Schmuck, Philip Runkel, and several of their colleagues developed what has been subsequently labeled Cadres of Organization Specialists. These University of Oregon researchers trained school district personnel to perform organizational training and consulting functions. Cadre members are drawn from various role groups within school districts; most of the time they are full-time teachers, principals, or counselors. Organized into teams, part-time cadre members are available to consult with school faculties who want to study school improvement or launch specific school improvement projects. Cadre members do not work with a faculty for which they are a member; they are, in effect, outsiders. This allows them to have an unbiased perspective and to act in supporting and helpful ways. Services of cadre members include training faculties in problem-solving and decision-making skills, helping resolve conflicts, connecting faculty to research and exemplary practices, and helping faculties understand the complexity of educational change.

Today, cadres exist in many locations in North America and Australia. Examples include Buffalo, New York; Cupertino, California; St. Johns, Newfoundland; and New South Wales, Australia. Cadres become a legitimate part of the local educational agency and become institutionalized over time, with their own administrative and budgetary support. In most instances, however, they have remained tightly connected to a local university for advanced training and for professional colleagueship. The original cadres trained by Schmuck and Runkel, for example, hold yearly conferences at which both university and public school organizational specialists meet to discuss mutual concerns and to study new training and consultative strategies.

PSINET. In 1985, the National Education Association initiated a nationwide effort known as the Mastery in Learning Project, aimed at improving education through teacher empowerment and the restructuring of schools. The 27 participating schools agreed to appoint a school improvement steering committee made up of the principal, teachers, parents, and students. This group followed a four-step school improvement process that included: (1) describing what was currently happening at the school, (2) setting priorities for teaching and learning, (3) exploring school improvement options and examining research-based approaches to teaching, learning, and school organization, and (4) designing a plan for implementing comprehensive improvement projects.

Through a grant initially from IBM, and more recently from OERI, teachers in the NEA schools have been connected to one another through a new telecommunication network called People Sharing Information Network (PSINET). Several universities, as well as each of the regional educational research and development laboratories, have been linked to the 26 schools through PSINET. PSINET allows participants in the various locations to share information with one another as they pursue their school renewal work. It also enables them to connect directly to the knowledge base on school renewal through interaction with faculties in institutions of higher education and personnel in the research and development laboratories.

Supporting Districtwide Initiatives.

Many of the improvements in schools require systemwide initiatives and the resources that only the larger educational agency can provide. Most improvement efforts initiated at the district level demand extensive attention to human resource development. Just as a university can support faculty study at the school level, so too can it support larger system efforts. This support, however, must remain under the governance structure and agenda of the local educational agency; and as with supporting faculty study of school improvement, classes and workshops are insufficient delivery mechanisms. Here are examples of how some universities are currently working with school districts who want to recruit and train teachers to work in multicultural settings.

The Houston Teaching Academy. In 1987, the University of Houston and the Houston Unified Public Schools became "partners" in creating the Houston Teacher Academy. The Academy focuses on the preparation and renewal of teachers for inner-city schools. The rationale of this partnership was a need of each organization for the other. Stallings (1988) reports that "the Houston schools needed teachers prepared to teach successfully in schools serving a wide variety of cultural groups and economic levels." The School of Education at the University of Houston needed placements in "supportive environments where their students could develop the skills, sensitivities, and wisdom to work in inner-city schools." Over time, this project has evolved to the point that a fully developed professional development school exists with extensive teacher education programs for both beginning and experienced teachers and that university faculty and Houston teachers engage in joint inquiry exploring questions about teaching and teacher education in inner-city environments.

Montgomery County Minority Teacher Education Project. To address the problem of insufficient minority teachers, the Montgomery County Public Schools, the University of Maryland, the Maryland State Department of Education, and the State Board for Higher Education have worked out a cooperative project that includes the following features: (1) Montgomery County hired 12 persons who already had bachelors degrees and who represented various racial backgrounds. The persons have been employed as instructional aides but are given time off their regular work to pursue a teacher preparation program. (2) The University of Maryland, in cooperation with the Montgomery County Staff Development Department, has designed and is currently providing training planned to extend over two summers and four academic semesters. (3) The Maryland State Department of Education and the State Board for Higher Education have provided this program experimental status and agency support.

The program is characterized by a carefully constructed multicultural learning community (an innovative professional core tailored to the unique needs of this student population), along with special support mechanisms to ensure a high degree of success. The University of Maryland and the Montgomery County Staff Development Department teach on-site classes and provide needed personnel for all training and supervision activities, including an extended internship. Successful graduates will receive a master's degree, will be certified to teach in grades 1-8, and are guaranteed jobs with the Montgomery County Public Schools.

Restructuring the University Connection

The preceding discussion provides many examples of special programs and projects that illustrate how universities can connect more tightly to the education profession to expand the knowledge base on teachers and learning and to ensure the initial and continuous growth of teachers. Informative and exciting as these special projects may be, they currently only provide a glimpse of what might be; in no way do they represent higher education's full commitment, nationwide, to prepare professionals or to find powerful linkages to the profession. The special projects have not become an integral part of the total fabric of the schools of education within universities where they exist, nor have they been disseminated very widely to other places. These things will not happen until a significant restructuring of purposes and activities occurs. In this final section, I will provide an analysis of the problems we face in universities, a set of purposes toward which I think universities (schools of education) should move, and a set of activities to consider for getting things started.

The Problems We Face

In 1987, Robert Bush, Emeritus Professor at Stanford University, described decade-by-decade attempts to reform initial and continuing teacher education since the 1920s. From a study of this historical record, he concluded that "the first sobering lesson to be learned from the past 50 years of attempted reform of teacher education is that there has been no fundamental reform during that period" (p. 15). I wish I could write with optimism that the current reform will be more successful or that the problems we face are clearcut and ready solutions exist. That is not the case. The problems facing schools and colleges of education in universities are incredibly complicated. Even though myriad remedies abound, none are close to being implemented.

Nonetheless, I start with the premise that knowledge production and use, the initial preparation of professionals, and work with experienced teachers and schools all exist in an intricate reciprocal relationship to each other. Success and strength in one area cannot be effectively accomplished without corresponding strength in the other two. For instance:

● To make contributions to staff development for experienced teachers, teacher education has to be strong. Yet it is weak.

● To make teacher education strong requires strong, well-articulated staff development programs so that preservice can be designed with a view of life-long learning. Yet these programs, although sufficiently strong in many places, remain disconnected to preservice efforts.

● To make both teacher education and staff development strong requires tight connections to the knowledge base on teaching, learning, and schooling, and to the processes of inquiry. Yet, most of the institutions that prepare teachers have low connections to inquiry and lack consensus about a common core of knowledge required for teachers.

● To make the problem even more complicated, the functions of knowledge production and use, the initial preparation of teachers, and continuing professional growth are conceptually and structurally separated and disconnected from one another within the loosely coupled university system and across the various other stakeholders who have legitimate concerns about teaching and teacher education. This disconnectedness creates enormous problems for would-be educational planners and reformers who try to initiate internal change. Furthermore, governing bodies such as state departments of education, certification and accreditation agencies, and numerous professional organizations have an array of policies that, although designed with good intentions, present fragmented and contradictory messages and have not been very successful in accomplishing externally imposed reform. Real reform will require initiatives and commitments from within and outside the university. They probably need to be characterized by smaller and more concise efforts than some of the more dramatic reforms proposed in the past.

Actions Possible from Within Universities

Issuing a Commitment for Change. Within the university, the beginning of reform must come with deans and a critical mass of their faculties in departments or schools of education issuing a commitment that they will orient their research and training toward the schools and the interests of teachers. Past practices of creating distance from teaching and teacher education in favor of other activity is dysfunctional and will not allow survival in the current environment. This commitment will explain how the initial and continued preparation of teachers and other professional educators is the school of education's central and overriding objective. It will describe how the research agenda for faculty, individually and collectively, will be formed around topics that will inform practice and enhance the wisdom of practitioners. Indeed, the faculty will go on record with a clear commitment for helping to build a common knowledge base to inform teaching, learning, and schooling.

Issuing this commitment—and meaning it—will be no easy task. Perhaps the difficulty explains why no single instance of such an act can be found in the almost 1,200 institutions in the United States that have departments or schools of education. The only word of advice is to remind deans and faculty of education that our work is currently under intense scrutiny and debate and that choosing to ignore or underestimate the prevailing criticism will place us at a disadvantage from which we may never recover.

Fostering a Culture for Innovation and Interdependence. American colleges and universities have an intricate set of cultural norms and legacies that both promote and retard innovation and change. On the one hand, norms and legacies of academic independence and institutional autonomy, along with a very decentralized organizational structure, allow individual faculty to do pretty much what they want. This has been a positive force for encouraging individual viewpoints and for creativity. On the other hand, these same norms and legacies insulate universities from important stakeholder groups and prevent coordinated and consensual responses to important problems. Some steps a faculty of education could take to remedy this situation would be to forsake voluntarily some aspect of academic independence so that coordinated and articulated programs could evolve, modify course approval structures so that change and experimentation could occur more readily, and organize for dealing with and responding to external demands and pressures in responsible and creative ways.

Reorganizing for Action. In universities, the teacher preparation curriculum and the administrative arrangements for connecting to schools have traditionally been characterized by decentralization and diffusion of control. It is not usual to find one course in a teacher preparation program under the auspices of an educational psychology department, another under the educational foundation department, and still others in the department of curriculum and instruction. Field experiences are normally administered under another unit such as an Office of Student Teaching or Laboratory Experiences. Offerings for experienced teachers, likewise, are administered in uneven and disconnected ways. Although these arrangements have kept relative peace in academic turf wars, they have not allowed for the development of well-articulated teacher preparation programs, nor for ways of becoming part of a coordinated human resource system.

It will be a complex undertaking, but if a school of education wants to make professional preparation central to its mission, it needs a group who will assume responsibility for this task. Leaving it as everyone's responsibility, in essence, makes it no one's responsibility. The structure I have in mind would be a unit (it could be an institute; it could be a department) where a professional development faculty will be chosen through nomination and application similar to procedures used currently to select faculty who wish to become members of a university's graduate school. Criteria for selection would include: (l) willingness and ability to teach in research-based professional preparation programs; (2) willingness and ability to provide courses, workshops, and other school-based activities for experienced teachers; (3) willingness and ability to structure a research agenda around practitioner interests in teaching, learning, and learning to teach.

This unit would constitute a faculty in which about 50 percent would hold more traditional academic appointments and 50 percent would hold clinical appointments. This arrangement will require differentiation of responsibility, but status differences between academic and clinical faculty will be minimized by making all members eligible for tenure. Once constituted, this faculty would be given complete autonomy over the governance of initial and continuing professional preparation programs, including doctoral programs in teacher education and staff development. This faculty, however, would be held accountable by a policy board or board of visitors consisting of members from academic and practitioner groups.

Curriculum Redesign. A consensus simply does not exist about what should be a common core of knowledge for teachers and other educational professionals. Without some type of agreement, the reciprocal relationship between preservice and inservice education and the connections between the university and schools will remain weak. Furthermore, there are faulty design problems that must be corrected.

The basic paradigm for the initial pedagogical preparation of teachers took hold in the early part of the 20th century and has persisted. Teacher candidates take one or two foundations courses that include content from human development, educational psychology, and the philosophy, sociology, or history of education. Secondary teacher candidates take a general and discipline-specific methods course, while prospective elementary teachers take five to ten discipline-specific methods courses. All programs cap off preparation with student teaching. This simply is not enough time. It forces covering too much in a superficial manner resulting in the well-known "Mickey Mouse" judgment made by far too many teacher candidates.

Although the course names are the same (probably because of standards for accreditation), when one looks inside the courses to see what is taught, few commonalities across courses within or among various institutions can be found. In a recent analysis (Christensen 1989) of the educational psychology and general methods course syllabi from 18 institutions in the state of Maryland that prepare teachers, few instances could be found of the same course objectives, the same teaching processes, or even the use of the same textbook. Similar results have been reported by others such as Raths and Ruskin (1984), who studied methods courses in Illinois.

It would be easier to understand and accept this situation if the knowledge bases on teaching, learning, schooling, and learning to teach were weak or inadequate. That simply is not the case. Inquiry on teacher effectiveness, on effective schools, and from the cognitive sciences, has provided a powerful set of concepts and teaching behaviors that can guide teaching and help teachers learn and grow as professionals. What remains to be done is assembling and synthesizing this knowledge, reaching agreement about what is essential for the novice teacher as well as the more experienced teacher, and then finding processes of delivery to ensure effective, life-long learning for teachers. The process of curriculum redesign is going to be difficult because we lack a common paradigm to guide curriculum development in higher education.

Building Linkages and Relationships. Once constituted, a professional development faculty will start building linkages to its various constituencies. This will take some time because connections have been so weak. Discussions will proceed simultaneously with superintendents and other leadership personnel in local school agencies, with leadership personnel in the teachers and administrators' professional associations, and with practicing principals and teachers. Obviously, university personnel will need to convey their new vision of themselves and their new commitments. They should expect not to be believed at first.

After initial discussions, extended dialogue can commence with the aim of identifying projects mutually beneficial to a variety of constituencies. These projects will vary according to the local situation and will be influenced by past histories. In some settings, first projects may be as small as the university's agreeing to pay cooperating teachers to attend a two-day workshop where ideas about the best ways to prepare beginning teachers are discussed, or by a faculty member's agreeing to team teach (pro bono) a course or workshop offered by the school's staff development department. In other settings, say where teacher education centers already exist and where the university has a history of offering an array of workshops and courses for teachers, first projects might be experimenting with having teachers team teach with faculty in the teacher preparation program, or with having a member of the university join the faculty at a local school for the purpose of study and implementation of a particular school improvement project.

To build effective relationships will require not only joint projects, but also joint dialogue in informal settings. University faculty and schoolteachers have few opportunities to talk to one another. They do not attend each other's professional meetings, read the same journals, go to the same parties, conduct research jointly, or serve as advocates for the same educational issues. University faculty can take some important first steps to change this situation. They can join and attend meetings where teachers are likely to go; they can initiate joint research projects; and they can invite teachers to join them at their conferences.

Realigning Resources. Historically, insufficient resources have existed to support initial and continuing education of teachers. Yet, in many instances, the lack of resources has not been the major barrier to accomplishing needed reform. It is the realignment of resources that is required.

The major resources that now exist in universities are the number of faculty lines (positions) that a particular academic unit commands. Faculty lines translate into courses taught and ultimately weighted-credit hours. Few resources are committed to funding clinical faculty or other roles needed to prepare teachers and for making the connections to schools, particularly if these do not produce credit hours. However, to do the type of work described in this chapter requires more than just faculty who teach courses for credit. It requires a strong clinical faculty, and it requires persons to plan and coordinate delicate interorganizational relationships and activities.

Reallocation of faculty lines can be the most attractive route for a faculty wishing to find resources for building stronger relationships with the professional field. Take the following situation as an example of what could be done. Suppose four senior faculty retire over a two-year period. All four are making salaries in the $50,000 range. Also assume that each faculty member was teaching four classes per year. A faculty and administration that wanted to reallocate these resources could buy the following with $200,000: one faculty replacement to teach four classes ($30,000); one person to coordinate school-university activities and teach one class ($35,000); one field agent to assist local school faculty on school improvement projects and to link teachers to research ($35,000); ten experienced teachers to teach the remaining ten classes at $3,000 each ($30,000); six experienced teachers interested in working on their doctorates, who would study and do school-based research at $10,000 each ($60,000); one secretary for clerical and logistical support ($10,000).

Reaching consensus on the core content for teachers is another way resources can be reallocated. Donald Cruickshank (1985) analyzed the courses and seminars offered by the Ohio State University College of Medicine and those offered by the College of Education. He reports that the College of Medicine offered slightly more than 20 courses and seminars, whereas the College of Education listed well over 300. This situation is true for other institutions as well. It would seem that systematic thought about a common core of knowledge for teachers could reduce the overall number of courses required, with significant savings to be freed for other purposes.

Engaging in Inquiry and Testing It with Practitioners. A final task a professional development faculty will want to accomplish is to make their own work the subject of inquiry. Programs of research would be designed to examine the match between teacher education processes and outcomes and the underlying beliefs and assumptions behind these processes. Programs of research will examine the effects, both positive and negative, of the faculty's effort to link more closely with the schools.

Actions Possible Outside the University

Neither the initial nor the continuing preparation of teachers can be strengthened extensively by the actions of university faculty alone. Help and assistance from a variety of stakeholder and governing bodies are also required.

Moratorium on Regulations from Accrediting Agencies and Legislatures. There has been a common perception that the only way to reform teacher education in universities is through regulation by external agencies. Most states, over the last decade, have initiated legislation requiring testing of teacher candidates prior to entry into preparation programs and testing for certification. These actions, although they may relieve some anxieties held by the larger public about the quality of teacher candidates, have had little actual impact on the quality of preparation, the more far-reaching and important problem. Under the guidelines set forth by the National Association of State Directors of Teacher Education and Certification (NASDTEC) and that association's program approval process, universities have also been required to include in teacher education programs curriculum topics such as working with handicapped children and working in schools with multicultural student populations. As well intentioned as these regulations have been, they have not addressed the more fundamental organizational and curriculum issues. In fact, dealing with these specific topics in piecemeal fashion may have hindered faculties from responding to the larger changes needed in teacher preparation. Some states, such as New Jersey and California, have passed legislation allowing alternative routes into teaching; others, such as Texas and Virginia, have restricted severely the number of hours in pedagogy. Again, neither of these actions does anything to promote reform in higher education, to help codify and reach a consensus of a knowledge base for teaching, or to expand opportunities to bring universities and schools closer together.

External agencies could better serve higher education attempts to prepare beginning teachers and to work with experienced teachers, by declaring a moratorium on regulations. This moratorium would exist only for a specified period of time and be granted only to institutions that could demonstrate serious internal commitment to change. Innovativeness in programs will only be constrained by more rules and regulations.

Support for Improvement Efforts. For the past three decades, a multitude of reforms in education in general have been proposed and promoted. For instance, Berliner reported the following examples:

Since 1975, 37 states developed programs to foster school or district planning; new curriculum and local district technical assistance initiatives were funded in 47 states; effective schools programs were created in 15 states; staff development programs for teachers were begun in 44 states; staff development programs for administrators were begun in 31 states; and new incentive programs for teachers were begun in 29 states (1984, p.4).

Except in rare instances such as Teacher Corps, comparable programs for school improvement, technical assistance, and incentives for the staff development of university-based teacher educators have not existed. Almost a decade ago, Hyde and Moore (1982) estimated that large school districts spent from $1,000 to $1,700 per teacher per year on staff development. In the AACTE studies cited previously, faculty in departments and colleges of education report getting from $200 to $400 per year for their development. Finally, the substantial research literature showing how to get successful improvement and curriculum implementation in K-12 schools (Berman and McLaughlin 1978; Fullan and Pompret 1977; Fullan 1982; Joyce, McKibbin, and Hersh 1983) does not exist for higher education. Substantial resources are needed in the future to study and foster educational change and innovation in departments and colleges of education.

Bringing the Connection Full Circle

Two scenarios about the university's role in the initial and continuing preparation of teachers can be imagined for the future. One is that institutional insularity and lack of connectedness to the larger profession, along with slowness and inability to respond to criticism, have so disadvantaged us that newly emerging organizations and forms will take over training for the teaching profession. Teacher preparation of the future could be under the auspices of inspired and well-funded district-based human resource development units or state-based special academies for teachers. Perhaps teachers themselves, through their professional associations, will reach out and assume this responsibility. Actions in such states as California, New Jersey, and Texas already provide models on which others could build.

Another scenario is that, indeed, internal and external forces will join together to accomplish meaningful reform. Although the outcomes are not yet known, perhaps initial efforts of the 94 major research universities who are members of the Holmes Group will produce new commitments and new forms and structures for the initial and continuing education of teachers. Perhaps, through continuing efforts such as those found in the recent publication of the Knowledge Base for Beginning Teachers (Reynolds 1989), a consensus will be reached on the core content for teacher preparation, and a professional community of teachers and teacher educators will be built.

After World War II, Americans invested substantially in rebuilding Japan and Germany, the two countries it devastated during the war years. Today, it is commonly believed that the economies and infrastructures of these two countries are much stronger than our own, and some have proposed that economic aid should begin to flow in the other direction.

During the past three decades the university has provided the profession with the beginnings of a codified knowledge base of which it can be proud. Today the university finds itself in a weakened position for initiating the type of change required in its own programs. Perhaps it is time for school systems and their human resource development units to consider aid and assistance that flows the other direction. Could we conceive of an "adopt a college" program in the near future?

References

American Association of Colleges for Teacher Education. (1987). *Teaching Teachers: Facts and Figures*. Washington, D.C.: AACTE.

American Association of Colleges for Teacher Education. (1988). RATE 11, *Teaching Teachers: Facts and Figures*. Washington, D.C.: AACTE

Anderson, D.P., D. Asbury, J. Grossman, K. Howey, V.M. Rentel, N. Zimpher. (1988). "Partnerships in the Professional Development of Teachers: The Columbus School District, The Columbus Education Association and the Ohio State University." Paper presented at the National Holmes Group Meeting in Washington, D.C.

Bahn, J. (1988) *Staff Development Programs in American Universities*. College Park: University of Maryland.

Berliner, D.C. (1987). "Knowledge is Power: A Talk to Teachers About a Revolution in the Teaching Profession." In *Talks to Teachers*, edited by D.C. Berliner and B.V. Rosenshine. New York: Random House.

Berliner, D.C. (1984). "Contemporary Teacher Education: Timidity, Lack of Vision and Ignorance." Paper presented to the American Academy of Education, Washington, D.C.

Berman, P., and M. McLaughlin. (1978). *Federal Programs Supporting Educational Change*. Santa Monica, Calif.: The Rand Corp.

Bush, R.N. (1987). "Teacher Education Reform: Lessons from the Past Half Century." *Journal of Teacher Education* 38: 13-19.

Carnegie Forum on Education and the Economy. (1986). *A Nation Prepared: Teachers for the 21st Century*. New York: Carnegie Corporation.

Christensen, P. (1989). "Content Analysis of Selected Courses in Teacher Education." College Park: University of Maryland.

Conant, J.B. (1963). *The Education of American Teachers*. New York: McGraw Hill .

Clark, D.L. (1978). "Research and Development Productivity in Educational Organizations." (occasional paper) Columbus: Ohio State University.

Clark, D.L., and E.G. Guba. (1975). *A National Study of the Role of Schools, Colleges and Departments of Education in Knowledge Production and Utilization*. Bloomington: Indiana University.

Clifford, G., and J. Guthrie. (1988). *Ed School*. Chicago: University of Chicago Press.

Cruickshank, D.R. (1985). *Models for the Preparation of America's Teachers*. Bloomington, Ind.: Phi Delta Kappa Educational Foundation.

Feistritzer, C.E. (1988). *Profile of School Administrators in the U.S.* Washington, D.C.: National Center for Education Information.

Fullan, M. (1982). *The Meaning of Educational Change*. New York: Teachers College Press.

Fullan, M., and A. Pompret. (1977). "Research on Curriculum and Instruction Implementation." *Review of Educational Research* 47: 335-397.

Holmes Group. (1986). *Tomorrow's Teachers*. East Lansing, Mich.: Author.

Hopkins, D. (1985). *A Teacher's Guide to Classroom Research*. Philadelphia: Open University.

Hyde, A., and I. Moore. (1982). *Making Sense of Staff Development: An Analysis of Staff Development Programs and Their Costs in Three Urban School Districts*. Washington, D.C.: U.S. Government Printing Office.

Joyce, B., and R. Clift. (1984). "The Phoexis Agenda: Essential Reform in Teacher Education." *Educational Researcher* 13: 5-18.

Joyce, B., M. McKibbon, and R. Hersh. (1983) *The Structure of School Improvement*. New York: Longman.

Joyce, B., and B. Showers. (1988). *Student Achievement Through Staff Development*. New York: Longman.

Joyce, B., S. Yarger, and K.R. Howey. (1977). *Pre-service Teacher Education*. Palo Alto, Calif.: Consolidated Publications.

Judge, H. (1982). *American Graduate Schools of Education: A View from Abroad*. New York: Ford Foundation.

National Education Association. (1987). *Status of the American Public School Teacher*. Washington D.C.: NEA.

Reynolds, M.C., ed. (1989). *Knowledge Base for Beginning Teachers*. New York: Pergamon Press.

Stallings, J. (forthcoming). "Professional Development Schools." In *Research on Teacher Education*, edited by R. Houston. Reston, Va: Association of Teacher Educators.

Stallings, J. et. al. (1988). "The Houston Teacher Academy." Paper presented at the Annual meeting of the American Educational Research Association in New Orleans.

Watson, N. (1988). "The Learning Consortium: A Partnership of Equals." *ORBIT* 14-15.

PART III
Changing Roles of the Shareholders in England, Wales, and Australia

8

Recent Developments in England and Wales

Ray Bolam

The purpose of this chapter is threefold: first, to summarise the main recent changes in national education policy and staff development in England and Wales; second, to analyse their consequences and implications for various system levels and protagonists in the country; and, third, to explore some of the emerging issues in a wider, international context.

I use the following working definition of staff development:

> Staff development is a deliberate and continuous process involving the identification and discussion of present and anticipated needs of individual staff to further their job satisfaction and career prospects and of the institution for supporting its academic work and plans, and the implementation of programmes of staff activities designed for the harmonious satisfaction of those needs (Billings 1977).

Ray Bolam is Director of Further Professional Studies, School of Education, University of Bristol, England.

As McMahon and Turner (1988) comment, this definition also

encompasses the concept of management development, i.e. development and training for the large proportion of the teaching force who either already have, or are preparing for, specific responsibility for managerial tasks in school in addition to their classroom work. They are headteachers, deputy headteachers, senior teachers, heads of house/year, heads of department, curriculum post holders, etc. As such they can be described as managers of other adults and they are likely to have particular needs as individuals and groups to develop their management skills (e.g. chairing meetings, working in a team).

However, this definition is by no means unproblematic—partly because, as discussed in a later section, it ignores tensions with professional development and partly because, as indicated in recent work by the European Commission (Blackburn and Moisan 1987), such definitions are inevitably culture bound.

Recent Policy Developments

Staff development policies and practices can only be understood within their particular national settings; therefore, a brief account of the context in England and Wales follows. The top political post in the educational system of England and Wales is the Secretary of State for Education and Science, working in consultation with Secretary of State for Wales. The Department of Education and Science (DES) helps to formulate and implement governmental policies on, for example, the aims, structure, and finance of the educational system, curriculum, and examinations and the supply, education, and training of teachers. Ministers and DES administrators receive advice and information from Her Majesty's inspectors (HMI), who number over 500. At the local level, the 116 local education authorities (LEAs; including 8 in Wales) are controlled by locally elected politicians and run by a team of professionals—administrators, inspectors and advisers—led by a Chief Education Officer.

There are over 400,000 teachers in England and Wales. Virtually all new teachers are graduates, although the profession still contains a substantial proportion of nongraduates, especially in the primary sector. There are two main routes to becoming a teacher: a three-year academic degree followed by a one-year, postgraduate professional training course or a four-year B.Ed. course of concurrent higher education and professional training. Both types of courses include a substantial period of school-based teaching practice, which is observed and evaluated by the school and the training institution. Higher education staff engaged in initial teacher training are required to teach regularly in schools to update their professional knowledge and experience. Beginning teachers are required to complete a probationary year during which their teaching is normally observed by the headteacher, head of department, or an LEA inspector.

Profound changes in the staff development framework have resulted from the Thatcher government's commitment to the view that the teaching force should be managed and developed in order to achieve its policy goals of improved teaching quality (DES 1983) and better schools (DES 1985). These goals are being realised through an education reform programme, embodied in the 1986 and 1988 Education Acts. The main components of this programme, to be implemented over a five-year period, include a national curriculum plus national testing and examinations; headteachers and school governors to be responsible for the local management of schools, including the budget and the hiring and firing of staff; the opportunity for schools to opt out of LEA control; government-imposed national salaries, conditions of service, and career ladders for all teachers; a national teacher appraisal scheme that includes classroom observation; school-level budgets for staff development, plus five days available for training each year; and regular monitoring and evaluation of school performance by LEA inspectors.

These changes are not simply technical. They embody values that are highly controversial, professionally as well as politically: the establishment, for the first time, of a framework of national objectives, standards, and priorities, hitherto the responsibility of schools and LEAs; the redistribution of power by decentralising as many decisions (e.g., on finance and the hiring and firing of staff) as possible to the school level and by requiring local education authorities both to act as "enabling" agencies and to evaluate the outcomes of school-level decision making within the framework of national objectives and standards; the creation of a market-oriented culture for schools whereby clients (parents) are empowered (via governors, open enrollment, published assessment scores, and the possibility of opting out of LEA control) to choose which schools to support and whereby schools are compelled to compete with each other for their clients and thus, in theory, to raise their teaching and learning standards by using their financial, human, and physical resources more cost effectively; the requirement that LEAs should hold school heads and governors accountable for the planning and delivery of the national objectives and standards by evaluating and inspecting their work according to specified performance indicators.

Thus, the implementation of multiple and complex innovations is now central to the professional lives of all involved in education. The implications for staff development are considerable, and key issues therefore arise about the capacity of the inservice education and training (INSET) system to support the implementation of this massive agenda. The national INSET system has itself been the target for reform. In 1983, the government made categorical funding available to LEAs for school management training in an initiative that had three elements: 20-day (or "basic") courses aimed at enhancing the management skills of new headteachers and deputy head-teachers; 50 day (or 1-term) courses with the additional aim of equipping senior heads with management training skills; the establishment of a small National Development Centre (NDC) for School Management Training to monitor and improve these 20- and 50-day courses and to promote the adoption of systematic management policies by LEAs. This attempt to improve school management training undoubtedly had positive effects. From 1983 to 1987, over 6,000 heads and senior staff from primary, middle, secondary, and special schools attended 95 1-term and 20-day courses in 45 institutions. Progress has also been made on the introduction of management development policies and programmes at LEA and school levels (McMahon and Bolam 1989; Poster and Day 1988; Wallace 1988)

During the 1980s, the use of categorical funding for national priorities in INSET was extended. The 1984 Education (Grants and Awards) Act empowered the Secretary of State to pay categorical funds to LEAs to promote particular improvements in the education service. For example, in 1985 the grant was used to support the introduction of a highly innovative national examination—the General Certificate of Secondary Education (HMI 1988). In 1989-90, a total Education Support grant of £81.5 million was payable to support LEA expenditure of £125.5 million, the bulk of which was spent on the salaries of advisory staff and a much smaller proportion on staff development activities. Priority topics included science and technology in primary schools, action to combat drug misuse, information technology, financial delegation to schools, training of school governors, the national curriculum, and LEA inspection.

In 1983 the government provided substantial funding for the Technical and Vocational Education Initiative (TVEI), which led to the TVEI-Related Inservice Training (TRIST) programme. From 1985 to 1987, this made £25 million available for LEAs to support staff development for teachers in secondary schools and further education colleges. TRIST had several innovative features: a contract that required LEAs and schools to be accountable for the achievement of carefully specified objectives negotiated at the outset; the use of training methods and trainers from industry and commerce; training conducted by teachers; access to high-quality facilities and accommodation, made possible by the high level of funding; production of a substantial number of practical manuals (e.g., Hall and Oldroyd 1988, Oldroyd and Hall 1988), and evaluation reports (e.g., Eraut et. al. 1987, Evans et al. 1988). TRIST also acted as a pilot scheme for the next stage in the reform of INSET.

In 1987, the government introduced the LEA Training Grants Scheme (LEATGS) with these aims: "to promote the professional development of teachers, . . . to promote more systematic and purposeful planning of inservice training, . . . to encourage more effective management of the teacher force, . . . to encourage training to meet selected needs which are accorded national priority" (Circular 6/86, 1986). The scheme requires each LEA to submit annually (usually in September) to the DES a plan showing how these aims are to be achieved, their training strategy, and their planned expenditure on designated national priority areas and their own selected local priority areas. National priorities now receive 65 percent, and local priorities 50 percent, support from the DES. For 1990-91, the national priorities included training in school management, teacher appraisal, the national curriculum, national testing, new technologies across the curriculum, managing student behaviour, school-based initial teacher education, meeting the needs of children with hearing and sight disabilities, and meeting the needs of four- and five-year-olds. In the financial year 1988-89, the approximate total national expenditure was £282 million (or £548 per teacher). This paid for 4.7 million training days, about one-third of which were devoted to the national priority areas, and also for the replacement teacher costs involved in 50 percent of those days. About half the training lasted one or two days; 31 percent lasted up to four weeks; 11 percent lasted from four weeks to one year; and 9 percent lasted one year or more. About 20 percent of the training took place in higher education institutions.

Consequences and Implications

In summary, government reforms in the 1980s led to fundamental changes in the ways in which staff development was funded, organised, delivered, and monitored in England and Wales. The levels of funding and training activity increased, but the demands placed upon the INSET system by the scale and pace of wider education policy initiatives have been considerable, with several evident consequences.

Features of Successful Staff Development and Training Courses

As a result of the intensive activity of the 1980s, LEAs and schools are now much more experienced in staff development. Overall, they are probably much more effective in using it to achieve their policy goals. The underpinning technical knowledge that is now being codified and disseminated (e.g., Hall and Oldroyd 1988, Oldroyd and Hall 1988, McMahon and Bolam 1989, Niblett 1987, Wallace 1986 and 1988) is remarkably consistent with comparable work from elsewhere (e.g., Loucks-Horsley et al. 1987). A rough synthesis of the current state of accepted good practice would probably run as follows (adapted from McMahon and Bolam 1989).

Each school and LEA should plan, implement, and evaluate a staff development plan that includes management development and that is based on their broader institutional or educational development plan and budget. Staff development (a) is a long-term dynamic process, (b) consists of more than external courses, and (c) is concerned with the effective functioning of the staff as a whole, not just the development of individual heads and senior staff. Hence, it embraces, for example, team building and aims to promote performance improvement, not only individual learning or career development. The ultimate aim of staff development is to improve the quality of teaching and learning. The immediate aim is to improve the performance of those with teaching and management responsibilities, using the following techniques: on-the-job (e.g., job enhancement, job rotation, classroom observation, coaching, team teaching, and performance review); close-to-the-job (e.g., team development, self-development, consultant support, and school-based INSET courses); and off-the-job (e.g., external training courses, award-bearing courses, and secondments). If external courses, and indeed the whole staff development process, are to be effective, then certain basic requirements are essential. Each school should have a policy and programme that balance the professional development needs of individual heads and teachers (as identified, for example, in a teacher appraisal process) with the institutional development needs of the school or college as identified in a development plan (e.g., as a result of using GRIDS, McMahon et al. 1984, or some other school review process).

Similarly, each LEA should have a policy and programme that balance the needs arising from particular heads and teachers, schools' development plans, groups across an LEA (see below), and the LEA's policy goals (e.g., on the national curriculum or school amalgamations). This could necessitate the use of surveys, group interviews, and a data bank. Each school and LEA must also recognize that the staff development needs of individuals and groups of individuals may vary significantly according to

their age, gender and ethnic background, school type (primary, secondary, etc.), and job stage. Job stages are classified as follows:
- Preparatory stage (when they wish to apply for a new job);
- Appointment stage (when they are selected or rejected);
- Induction stage (first two years in post);
- Inservice stage (3-5, 6-10, 11 + years in post);
- Transitional stage (promotion, redeployment, retirement).

Fundamentally, staff development programmes should be policy-led. The planning, implementation, and evaluation of such programmes at school level must take account of the school's policy priorities and its available resources. Similarly, at the LEA level the programmes must take into account LEA resources, values, and priorities, including its equal opportunities policy (e.g., on race and gender). Each LEA and school should see its staff development policy and programme as part of its overall human resource strategy. Such a strategy should include its recruitment and appointment procedures, its personnel system, and its appraisal system. Schools and LEAs must recognize that their human resource strategy is rooted in the organisational structure and therefore requires appropriate staff and organisational arrangements for its implementation.

Within this broad consensus, issues associated with the design and implementation of good training courses have been the focus of several British research and development studies (e.g., Bailey 1987, Rudduck 1981, Wallace 1988). A rough synthesis of their conclusions suggests that good courses have the following features:
- collaborative planning involving course leaders, LEA sponsors, and former or prospective participants;
- a clear focus on participants' current and future needs;
- careful preparatory briefing for participants several weeks ahead of the course, with opportunities for pre-course work where appropriate;
- a structured programme with enough flexibility to allow for modifications in the light of monitoring and formative evaluation;
- a programme oriented towards experience, practice, and action;
- using, when appropriate, methods like action learning, action research, performance feedback, and on-the-job assistance or coaching;
- a "sandwich" timetable, including course-based and job-based experiences to facilitate this approach;
- careful debriefing after the course and sustained support, ideally including on-the-job assistance and coaching, where new skills are being implemented.

The experience of the 50-day and 20-day school management courses was illuminating in this context. Although many of the participants' early criticisms (1983-84) were directed at the courses themselves, these diminished as the "teething troubles" were sorted out by course organizers and tutors. However, criticisms directed at LEAs have continued (Wallace 1988). They mainly concern two areas: first, poor and tardy preparatory briefing, which still leads too many participants to say things like, "I only found out I was coming on this course two days ago," and "I don't know why I'm here—I was just told by phone that I should turn up"; and, second, poor or nonexistent debriefing and follow-up support.

LEA Level

According to a recent survey of the first year of the LEA Training Grants Scheme (HMI 1989), all LEAs now have an explicit staff development policy and a designated professional (e.g., an inspector) responsible for LEA-wide coordination, usually supported by a steering group representing teachers and other interest groups. The nature and scale of the scheme is illustrated by one LEA's experience. Located in outer London, this LEA has a population of 319,000, 23 secondary schools, 100 primary schools, 41,300 pupils, and about 2,300 teachers. It has an advisory and support service staffed by 30 inspectors and advisers responsible for about 250 advisory and support teachers (an unusually high number), all working on various aspects of staff development and school improvement. In 1988-89 these staff were responsible for 16 major curriculum and related projects, with a total budget of £1.7 million derived from a range of Education Support Grant, LEA, and private foundation sources, and involving most schools in the LEA. In addition, under the LEA training grants scheme, £880,000 was spent on 26,000 training days. These total budget figures include the salary and other costs of support staff and central administrators.

The general impact on LEAs across the country has the following main features:
• much greater emphasis on staff development, which is directly relevant to immediate perceived needs;
• greater reliance by LEAs on in-house provision;
• an increase in take-up for short courses, usually at the expense of long courses and secondments;
• considerable variation in the extent to which the LEATGS budget is devolved to schools and growing recognition that substantial devolution may constrain LEA strategic planning and reduce its overall capacity to take up long courses;
• the creation of area-based clusters, especially for primary schools, to coordinate and manage LEATGS;

• increasing recognition of the problems of strategic planning, administration, and financial management arising from the annual LEATGS process and budget;

• continuing frustration with the problems of inadequate supply cover and the associated problem of disruption to teaching and learning;

• a wide variety of practice in ways of using the five INSET days (e.g., whether LEA or schools should decide on their purpose; how to deal with the resource, logistical, and provider availability implications when schools take them simultaneously);

• growing recognition that the various funds and resources (e.g., ESG, TVEI and LEATGS, and the five training days) should be managed together rather than independently in order to achieve a coherent programme and value for money.

School Level

A well-established tradition of school-based, school-focused, or school-centred INSET in England and Wales goes back to the 1960s (Baker 1980, Bolam 1982, Chambers 1982, Hopkins 1986, Oldroyd et al., 1984), which experience up to 1987 confirmed and extended (Hewton 1988, Oldroyd and Hall 1988, O'Sullivan et al. 1988). The 1987 LEA Training Grants Scheme, together with the new teachers' conditions of service and other aspects of the government's education reform programme, are having a dramatic impact, as the following summary of key features indicates:

• Schools have five days per year available for staff development when teachers are required to be present and students stay at home.

• Most have a staff development budget, devolved by the LEA. According to a 1989 DES survey,

> Most authorities offered a fixed sum per school with different amounts for primary, secondary and special schools plus a fixed sum per full time equivalent teacher. In addition all authorities said that small schools were given a minimum allocation as a protected base. Examples ranged from £150 per institution plus £50 per member of staff to £400 per school plus £25 per member of staff. These sums represented anything from 10% of the total INSET budget to 80% of the total funding available for local priorities within LEATGS (DES 1989).

• All will soon have a general budget that can be used to supplement the staff development budget.

• Many schools are required by the LEA to produce an annual institutional development plan to underpin their staff development programme; this is often based on a self-review process (e.g., McMahon et al. 1984).

• Many LEAs require schools to designate a staff development co-ordinator—usually the head in primary schools and a deputy head in secondary schools.

• Most schools run a programme of school-based activities led by teachers and external advisers and consultants.

• All schools will be required to have a teacher appraisal scheme operating by 1993-94.

Individual Teachers

The implications of these developments for individual teachers and headteachers are considerable and complex. On the positive side, the substantial increase in the sheer volume of activity means that far more teachers have had some form of staff development experience in school time, especially in the secondary sector. The devolution of funds to schools, together with the introduction of five annual INSET days, has led to a greater involvement of teachers in decision making about programmes and in the actual delivery of particular activities. Furthermore, professional confidence has grown in respect to needs analysis, including appraisal and evaluation techniques. On the negative side, the sheer volume of staff development, together with the initiation of the government's reforms, has led to severe staff development and innovation overload for schools and teachers, characterised by too many classes' being without their regular teachers when the latter are out of school on a course. There has also been a sharp drop in the number of opportunities to attend longer, credit-bearing courses in school time.

In the context of management development, great stress is now being placed on the notion of

> individual responsibility for personal development [as] a care concept in all professions. School management training and development must harness this major resource. Personal commitment and an ability to adjust to changing professional circumstances through systematic reflection, analysis of personal performance and the acquisition of new knowledge and skills are fundamental to the process of development (Styan 1989).

It is probable that these ideas about individual responsibility will be taken further and that links with individual appraisal will be made.

External Providers in the Marketplace

The most dramatic consequence of the LEA Training Grants Scheme for providers and trainers, particularly those based in universities, polytechnics, and other higher education institutions, has been the creation of a market economy in staff development. Whereas, prior to 1987, substantial funds were earmarked by LEAs for accredited INSET courses (i.e., master's degrees, advanced diplomas and certificates), this is no longer the case. Schools and LEAs both have their own staff development budgets for which they are held accountable, and they now select courses and consultancies with much greater care and with the aim of getting value for money. Pre-1987 INSET was, effectively, a seller's market, controlled by higher education (HE) institutions; now it is a buyer's market, controlled by schools and LEAs.

Recent data confirm the marked negative impact of this change on the take-up of long courses. One survey asked 38 university and public sector HE institutions to compare the take-up of school management courses in 1987-88 with 1986-87. Wallace (1988) reported on the outcomes as follows: short courses—23 percent increase; 2-day basic courses—10 percent decrease; 50-day courses—67 percent decrease; 1-term fellowships—52 percent decrease. Another survey of 27 university departments of education, comparing the same two years for INSET in general, reported a reduction of 68 percent in full-time secondments for certificates, B.Phils., D.Eds., and M.Eds.; a reduction of 14 percent in part-time secondments; and an increases of 14 percent in short non-award-bearing courses. Taught master's degrees have been particularly badly affected (UCET 1987). One eminent university professor (Turner 1987) argued that university departments of education were having to respond to the INSET market economy while being required to charge full-cost fees under new university financial arrangements that do not give weight to INSET students. In response to these powerful dual pressures, university departments had attempted to modularize diploma and degree programmes; introduced credit transfer systems; created modules taught by LEA staff; spent more time on "selling" and on consultancies; and emphasized part-time courses and "problem-solving" research degrees. He concluded,

> I believe therefore that the continuance of faculties, schools and departments of education as teaching and research institutions is under severe threat and that the next five years may well determine the future of scholarship in the field of education for the next fifty years. (Turner 1987, p.9)

Competition in the INSET marketplace has been further increased by the advent of new providers and modes of provision. First, industrial and commercial trainers and consultants have entered the fray, particularly in school management training. Second, the many recent early retirements among headteachers, inspectors, advisers, and administrators have produced a growing number of private education consultants and trainers.

Third, LEAs have created their own in-house training teams. Fourth, schools often prefer to use their own staff, or someone from a neighbouring school, to lead their training. Fifth, the Open University and the Open College are producing a great deal of open learning material aimed at teachers, as are a growing number of other private, commercial consultants.

Research

The impact of these developments on research into staff development has been significant (Bolam 1989). They have generated a great deal of nationally and locally funded development and evaluation research. Most national funding bodies, especially the DES and the Training Agency, have adopted immediate relevance to policy as the main funding criterion. Most Projects were, therefore, aimed at providing solutions to immediate problems rather than at theory testing. Given their institutions' uncertain financial and recruitment situation, caused by the vicissitudes of the INSET market, researchers based in higher education have, sometimes reluctantly, felt compelled to bid for these research funds and accept them when offered. In consequence, most of the academic research community's time and energy appears now to be devoted to obtaining funds to carry out research of an important but severely restricted nature. It is largely left to graduate students to carry out research that is not immediately relevant to current national and local policies.

Appraisal and Management Development

Two major initiatives recently started have significant potential consequences for staff development. First, teacher appraisal pilot schemes being run in six LEAs should provide answers to the following major questions (McMahon 1988):

1. What should be the purposes of appraisal?
2. What principles should guide the appraisal process?
3. Who should be the appraisees and appraisers?
4. How frequently should appraisal take place?
5. What kind of preparation and information is needed for an appraisal interview?
6. What part should classroom observation play in appraisal?
7. What form should the interview take?
8. What should happen after an appraisal interview?
9. What are the particular problems of headteacher appraisal and how can they best be resolved?

10. How can appraisal best be managed, resourced, and implemented at school level?
11. What kind of support and training should the LEA provide?
12. How can appraisal best be managed, resourced, and implemented at the LEA level?

The expectation of all three protagonists at the national level—LEA employers, teacher associations, and the DES—is that a nationally agreed-on scheme of teacher and headteacher appraisal will be implemented in all LEAs and schools over four years, starting in 1989-1990. This will seek to balance two purposes—individual development and school improvement. Its main stages are summarised in Figure 8.1.

The second initiative, on management development, continues to be a high priority mainly because the sheer scale and pace of the current educational reforms mean that the main task facing headteachers and teachers is the management and implementation of multiple changes. The government has acknowledged this, first, by setting up a task force to identify the implications for management training and development (Styan 1989) and, second, by requiring each LEA to adopt a systematic approach to

Figure 8.1
The Appraisal Process

Planning Stage
Appraiser and appraisee meet to review purposes of scheme and agree timetable and data to be collected.

Data Collection Stage
• Classroom observation data
• Appraisee's self-appraisal
• Data from colleagues

The Interview Stage
Appraiser and appraisee:
• discuss data
• set action targets
• agree record

Follow-up Stage
• Action by appraiser and appraisee
• Professional development activities
• Short meetings to monitor progress

management development (Circular 5/89) along lines advocated by the NDC (McMahon and Bolam 1989). A key short-term aim for LEAs is to ensure that the numerous and diverse activities that make up their training programme to support the implementation of the various components of the Education Reform Acts have coherent and consistent aims and methods, avoid duplication of content, and are delivered as cost-effectively as possible. At present, this aim is proving difficult to achieve, although a number of techniques are being developed—including the use of in-house training teams, open learning packages, and modules and annual development plans at LEA and school levels.

The longer-term aim for LEAs and schools is to base their management training strategies on their annual development plans (i.e., to adopt a policy-based approach). This would involve giving appropriate weighting to the following three main components of management development:

• "Management training," which refers to short conferences, courses, and workshops that emphasise practical information and skills that do not normally lead to an award or qualification and that may be run by LEAs, schools, or external trainers and consultants from higher education or elsewhere.

• "Management education," which refers mainly to secondments and to long, external courses that often emphasise theory and research-based knowledge and that lead to higher education and professional qualifications (e.g., specialist school management diplomas and M.Eds.)

• "Management support," which refers to job-embedded arrangements and procedures for such things as selection, promotion and career development, appraisal, job rotation, job enhancement, on-the-job assistance and coaching, team building, retirement, redeployment, and equal opportunities, which are the responsibility of the LEA and the school.

General Issues

The previous sections have already raised issues significant for other countries as well as the United Kingdom: the dilemmas for higher education institutions operating in a market economy for staff development; the pressures on researchers to concentrate on policy-related studies; and the linkages between staff and management (or leadership) development. These issues will all surely find echoes in the United States and beyond. In this final section, some additional key issues of wider significance are considered in the context of two broad questions.

The first of these is "How can we make better use of what we know?" A considerable body of technical knowledge now exists about effective staff development that is insufficiently utilised in England and Wales. For example, two major studies (Mortimore et al. 1988, Rutter et al. 1979) produced well-researched conclusions about effective processes of classroom teaching and school leadership; but, as yet, they have not informed the design of staff and management development programmes to any noteworthy extent. Similarly, there is now a soundly based body of professional knowledge about effective training practice (Oldroyd and Hall 1987, Wallace 1988) that is entirely consistent with current thinking in the United States (Joyce and Showers 1980, 1988) yet is insufficiently used. As a third example, we may cite the inadequate use being made of available technical knowledge about evaluation: policymakers and administrators are too often satisfied with weak evaluation designs, while rigorous studies of impact on pupil learning are noticeable by their absence (Bolam 1988).

Why should this be so? The following reasons and ways forward are worth consideration. First, staff development organisers, trainers, and evaluators are themselves inadequately trained. Thus, we should explore ways of helping them to strengthen their individual knowledge and skills. Second, for a mix of technical, micro-political and logistical reasons, the organisations of which they are members—LEAs, schools, and higher education institutions—find it difficult to build upon and use available knowledge. Thus, we should explore ways of helping them learn and develop as organisations. Third, at national and LEA levels, the pressures to change are so massive that they have arguably outstripped the system's implementation capacity. Thus, we need to explore ways of educating policymakers about effective change strategies while recognising the political values and context within which they operate.

The second broad question is, "Does staff development differ significantly from professional development and, if so, what are the implications?" In earlier work, carried out in an OECD context (Bolam 1982, Hopkins 1986), five main purposes of continuing professional development were distinguished:

1. Improving the professional knowledge, skills, and performance of the whole staff or a group of staff in a school or schools (e.g., a school-based training course to support an externally imposed curriculum innovation);

2. Improving the professional knowledge, skills, and performance of an individual teacher (e.g., a short, practical training course on the teaching of reading);

3. Extending the experience of an individual teacher for career development or promotion purposes (e.g., a training course on preparation for headship);

4. Developing the professional knowledge and understanding of an

individual teacher (e.g., a master's degree specializing in child development or the sociology of schooling);

5. Extending the personal or general education of an individual teacher (e.g., an Open University degree course in history or mathematics).

In England and Wales during the 1980s, the trend has undoubtedly been towards staff development of a relatively narrow, instrumental kind aimed primarily at meeting Purposes 1 and 2, rather than Purposes 3–5. Whatever the government's intention, the inescapable logic of the market mechanism is pressuring LEAs to make the most of their limited budgets by concentrating on short, often in-house, courses and by reducing their take-up of long courses. This is especially true where a substantial proportion of the budget is devolved to schools: Few head teachers, or their staffs, are prepared to spend most, if not all, of their budget on long courses for just one or two teachers. They prefer to spread their resources more thinly by funding short workshops and conferences for the whole staff. Furthermore, although LEAs do allocate a proportion of their budgets for long, award-bearing courses, this proportion is far smaller than it was prior to 1987.

Whether or not this can reasonably be interpreted as contributing to the deprofessionalisation of teaching (Bolam 1988) turns on one's view of what it means to be a professional, of what constitutes professional development, and of the contribution of advanced educational studies to professional development. According to Hoyle (1988):

> The most fundamental characteristic of the school as a workplace for the teacher-as-professional is the endemic tension between professionality and organization. A professional person can be described as someone who, on the basis of a lengthy period of training, exercises knowledge and skills thus acquired in accordance with perceived needs of clients in a context in which autonomous judgments are made. An organization such as a school is characterized by centralized authority, hierarchy, rules and routines. Thus the professional's autonomy is offset by hierarchical authority and managerial control.

On this definition of a professional, one important and distinctive aim of professional development should surely be to inform the autonomous judgments of individual professionals about the strengths and weaknesses of various ways of meeting their clients' needs. It follows that the consideration of professional and educational values ought to be a core component of any professional development activity, but also that those values ought to be professionally and empirically validated and not simply based on individual idiosyncrasies or ideologies. A professional development activity of this kind could legitimately lead to teachers' being actively critical of aspects of school or LEA policy and practice and, in extreme cases, to their resignation from that school or LEA if, in their professional judgments, those policies and practices did not adequately meet client needs.

Most recent activities going under the name of staff and professional development in England and Wales arose primarily from the obligations of LEAs and schools to meet their legal obligations to their clients as effectively and efficiently as possible: Understandably, they see their professional staff, and hence staff development, as one important means of achieving these aims. Accordingly, they normally regard professional and educational values as unproblematic because these are "given" in the national curriculum and assessment systems or in the financial and organisational arrangements that result from legislation and regulations. The main purpose of "staff" development is, on this model, essentially to train professionals to implement these arrangements and systems as cost-effectively as possible. In consequence, an instrumental approach to individual and group training has become the norm. It is unsurprising that training and development activities paid for and delivered by LEAs and schools emphasise "staff" development aims to meet system needs. However, although universities and other higher education institutions, are, for all practical purposes, compelled to opt into this process, because of their independence from particular schools and LEA employers and because they traditionally offer master's degrees and other professional education courses, they are also the most likely source and location of "professional" development. But, in England and Wales, if they are to persuade teachers, schools, LEAs, and the government to pay for this, they will have to demonstrate the practical utility of advanced educational studies courses, a process that will not be helped by the fact that higher education institutions have produced few, if any, evaluation studies of their advanced educational studies programmes to support their case. It will be even more difficult but arguably even more important to convince them of the necessity for a "critical" component in advanced educational studies courses.

Of course, considerations of this kind must be set alongside more technical arguments. There appears to be a broad, emerging consensus that learning and organisational change require a range of development, training, and learning approaches; that the traditional external course, while reasonably effective as a briefing device for promoting awareness, is poor at promoting behavioral and organisational change; that change is more likely to be achieved via techniques specifically aimed at particular learning targets related to the individual's practical tasks and experience;

and that development, training, and coaching should, when appropriate, take place as close to the work situation as possible. Fundamental to this emerging theory is the belief that, although professionals must acquire a repertoire of techniques and skills, they are, in the final analysis, required to exercise them in complex, dynamic, and unpredictable situations for which specific training cannot be provided. The concepts of action research (Elliott 1980) and, more recently, reflective practice (Schon 1983, 1987) have stimulated two sets of responses to these dilemmas, some researchers emphasising their potential as methods for improving technical competence and others their potential for empowering teachers to be critical professionals. The issues generated by these emphases are similar to those that have arisen in Australia and the United States (Smyth 1989, Killen 1989), but although action research has undoubtedly grown in popularity during the 1980s (see Hopkins 1985, McNiff 1988, and Wallace 1987, for useful accounts), one may reasonably infer that, here too, LEAs and head teachers authorise payments for it from staff development funds mainly because they regard it as being of practical relevance (i.e., they are attracted by its technical rather than its critical aspect).

The broad questions raised in this section are two sides of the same coin. It is vital for the long-term health of the education profession and, ultimately, of the educational process itself, that an appropriate balance be struck between the technical and the critical dimensions of professional development. At present there is a serious risk that teachers in England and Wales will become little more than bureaucratic functionaries with neither the time nor the support to engage in professional development or contribute as informed professionals to the education of their clients, because they are too busy being trained to implement government reforms.

These issues are beginning to be debated in the context of certain European Commission activities. It is critically important that this debate also be informed by professional dialogue across the Atlantic.

References

Bailey. A.J. (1987). *Support for School Management*. London: Croom Helm.
Baker, K. (1980). "Planning School Policies for INSET: the Site Project." In *World Yearbook of Education 1980: Professional Development of Teachers* edited by E. Hoyle and J. Megarry. London: Kogan Page.
Billings, D.E. (1977). "The Nature and Scope of Staff Development in Institutions of Higher Education." In *Staff Development in Higher Education* edited by L. Elton and K. Simmonds. London: Society for Research into Higher Education.

Blackburn, V. and C. Moisan. (1987). *The In-Service Training of Teachers in the Twelve Member States of the European Community.* Maastricht: Presses Interuniversitaires Europeenes Maastricht.

Bolam, R. (1982). *In-Service Education and Training of Teachers: A Condition for Educational Change.* Paris: OECD.

Bolam, R., ed. (1982). *School Focused In-Service Training.* London: Heinemann.

Bolam, R. (1988). "What is Effective INSET?" In *Professional Development and INSET: Proceedings of the 1987 NFER Members Conference* edited by the National Foundation for Educational Research. Slough: NFER.

Bolam, R. (1989). "Recent Research on the Management and Development of Staff." In *Research in Education Management and Policy: Retrospect and Prospect* edited by R. Saran and V. Trafford. Lewes: Falmer Press.

Chambers, P., ed. (1982). *Making INSET Work: Myth or Reality?* Bradford: Bradford College of Higher Education.

Circular 5/89. (1989). *LEA Training Grants Scheme 1990-91.* London: DES, Teachers' Supply and Training Branch.

Circular 6/86. (1986). *LEA Training and Grants Scheme: Financial Year 1987-88.* London: DES.

Department of Education and Science. (1972). *Teacher Education and Training.* London: HMSO.

Department of Education and Science. (1989). *LEA Training Grants Scheme 1989-90: Summary of LEA Responses to DES Questionnaire on INSET Management.* London: DES Teachers' Supply and Training Branch.

Department of Education and Science and the Welsh Office. (1983). *Teaching Quality.* Cmnd 8836. London: HMSO.

Department of Education and Science and the Welsh Office. (1985). *Better Schools.* Cmnd 9469. London: HMSO.

Elliott, J. (1980). "Implications of Classroom Research for Professional Development." In *World Yearbook of Education 1980: Professional Development of Teachers* edited by E. Hoyle and J. Megarry. London: Kogan Page.

Eraut, M., D. Pennycuick, and H. Radnor. (1987). *Local Evaluation of INSET: A Meta-evaluation of TRIST Evaluations.* Bristol: NDCSMT.

Evans, K., J. Yates, S. Battle, P. Davies, P. Lloyd, and V. Dovaston. (1988). *National Evaluation Report: An Evaluation of TRIST Management.* London: Manpower Services Commission.

H.M.I. (October 1988). *A Critique of the Implementation of the Cascade Model Used to Provide INSET for the Introduction of the GCSE.* London: DES NS.

H.M.I. (1989). *The Implementation of the Local Education Authority Training Grants Scheme (LEATGS): Report on First Year of the Scheme 1987-88.* Stanmore: DES.

Hall, V. and D. Oldroyd. (1988). *Managing INSET in Local Education Authorities: Applying Conclusions from TRIST.* Bristol: NDCSMT, Bristol University School of Education.

Hewton, E. (1988). *School-Focused Staff Development.* Lewes: Falmer Press.

Hopkins, D. (1985). *A Teacher's Guide to Classroom Research.* Milton Keynes: The Open University Press.

Hopkins, D., ed. (1986). *In-Service Training and Educational Development: An International Survey.* London: Croom Helm.

Hoyle, E. (1988). "Teachers' Roles and Careers." *O.U. Course E325: Managing Schools: Block 4—Managing Staff in Schools*. Milton Keynes: The Open University Press.

Joyce, B. and B. Showers. (1980). "Improving In-Service Training: The Messages of Research." *Educational Leadership* 37, 5: 379-385.

Joyce, B. and B. Showers. (1988). *Student Achievement Through Staff Development*. London: Longman.

Killen, L.R. (1989). "Reflecting on Reflective Teaching: A Response." *Journal of Teacher Education* 40, 2: 49-52.

Loucks-Horsley, S., C. Harding, M.A. Arbuckle, L.B. Murray, C. Dubea, and M.K. Williams. (1987). *Continuing to Learn: A Guidebook for Teacher Development*. Andover, Mass: The Regional Laboratory for Educational Improvement of the North East and Islands and the National Staff Development Council.

McMahon, A. (1988). "School Teacher Appraisal Schemes in England. The Pilot Scheme Experience." In *Assessment for Teacher Development* edited by J.D. Wilson, G.O.B. Thomson, R.E. Millward, and T. Keenan. Lewes: Falmer Press.

McMahon A., and R. Bolam. (1989). *Management Development and Educational Reform: A Handbook for LEAs*. London: Paul Chapman.

McMahon, A., R. Bolam, R. Abbott, and P. Holly. (1984). *Guidelines for Review and Internal Development in Schools: Primary and Secondary School Handbooks*. York: Longman for the Schools Council.

McMahon, A., and G. Turner. (1988). "Staff Development and Appraisal." *O.U. Course E325: Managing Schools: Block 4—Managing Staff in Schools*. Milton Keynes: The Open University Press.

McNiff, J. (1988). *Action Research: Principles and Practice*. Basingstoke: Macmillan Education.

Mortimore, P., P. Sammons, L. Stolle, D. Lewis, and R. Ecob. (1988). *School Matters: The Junior Years*. Wells, Somerset: Open Books.

Niblett, B.S. (1987). *Managing INSET: Annotated Bibliography No. 5*. Bristol: NDCSMT, Bristol University School of Education.

O'Sullivan, F., K. Jones, K. Reid. (1988). *Staff Development in Secondary Schools*. London: Hodder and Stoughton.

Oldroyd, D. and V. Hall. (1987). *Managing Professional Development and INSET: A Handbook for Schools and Colleges*. Bristol: NDCSMT, Bristol University School of Education.

Oldroyd, D., K. Smith, and J. Lee. (1984). *School-Based Staff Development Activities: A Handbook for Secondary Schools*. York: Longman for the Schools Council.

Poster, C. and C. Day, eds. (1988). *Partnership in Education Management*. London: Routledge.

Rudduck, J. (1981). *Making the Most of the Short In-Service Course: Schools Council Working Paper 71*. London: Methuen.

Rutter, M., B. Maughan, P. Mortimore, and J. Ouston. (1979). *Fifteen Thousand Hours: Secondary Schools and their Effects on Children*. London: Open Books.

Schon, D. (1983). *The Reflective Practitioner: How Professionals Think in Action*. London: Temple Smith.

Schon, D. (1987). *Educating the Reflective Practitioner: Toward a New Design for Teaching and Learning in the Professions.* San Francisco: Jossey-Bass, Inc.

Smyth, J. (1989). "Developing and Sustaining Critical Reflection in Teacher Education." *Journal of Teacher Education* 40, 2: 1-9.

Styan, D. (1989). *School Management Task Force: Interim Report.* London: DES.

Turner, J. (1987). *GRIST and University INSET.* Paper presented at the annual UCET Conference. Manchester: University of Manchester Department of Education.

Universities Council for the Education of Teachers. (1987). *Survey of the Impact of GRIST on University INSET.* London: UCET.

Wallace, M. (1986). *A Directory of School Management Development Activities and Resources.* Bristol: NDCSMT, Bristol University School of Education.

Wallace, M. (1987). "A Historical Review of Action Research: Some Implications for the Education of Teachers in Their Managerial Role." *Journal of Education for Teaching* 13, 2: 97-115.

Wallace, M. (1988). *Toward Effective Management Training Provision.* Bristol: NDCSMT, Bristol University School of Education.

9

Perspectives from Down Under

John M. Owen

I n Australia, pressure on schools is higher than ever before. We can identify several major factors associated with this situation. First, the government sees schools as key agencies in the "skilling" of the work force, a strategy designed to redress the current economic plight of the nation. Second, schools are expected to deal with an increasing range of social issues (such as parental participation and pastoral care), which add to the more conventional needs to improve teaching and learning. Third, teachers are required to absorb an expanding educational knowledge base and to incorporate new subject matter or content into school programs. Finally, students and parents are expecting teachers to develop more challenging and relevant learning experiences.

These pressures operate within a context of curriculum devolution. While broad guidelines and priorities for education are developed by central authorities, such as state education departments, most schools are re-

John M. Owen is Senior Lecturer, Centre for Program Evaluation, Institute of Education, the University of Melbourne, Australia.

quired to develop a policy, assemble programs, and determine teaching strategies for each area of the curriculum. Teachers are thus at the very front line of curriculum improvement.

A recent review of needs suggested that teachers should be able to accomplish the following with confidence and competence:

• Respond to changing educational policies and priorities, such as new calls for teaching about the world of work;

• Keep abreast of developments and changes in emphasis in their own teaching fields;

• Assume broader responsibilities in curriculum planning, implementation, and evaluation;

• Adapt to the introduction of new syllabuses, materials, and equipment;

• Adopt new teaching methods, including cross-disciplinary approaches, and new strategies for classroom management;

• Assume a more significant role in student assessment with the change in emphasis from external to school-based assessment;

• Be capable of diagnosing learning difficulties among students and developing appropriate remediation strategies;

• Participate in cooperative educational decision making with the various groups constituting the whole school community (Department of Education, Employment and Training 1988, p. 2).

Teachers and school administrators need ongoing professional development to acquire confidence, knowledge, and skills. As a contribution to the organisation of professional development in the future, this chapter reviews briefly trends in professional development in Australia, identifies encouraging practices that have been used, and enunciates a set of principles on which professional development should be based.

Recent Trends in Professional Development

Only during the last 15 years have Australian education systems acknowledged seriously the need for the professional development of teachers. Coinciding with a massive effort to improve education by a reformist Commonwealth Labor Government, there was a huge increase in the funds made available for award and non-award courses for teachers from 1974. Combined with state-level funding, the level of activity in professional development markedly increased after 1974.

By the end of 1975, all States reported a substantial increase in inservice activities. In 1975, the funds provided by the [Commonwealth] Schools

Commission were used to provide over 500,000 teacher days of non-accreditation inservice education, that is 3.5 days per teacher. In the State of New South Wales in 1976, 69 percent of teachers in the State attended at least one inservice course (Cameron 1977, p.3).

Commonwealth and state funding for professional development reached its peak in 1976, after which it declined in real terms (Coulter and Ingvarson 1985, p.15). There was a decline by 65 percent in the 1984 level of professional development funding from the commonwealth over the 1975 levels.

Within an unchanged overall allocation to education in this period, the commonwealth chose to increase allocations to special purpose curriculum programs at the expense of professional development. Many of these programs focused on whole-school change, which relied, in turn, on teachers' acquiring new knowledge and skills. However, planning for whole-school change programs often stopped short of providing a detailed plan of action for the professional development of teachers, which was needed to accompany the provision of policies and the change rhetoric. There was what Coulter and Ingvarson (1985) described as a "reluctance to analyze in detail the knowledge and skills which teachers will require in order that [these] programs may be effectively implemented."

In summary, much criticism has been leveled at the planning of professional development in Australia up until very recent times. To some extent this has been due to the paucity of relevant research knowledge available. Through reflection on the mistakes made and through an increase in interest in professional development among educational planners and academics, a knowledge base on which to plan professional development practice is emerging (e.g., Hughes 1987). One positive side to the present funding situation is that parsimony has encouraged a more reflective approach to the implementation of teacher and school improvement programs. Two examples of current "good practice" from a wider repertoire are outlined below.

First, from 1984, the commonwealth and states have combined to provide professional development programs designed to improve elementary teacher classroom performance in literacy or mathematics (Basic Learning in Primary Schools, or BLIPS). Teachers from a small number of schools meet for a series of inservice sessions (from 5 to 12) led by a trained tutor. The sessions are spaced to allow teachers to test new ideas in their own classrooms. Generally, groups of two or three teachers from one school attend the sessions. It is expected that they will assist one another in trying new ideas in the school, even after the formal sessions have been completed. The approach is thus relatively consistent with the literature on effective change strategies (Showers 1984). Since 1984, BLIPS programs have involved 40 percent of elementary teachers in the state of Victoria (Stephens 1989).

The second example is the national Mathematics Curriculum and Teaching Program (MCTP). As a professional development initiative, the MCTP has distinctive content and process change components. A concerted attempt is made to expand the teaching repertoire of mathematics teachers through the collection of innovative approaches to teaching. It is important to note that many of the ideas put together by the MCTP team are based on good practice from the field, that is, on the craft knowledge of teachers.

Because the MCTP is national in scope, it is difficult to estimate its effect at the individual school level. However, during the 1986-88 period, members of the MCTP team visited all states and conducted workshops with a majority of mathematics curriculum consultants.

A notable aspect of the MCTP has been an attempt to help consultants and curriculum leaders in schools by codifying the following series of approaches to professional development (Owen et al. 1988).

Structured Course Outside Schools

Here, many of the processes are formalized into an organised course over a fixed time. Teachers are released on a regular basis from school responsibilities to attend sessions devoted to presentations and reports on trials and developments. Opportunities for teachers to be engaged in developmental or teaching activities between the formal sessions are assumed. Normally, a course of this nature would be held outside the schools represented by teachers in the course. In its most extended form, this approach could describe subjects in a formal graduate structure offered by a tertiary institution.

Sandwich Course Outside Schools

This has a format similar to the structured course, but shorter in duration. It involves the opportunity for trials between two formal sessions. The sandwich was suggested as a means of taking a small but important extension beyond the limitations inherent in the "one-shot" inservice course.

In-school Intensive Course

Approaches of this nature are conducted within a school with a group of staff, preferably engaged on a common mission (e.g., trying out inductive teaching in the junior elementary school). The arrangements for conducting such an approach are flexible and vary according to factors such as the needs of the group and the availability of common times to meet. Similarly, the extent of the commitment varies according to these factors.

Features of this approach are that teachers have a large say in determining the agenda and that there is an opportunity to start where the teachers are before moving on. Nevertheless, the presentation of theory, trial results, and feedback are important features in later stages of the process.

Course for School Clusters

The approach is similar to the in-school intensive course, except that the participants include teachers from a small number of schools where a common issue in curriculum and teaching has arisen. One obvious issue is transition from elementary to secondary school. Another might be the implementation of a common discipline policy.

Teachers meet at mutually suitable times to consider the issue. If it is appropriate, trials of a new technique are made by teachers in individual schools and brought back to the cluster for analysis.

Postal Course

Some Australian teachers working in remote parts of the country have little opportunity to meet with consultants or other teachers with common professional development needs. The only viable approach in this case is for consultants and teachers to communicate through conventional and electronic mail. In these situations, consultants and other system-level educators are responsible for organizing ongoing inservice programs from a distance. While past attempts have used conventional mail approaches, the opening up of new forms of electronic interactions should encourage the use of more imaginative and interactive forms of communication.

In-school Peer Tutoring

This relies on the availability of a colleague within a school to provide ongoing support. Effective use of peer tutoring requires the collection of systematic information about teaching and classroom management. The approach is based on the action research principles of data collection, search for solutions, and monitoring of new practice. While there is no objection to the introduction of innovative practices based on educational research, it is more likely that peer tutoring concentrates on the craft and local knowledge of the teachers involved as the basis for making decisions about improved practice (e.g., Smyth and Strachan 1981, Thew 1987).

Activity Documentation

This involves the documentation of successful practice and its dissemination. Marsh (1987) maintains that the development of materials can be a most important vehicle for professional development. Teachers are working in the field at the "cutting edge," successfully implementing new approaches in their teaching. Tapping into this craft knowledge and showing others examples of quality practice is the purpose of activity documentation. The approach is, therefore, based on two assumptions: that craft knowledge is an important resource and that it is possible that such knowledge can be transferred successfully to other teachers.

Development of the manual reflects the need for immediately usable guidelines based on research into exemplary practice. The rationale is that consultants, in different conditions, will need to select an approach to fit those conditions. While some approaches are clearly preferable to others, the codification of alternatives recognizes that there will be circumstances where a less ideal approach is the only one feasible. All the approaches suggested are preferable to the "one-shot" inservice day.

The manual has applicability to professional development over and above its use in mathematics, and it is now being used widely by consultants with responsibilities in other areas of the curriculum.

Focuses for Professional Development

School-level curriculum responsibility means that, in practice, professional development needs exist at three levels, described as follows.

School Policy Development and Whole-School Program Change

Policy and associated change activities are designed to determine the general educational direction taken by the school. In practice, a school policy consists of a set of sub-policies on matters such as computer education and language across the curriculum. In well-organised schools, the school policy is not immutable, rather it is open to amendment from time to time in response to system initiatives.

The school administration is responsible for school policy. In theory, policy is developed after consultation across the school community, including parents and students.

Development of Curriculum Programs

These involve the development of documentation on what is taught across the school and are most likely to be organised according to conventional subject disciplines, for example, mathematics and social science. Programs will often be organised into units of less than a year in length, for example, on a semester (half yearly) basis.

The responsibility for curriculum programs generally rests with subgroups of teachers; for example, in an elementary school a committee might be responsible for science. In the secondary school, subject departments, such as the art department, have the equivalent responsibility.

Organizing Teaching and Learning

This involves refining existing teaching methods and extending the repertoire and is ultimately the responsibility of teachers for implementation. Extension of the repertoire includes the use of effective teaching models, such as inductive teaching, cooperative learning, role play, and enquiry approaches.

A central thesis of this chapter is that serving the needs of practising teachers in Australia requires offering forms of professional development to assist teachers in these three areas. Strategies for professional development must acknowledge that different groups of teachers have different priorities. While, for example, senior staff may need assistance with policy development, the priority of those who spend more time in the classroom is likely to be improvement of teaching techniques.

It is salutary to compare this range of concerns within professional development in Australia with those in the United States. There, the overwhelming concern of leaders in the field of professional development appears to be with improved classroom teaching (Joyce and Showers 1987). Little is made of teacher needs in curriculum or school policy development. This is probably due to the fact that policies and curriculum programs in the United States are often developed by a school district or a state department. More is expected of Australian teachers in terms of the range of tasks; consequently, concomitantly greater needs for professional development exist in Australia.

Professional Development as Empowerment of Teachers

Broadly, professional development can be delivered in two ways. The first is through short courses and ongoing in-school initiatives. Such approaches can be thought of as informal in that they do not lead to recognition by an authority for the purposes of gaining a formal education. The second is through formal courses offered by universities and colleges that lead to the awarding of a postgraduate qualification.

For both forms, we define *professional development* as a deliberate learning activity that has as its focus empowering teachers to effect improvement of policy and curriculum development and teaching with a view to providing better student outcomes.

Empowerment can be thought of as a mediating variable between professional development (as the independent variable) and the development of policies and programs and the use of better and more appropriate teaching techniques (the dependent variables). This view of professional development is outlined in Figure 9.1.

Figure 9.1
A Conceptual Overview of the Roles of
Professional Development in School Improvement

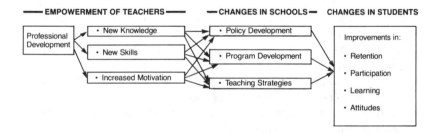

Why should teachers be empowered? Enhancing empowerment is based on an assumption that teacher acquisition of knowledge and skills ultimately influences student outcomes through changes in schools. These could include increased participation in the sense of involvement in class work, increased retention to higher levels of schooling, improved attitudes, and increased learning. In addition to student outcomes, it is possible to see the benefits to teachers themselves in terms of increased recognition among peers and promotion.

Outlining Principles

To this point, this chapter makes it clear that professional development programs must be planned to meet the needs of a given context or situation. Nevertheless, it is possible to identify a set of general principles as a basis for good practice.

In this section such a basis is put forward. In advancing these principles, we have made extensive use of recommendations developed through a recent national report on professional development (DEET 1988). The section is organised around five aspects of professional development: platform, leadership and support, strategies, setting, and outcomes.

Platform

Effective professional development is characterized by these attributes:

• It recognizes that teachers are learners who need to relate new knowledge to their existing curriculum and classroom experiences, who need to apply and critically evaluate new knowledge and practices in their own contexts, and who require support and encouragement throughout the process.

• It requires that educational planners acknowledge their responsibility for supporting the development of teachers and administrative personnel. This entails coordinated responsibility for inservice education, and a higher profile for inservice as a part of all major policy initiatives.

• It occurs when systems and institutions develop climates that commit people and resources to the pursuit of professional learning.

These points emphasize the prime importance of the human capital in the delivery of education and the need for greater commitment to professional development by systems to place it within the mainstream of teacher education. As a noted observer of professional development in Australia recently said:

> Talk about improving the quality of education is mere humbug unless inservice education moves from the marginal status of a cottage industry to become a central component of system-level planning and coordination of all resources relevant to the support of innovation, school improvement and professional development (Ingvarson 1987).

Leadership and Support

Effective professional development (a) is directly related to the commitment and support provided by the principals in schools and is enhanced through collaborative leadership and (b) provides teachers with ready access to and development of relevant internal and external support services.

These principles are predicated on the reality that change requires backing from those who exercise power within a school. An element of good leadership is to enable participants to feel a substantial degree of ownership and commitment. If teachers have a say in their professional development, a commitment to change will result from inservice activities. Teachers need to be involved in decisions about their professional development activities because in the long term they will be responsible for the implementation and continuation of the learning from these activities.

School leaders must show initiative in deciding priorities for professional development of the staff; that is, professional development becomes a whole-school issue rather than an issue concerning the individual teacher. Teachers should be involved in decisions that link the priorities of professional development with the development of the curriculum of the school. The implications of these procedures are that schools will concentrate on a few issues rather than many and that these issues will need to be addressed over time to come to satisfactory solutions.

In a recent review of exemplary school-based professional development projects, it was noted that all had well-informed, sensitive, and enthusiastic leaders whose vision emphasised the value of a quality education for students. All the leaders were "extended professionals" in that they had themselves upgraded their educational knowledge and skills through courses on leadership and curriculum development and were committed to continually upgrading their skills and knowledge.

Strategies

Effective professional development is derived from school priorities and addresses teachers' perceived needs. This is predicated on the assumption that inservice education should help teachers and others in schools to solve problems that they encounter in their work. Given the shortage of time and resources for professional development, schools need to develop policies for determining priorities.

The identification and selection of problems to be approached through professional development activities has been and will continue to be an issue. It is not clear how Australian schools choose the focuses of their professional development activities. Anecdotal evidence suggests (a) that selection is often done informally, rather than through more systematic methods such as needs assessments or Delphi techniques, and (b) that decisions about the focus for professional development are made by individuals or sub-groups in a school rather than at the school level.

A second issue in the selection of professional development activities is whose concerns should be of primary importance. What if the expressed needs of individual teachers or schools are in conflict with the needs for reform as seen by the school or the school system?

This argument brings into focus the distinction between two alternative orientations to professional development: the innovation-focused and action research models. The first is more appropriate when new policies, programs, and teaching strategies are introduced into the school. The second assumes that teachers should use their own contexts as the basis for improvement. Johnson and Owen (1986) see a need for both approaches to be used together in an effective inservice education program. They assert that starting where the teachers are and then selecting new ideas or strategies later in the program are essential complementary elements of effective inservice education. The implication is that a great deal of time is necessary for effective changes.

Effective professional development recognizes the contribution that innovation-focused and action research delivery models make to teachers' learning and balances and supports these modes over time. It includes material (content, teaching strategies, etc.) responsive to established and new knowledge fields and provides for participation in developments regarding them, in addition to using the services of an informed consultant or critical friend.

There is an increasing recognition of and demand for the services of informed consultants (or change agents) in schools. The relatively few consultants in Australia who have an overview of educational change, can assist teachers or schools in conducting responsive professional development programs, and can be involved in at least some of the processes, are in very high demand.

Effective professional development occurs when the design provides for recurrent participation of the learners. It is now almost a cliche that change is a process, not an event, and that the acquisition of educational knowledge and skills that result in lasting change is a complex process.

The implementation of this principle also allows opportunities for reflection and feedback. This is predicated on the assumption that participants learn by applying new knowledge and skills, that theoretical inputs must be accompanied by the opportunity to put such inputs into practice, and that the sharing of practice by participants further enhances learning.

From the little that is documented on exemplary professional development and whole-school change, it is clear that the principals or change agents emphasized the need for gradualism. Regular discussions, planning sessions, reviews of draft documents, and reports on trial implementations are strategies used to involve staff. These are designed to inform teachers about developments to encourage them to draw on their own ideas and to integrate newly acquired approaches into their classrooms.

Setting

Effective professional development offers a conducive setting and uses the school as its major focus because of its pivotal role in the development and application of ideas, the practice and sharpening of skills, and the critical appraisal of curriculum programs.

The implication of this principle is that professional development should relate closely to the participants' own work environment. This is predicated on the notion that the closer the match between the environment of the professional development program and that of the school, the more likely will be the transfer of the learning between the professional development and the curriculum of the school. The key notion is proximity, and it has both physical and psychological dimensions.

While the school may be the most ideal physical location for many activities, numerous professional development courses in Australia, with the support of teachers and funding agencies, are held outside the school.

Some of the features of exemplary programs of this form include having more than one staff member from a given school in the course, giving participants opportunities and time to try new ideas in their schools and to reflect on their attempts to use new practices, and ensuring that the programs focus on the day-to-day concerns of teachers (curriculum development, evaluation, and teaching strategies) rather than more general issues (e.g., the examination of schools in society).

Outcomes

Effective professional development encourages participants to consider outcomes when a professional development program is in the planning stage and goes beyond justificatory evaluation to conscientiously assess its impact on students and their learning, teachers and their teaching, and the educational enterprise as a whole.

It is here that Australian practice is particularly weak. Almost nothing has been published in this country on evaluating the impact of professional development on students. The modal form of self-evaluation of professional development programs is through the use of opinions, an approach roundly condemned by Joyce and Showers (1988).

* * *

Professional development in education in Australia is at a watershed. There are fewer commonwealth financial resources available now than at any time over the past 15 years. This places the ball back into the courts of state governments for the major funding of professional development exercises. One advantage of this is that there should be closer links between professional development policies and their implementation.

Ironically, because of reflection on past interventions from the commonwealth, there is now a greater appreciation than ever before of the seminal role of professional development in the maintenance and improvement of our schools.

While some observers view the present lack of resources in doom and gloom terms, there are a few promising signs. An example serves to illustrate this guarded optimism. Within the state of Victoria, the Ministry of Education has recently set up over 30 School Support Centres. Each one is responsible for between 30 and 60 schools and has a staff of curriculum and other support consultants. The centres are sufficiently close to schools to remain aware of the needs of teachers. At the same time, a central agency has been set up to support consultants in the areas of mathematics and science. The agency is also providing the more general research base on educational improvement (this is a temporary system with a 30-month life span). In the same state, every government school now has three pupil-free days for inservice education. There are strong moves to assist these schools in using these days for ongoing professional development projects. Practising teachers have become a little cynical about the role of educational systems in improving schools. The school support centre idea is an acknowledgement of a system-level resource provision of some magnitude. It is now essential that they provide appropriate support. The centres may be the last chance to convince teachers that knowledge from the world outside their own school environment can be useful and should be placed alongside their existing craft knowledge as a basis for actions to improve schools.

The arrangements in Victoria may be the start of a new age in professional development in Australia—one that acknowledges, for the first time, the consolidated research base on educational improvement and teacher change for its planning and delivery. Building future professional development programs on the principles outlined in this chapter is essential if we are to be efficient and effective in our attempts to empower teachers.

References

Cameron, P. (1977). *The Cost and Utilisation of Resources for the Inservice Education of Teachers in Australia.* Canberra, Australia: Commonwealth Schools Commission.

Coulter, F., and L. Ingvarson. (1985). *Professional Development and the Improvement of Schooling: Roles and Responsibilities.* Canberra, Australia: Commonwealth Schools Commission.

Department of Employment, Education and Training (1988). "Teachers' Learning: Improving Australian Schools through Inservice Training and Development." Report of the Inservice Teacher Education Project. Canberra: Australian Government Printing Service.

Hughes, P., ed. (1987). *Better Teachers for Better Schools.* Melbourne, Australia: The Australian College of Education.

Ingvarson, L. (1987). "Policy-Related Issues in School-Based Curriculum Development." Paper presented at the annual meeting of the Australian Association for Research in Education in Canberra.

Johnson, N.J., and J.M. Owen. (1986). "The Two Cultures Revisited: Integrating Messages from Models of Teaching and Clinical Supervision to Encourage Improvement in Teaching." Paper presented at the annual meeting of the Australian Association for Research in Education in Melbourne.

Joyce, B., and B. Showers. (1988). *Student Achievement through Staff Development.* White Plains, N.Y.: Longman.

Marsh, C.J. (1987). "Professional Development through Materials Production and Implementation." In *Better Teachers for Better Schools*, edited by P. Hughes. Melbourne, Australia: The Australian College of Education.

Owen, J.M., N.J. Johnson, D. Clarke, C.J. Lovitt, and W. Morony. (1988). *Guidelines for Consultants and Curriculum Leaders. The Mathematics Curriculum and Teaching Program.* Canberra, Australia: Curriculum Development Centre.

Showers, B. (1984). "Peer Coaching and Its Effects on Transfer of Training." Paper presented at the annual meeting of the American Educational Research Association in New Orleans.

Smyth, J., and J. Strachan. (1981). "Helping Teachers through Clinical Supervision." *The Practising Administrator* 3: 1, 12-13.

Stephens, M. (1989). Private telephone communication.

Thew, D.M. (1987). "Professional Development through Supervision." In *Better Teachers for Better Schools*, edited by P. Hughes. Melbourne, Australia: Australian College of Education.

PART IV

Opportunities to Learn: District Initiatives

10

The Pittsburgh Experience: Achieving Commitment to Comprehensive Staff Development

Richard C. Wallace, Jr.
Paul G. LeMahieu
William E. Bickel

T he other chapters of this yearbook give ample testimony to a few things that should be clear. First, America's schools need forms of professional development that break from the traditional patterns of inservice training that have been employed for so long. We need staff development that is dramatically different, not just in content, but in form of delivery and level of commitment. The change that has occurred in the various subjects we teach, in the forms of pedagogy that have been developed, in the ways of organizing schools and classrooms for effective teaching and learning, in the ways that schools are governed, and in technologies for making decisions about education all imply an urgent need for staff development. The scope of change that America's schools intend to

Richard C. Wallace, Jr., is Superintendent and Paul G. LeMahieu is Director of Research, Evaluation, and Test Development, both with the Pittsburgh, Pennsylvania, Public Schools. William E. Bickel is Associate Professor in the School of Education and Senior Scientist at the Learning Research and Development Center, University of Pittsburgh.

pursue will require comprehensive, innovative, and ongoing staff development. The old forms will prove inadequate.

As great a challenge as that may be, there are three others that may prove to be far greater. The first is the need to conceive of staff development as a necessary part of a comprehensive and thoughtful plan for the change that is desired for our schools. The second is to organize the school district to deliver a program that touches the lives of all professional personnel. The third (and perhaps greatest) challenge is to secure the support, political and financial, that is required to successfully carry out the necessary inservice professional development.

When board members ask, "If they're professionals, if they've had all this schooling, why do they need more?" or even more difficult, assert, "We know that staff development is important, but we just don't have the money for resources to support it," the challenge is posed. As resources grow scarcer, that challenge becomes a crisis. We will describe the ways in which one school district, the Pittsburgh Public Schools, took up and responded to these concerns. In the pages that follow, we present a case study of a comprehensive professional staff development effort. This program, the Schenley High School Teacher Center, was the first of three such programs (including elementary and middle school implementations) that address themselves to all educational professionals within the school district.

The Schenley High School Teacher Center opened in September 1983 with a truly complex and ambitious staff development program that existed within a fully operational and comprehensive urban high school. Secondary teachers from throughout the district, as well as principals, vice-principals, and other professionals, were required to participate in the program sometime during the four years set aside for the first stage of its implementation (1983-1987). For the visiting professionals, the staff development program entailed a full eight-week "mini-sabbatical" built around activities that addressed the refinement of instructional skills, sensitivity to adolescents as learners, knowledge within subject and content areas, individual professional enrichment; districtwide initiatives, and follow-through at home schools for continued professional growth.

Four times each year, cohorts of 45 to 50 teachers participated in a teacher center cycle, while trained replacement teachers took their place in the home schools. Among the resident Schenley staff were specially trained teachers who worked individually with one or two visitors within their own content areas. These teachers, called Clinical Resident Teachers (CRTs) assisted the visiting teachers in planning the lessons to be taught in the CRT's classroom, observed entire periods taught by the visiting teacher, and provided immediate and structured feedback to the observed teacher. (See Wallace et al. 1984 for more information on the Teacher Centers.)

The result was a program that was dramatic in scope and undertaking. It provided time that was rarely, if ever, realized in any other district-based staff development efforts. It represented a substantial commitment, both political and financial, on the part of the Board of Education and the Pittsburgh community. Over the period of time coextensive with the operation of the Schenley High School Teacher Center, student achievement in the district's secondary schools increased dramatically in both reading and language. In 1983, 45 percent of the district's secondary students were at or above the national norm in both subjects. By 1987, 53 percent of the high school students were at or above the norm in reading, and 69 percent were in language. Accepting normative performance in some national sense as a reasonable level of expectation, the target proportion of students at or above grade level would be 50 percent. In 1987, the district exceeded those expectations in both subjects for the first time.

At the Schenley High School Teacher Center itself, the increase in performance over the same period of time was even more dramatic. Student achievement went from 28 percent reading at or above grade level in 1983 to 56 percent meeting or exceeding that criterion in 1987. Similar increases were observed in the language test as well, where 27 percent were at or above the national norm in 1983 and 77 percent had achieved that stature in 1987. Such increases as those observed at Schenley are considerable in their own right. It must be noted also that they outstrip the increases in performance of the Pittsburgh Public Schools generally (which, as was noted earlier, was somewhat higher than national performance). Using the district as its own normative reference, it can be observed that in 1983 Schenley ranked 10th of 11 schools in reading. By 1987, it had improved that standing to 4th of the 11. Similar results were observed in the language domain. In 1983 Schenley was tied as the 11th of the 11 high schools, by 1987 the scores had risen to place it the 2nd highest of the 11 high schools.

This chapter focuses not so much on the particulars of the staff development program as on the way in which it was approached so as to secure those commitments and ensure its proper implementation. Three conditions, at least, must be addressed in order to realize an adequate and effective staff development program. First, both the substance and form for the staff development effort should be based upon a rational analysis and review of the needs of the school district. Second, the staff development effort must be comprehensive in scope, must be designed and addressed to all of the needs of the district, and must serve all professionals. Third, the broad participation of all of the involved parties is necessary to ensure the quality of the experience and the professionals' commitment, as well as their benefiting from and enjoying it. In short, the program must be responsive to the needs of those it serves and consonant with a vision of educational reform and change, rather than being predicated on the "passing fancies" of the education world.

Five sections follow in this chapter. The first of these, *Establishing the Need: The Data*, describes how a vision of staff development was crafted from a rational assessment of the needs of the district and the constituencies that it serves. Section 2, *Addressing the Need: Establishing Institutional Commitment*, describes the manner in which a carefully articulated staff development program was presented to secure the necessary public support for a sizable undertaking. The next section, *Organizing for Implementation*, describes the strategies that were employed to achieve effective implementation of a staff development effort far greater in scope than any that the district had previously undertaken. The section on *Institutionalization* describes how this program evolved over time, to ensure that ongoing professional development become a "fact of life" of service in the Pittsburgh Public Schools. It is this final achievement that should serve as the abiding goal of all genuine reform (see *Concluding Comments*). Genuine change is realized not when embodied in particular programmatic efforts but when the standard operation of the schools has been affected.

Establishing the Need: The Data

The support for the district's emphasis on staff development grew out of the program planning and development cycle by the Pittsburgh Public Schools (LeMahieu 1984, Wallace 1986). That cycle begins with a far-reaching assessment of needs. It includes both a comprehensive review and analysis of existing data, as well as the assessment of the perceptions of all major constituents regarding those conditions in the district that are most in need of attention or improvement. The results of the needs assessment are presented for review by the school board, typically at a retreat convened for that purpose. The board considers all relevant data, asks questions until it is satisfied of its understanding, and then establishes a set of priorities that serves as the guiding focus for the district's efforts for the ensuing years. Subsequently, the superintendent convenes committees to prepare plans to address the board's priorities, and program design is begun. From that point forward, all of the district's programming efforts and all actions submitted to the board must be justified in terms of the board's own priorities. Historically, this priority and planning cycle lasts for approximately five or six years before beginning anew (Wallace 1986; Hammond, LeMahieu, and Wallace 1989).

This approach to priority setting and program planning offers two very important benefits to the district. First, the district's own development efforts must focus on a manageable number of goals established by the board. This is extremely important inasmuch as any successful effort at educational reform must be of comprehensive view yet focused in its direction. The second and equally important outcome of the priority-setting process is that it secures the board's commitment to a set of common goals and implicitly to the activities that must be pursued to address them. The board's commitment to a set of priorities is expressed through its decisions to provide material support for the proposed programs. This was an important consideration in recruiting public endorsement for the staff development needs of the district.

In the manner of the planning cycle outlined above, one of the first acts of the then newly appointed superintendent, Richard C. Wallace, Jr., was to commission a districtwide needs assessment (Cooley and Bickel 1986). The primary purpose of this assessment was to determine the degree to which the Pittsburgh Public Schools were meeting the educational needs of their children. The needs assessment also sought to conduct analyses that would suggest priorities for improving the educational program throughout the district. The general objective was to identify conditions that could and should be improved. That is, the focus of the assessment was on identifying problems and solutions that were within the realm of the district's ability to influence and implement.

Two approaches were used to carry out the needs assessment. The first included the collection and analysis of existing school data, notably data on failure and dropout rates, student attendance, suspensions, and demographic descriptions of trends within the district, as well as student achievement. The second approach included a survey of every relevant stakeholder group regarding its perceptions of the conditions within the district. These groups included citizens and community leaders, students, parents, teachers, administrators, other professional and nonprofessional school staff, and especially the school board members themselves.

The districtwide needs assessment completed in January of 1981 suggested a number of conditions that could be adequately addressed only through a concerted and well-conceived program of professional staff development. Teachers in the district had an average of nearly 14 years' teaching experience, 11 of those in the same buildings in which they were then working. Moreover, their most recent formal educational experiences related to their teaching had come over 10 years before. The needs implied by those conditions were considerable. The district's leadership realized that the traditional means of staff development (e.g., after-school or Saturday training programs, often voluntary in nature) would simply be inadequate.

The districtwide needs assessment surveys were analyzed for each of the various respondent groups. While differentiated response patterns proved enlightening for the development of programs for various constituencies, a number of areas of need were consistently identified across all groups. The data relevant to staff development could be categorized as being of one of two types: those that substantiated the need for inservice staff development and those that offered direct commentary regarding the substance of those needs.

For example, the needs assessment documented the "lack of opportunity for building level inservice" (73 percent support). It also revealed the "lack of adequate districtwide inservice" (58 percent support), the "lack of inservice programming relevant to the staff's greatest professional needs" (56 percent support), and the "generally poor quality of inservice programming offered at that time" (44 percent support). Taken collectively, these data gave evidence of a broad-based concern about the quantity and quality of professional inservice training at that time. The data suggest that what was needed was a more comprehensive and relevant program for the schools that would be of considerably greater quality than what was being offered at that time.

In addition, there was very strong evidence suggesting the content of what might be considered an appropriate staff development program. Some of the data related to the nature and quality of instruction as well as its evaluation. The needs assessment cited "a lack of systemwide expectations regarding the instructional responsibilities of teachers" (80 percent support), "a lack of good criteria by which to evaluate teachers' instructional effectiveness" (79 percent support), and "a lack of definitive systems for evaluating the performance of teachers and other professional staff" (64 percent support).

These data suggested that a commonly held vision of instruction needed to be developed, along with a clear and expressive language for communicating about it. These, in turn, would have to be conveyed to all professionals within the district. Following that, an appropriate system for reviewing, evaluating, and offering commentary about instructional performance had to be developed. Again, once developed, the substance of these efforts had to be conveyed throughout the district.

A second area probed by the needs assessment concerned the management of an enrollment decline. On a per-pupil basis, costs were going up faster than one would expect from inflation alone. This occurred because fixed building and maintenance costs were being apportioned over consistently fewer students. Moreover, the reductions in school enrollments were very uneven. The needs assessment concluded that a comprehensive plan for managing the enrollment decline through school closings needed to be developed. While the enrollment-decline issue might seem unrelated to staff development concerns, in fact, it played an important role in obtaining support for the district's proposed professional development program. More will be said about this in the following section.

Finally, personnel evaluation was the most consistently mentioned problem by nearly all groups that responded (including *all* employee groups within the district). While this was not surprising when voiced by school board members, the fact that employees, too, identified personnel evaluation as a problem was particularly compelling. Few among the district's staff were happy with the existing evaluation procedures. Employees wanted their evaluations to stimulate the improvement of job performance. Many suggestions for the improvement of personnel evaluation became apparent throughout the needs assessment. They were summarized for the Board of Education as follows:

1. Clarify who is responsible for whom.
2. Establish and publicize performance expectations.
3. Follow up with corrective feedback.
4. Specify incentive and evaluation systems.
5. Take strong action when all else fails.

On February 25, 1981, the Pittsburgh Board of Education responded to the results of the districtwide needs assessment by adopting a resolution that specified six priority areas. A number of them (e.g., student achievement in the basic skills, student discipline, and increasing the effectiveness of individual schools) proved quite relevant to the determination of the district's inservice staff development needs. Two more, improving staff evaluation and managing an enrollment decline, were directly relevant both to the substantiation of staff development needs and the securing of school board and community support for them. In fact, in its resolution, the board agreed to assign resources and concentrate its efforts on the resolution of these identified areas of need. The district's program planning cycle could begin in earnest.

Addressing the Need: Establishing
Institutional Commitment

Following the board's approval of priorities in February 1981, the superintendent convened a task force of teachers and school-based and central office administrators. It was charged to explore how the district could address the board's priority for improved evaluation of personnel. The superintendent persuaded the task force that it should take a constructive as opposed to a punitive approach to personnel evaluation. The superintendent articulated the position that to evaluate professionals in the district effectively, each professional needed: (1) to know precisely what the district's expectations were with respect to their performance; (2) to have an opportunity to receive training in and practice any "new behaviors" implied by those expectations; (3) to be provided with feedback to ensure that performance would be consistent with the expectations; and (4) to be evaluated in a system that reflected the new expectations. The task force, and ultimately the Board of Education itself, agreed to this approach. Thus, the task force began to review a variety of approaches to staff development that dealt specifically with improving both teachers' and administrators' performance (Davis 1983).

For a period of five months, the task force on personnel evaluation deliberated about various approaches to staff development and then made specific recommendations to the board in June 1981. Among those recommendations were the following: employ four full-time staff development trainers; build a model of teacher and administrative effectiveness based on research findings; and provide specific training for principals in observing and conferring with teachers to bring improved instructional performance in the classroom.

During the summer of 1981, the staff development team was appointed and began to work with a variety of consultants to develop and implement its program called PRISM (Pittsburgh Research Based Instructional Supervisory Model). The superintendent, all central office educational personnel, and all school-based professionals participated in a training program related to PRISM beginning in the fall of 1981.

Simultaneous with the development of this approach to personnel evaluation through staff development, planning relevant to the board's priority of managing enrollment decline was also under way. It became evident to the board that the district needed to close a number of schools in response to the decline in the student population.

In addition to the obvious difficulties that attend school closings, the situation in Pittsburgh would require a number of staff reductions. The furloughs would most greatly affect teachers with the least seniority, many of them among the most able young minds in the district. No one was pleased with the prospect of seeing these young professionals lost to the district and possibly the teaching profession.

As the board reviewed the enrollment data with the superintendent, it became very clear that three city high schools should be closed. In November 1981, the superintendent recommended to the board that one of the high schools that was a candidate to be closed be used as a teacher center. At this center, the board's priorities of personnel evaluation and enhancing student achievement could be dealt with in a coordinated program. The superintendent recommended to the board that Schenley High School, an underenrolled (and at that time a low-achieving) school, be designated as a teacher center that would serve both as a comprehensive high school for a conventional student body and as the site of a clinical staff development center for secondary teachers.

The board was interested in the idea but expressed concerns about its cost and the need for more specific information. The superintendent agreed to convene a task force of teachers to prepare plans for the program and to present them to the board for their consideration within six months. Following this agreement, over 200 secondary teachers volunteered to work with the superintendent's steering committee to begin the design of the Schenley High School Teacher Center. Six months later, the board received and approved a general plan for the center and final detailed planning began.

In August of 1982, Judy Johnston, a member of the steering committee for the personnel evaluation planning task force, was appointed director of the Schenley High School Teacher Center. Johnston began working with 75 teachers in August 1982 to develop the final plans for the center. By the spring of 1983, the planning was completed, the faculty selected, and the intensive training of the clinical resident staff at Schenley was under way. The Schenley High School Teacher Center opened in August 1983.

Throughout the entire planning process, the union leadership was involved. The Pittsburgh Federation of Teachers became convinced that it was in their best interest to support the center and exercise a strong voice in shaping the revitalizing experience for teachers. It was also to its advantage for the union to be perceived by the general public as supporting professional development and promoting greater accountability of teachers.

Thus, the Schenley High School Teacher Center grew out of four major forces operating within the district in the early 1980s. First was the determination of the Board of Education to improve the quality of personnel evaluation; second, the desire of the union to enhance the professional capacities and status of its members and of teachers to increase opportunities for meaningful professional renewal; third, the desire of the superintendent to take a constructive approach to staff development as a necessary prelude to effective personnel evaluation; and fourth, the need to respond in a responsible manner to manage an impending enrollment decline.

The confluence of these forces paved the way for the comprehensive staff development program that has been successfully implemented at the Schenley High School Teacher Center. As further demonstration of its commitment to staff development, the board voted to open the Brookline Elementary Teacher Center in August 1985 and the Greenway Middle Teacher Center in August 1988. Both the Brookline and the Greenway Teacher Center programs have evolved from the Schenley model and its successes.

Organizing for Implementation

Three basic strategies were employed throughout the program's implementation. The first involved considerable effort to encourage teachers' planning and decision processes. For example, from the earliest stages of the center's development, teachers across the district played a central role in defining the basic goals, structure, and programmatic content of the program. The teachers were involved through their participation on the many planning committees charged to define the teacher center. In all, over 200 teachers participated in the planning process, nearly one-quarter of all of the secondary instructional professionals in the district. In addition, all teachers were invited to respond to a second needs assessment—this one focusing on the professional development needs and preferences of teachers. The sincere engagement of teachers in the shaping of the center was felt to be essential. It enhanced the likelihood that the program would have districtwide support from the teaching ranks. Moreover, such involvement was a critical mechanism for tapping the professional wisdom of teachers. This would prove to be a valuable resource to the program.

The engagement of teachers during the planning process was carried over into the actual implementation of the program. The center's faculty was involved in almost every aspect of program planning. This was done through numerous formal committees (e.g., the school's instructional cabinet), and perhaps more important, through a spirit of inventive collaboration that permeated the collegial interactions between the faculty and the program's administration. In addition, the teachers participating in the program (the "visiting teachers") had direct influence on the effort via an extensive program of documentation and formative evaluation research effort funded by the Ford Foundation. (More will be said later about this aspect of the center's development).

A second important feature of the planning/decision process involved a hybrid management model that combined program leadership with direct lines of communication with key central administrative personnel. The center's director and administrative staff were located on site and were integrated as part of the school's management team. In addition, the center's leadership organized and chaired weekly planning and implementation meetings over the first two years of operation. The meetings included key central office personnel, including the superintendent. The group was small, and membership in this "breakfast club" varied somewhat over the life of the program. The central theme was that any administrator with control over resources needed by the center was in attendance so as to ensure their involvement in and response to relevant deliberations. The documentation team kept formal minutes of "decisions reached" and "outstanding issues." The net effect of this "flat management model" was that it drastically reduced the administrative layers separating program needs, organizational decision processes, resource allocation, and policy or programmatic action. This enabled the center to "get things done" and to make mid-course corrections as needed.

The third major aspect of organizing the district for implementation involved significant redesign of personnel practices. The changes were numerous and substantive in their implications for both the program itself and for future district policies. For example, in order to ensure that a top-quality faculty could be attracted to the center, a Memorandum of Understanding was negotiated between the Pittsburgh Federation of Teachers and the school board. The memorandum enabled the center, in effect, to close down "Schenley High School" and then post all positions. The SHSTC could then open with a staff recruited from across the district. Numerous, complex contractual issues (e.g., building seniority) were addressed in the memorandum. In effect, this created an "experimental policy space" in the fabric of the district, jointly crafted by the union and district leadership, that enabled the center to recruit topflight faculty to implement the program.

Another area of personnel policy modification involved the creation of new roles for teachers at the center. The roles of CRTs, seminar leaders, and replacement teachers have been described here earlier and at length elsewhere (e.g., Bickel et al. 1987). Of importance here was the restructuring of personnel policies that enable these new roles. For example, the district, in effect, "overstaffed" SHSTC by approximately a 1.5:1 ratio of the normal staffing patterns for a secondary school with comparable enrollment. This "banked" enough real time in the schedule to permit the center's teachers to undertake the many staff development roles envisioned.

The normal district personnel and selection assignment process was drastically modified to staff the center. (The district's director of personnel sat in on the "breakfast club.") One outcome was the use of an interview process that integrated the center's leadership into the decision process. Final decisions about placement rested with the program's leadership (the director and the principal of the SHSTC). Similarly, decisions about selection for new roles within the center faculty were in the hands of center leadership.

The implementation of a districtwide staff development effort was critically shaped by the leadership's ability to influence traditional personnel policies and practices. The next effort was to integrate personnel issues into the program's planning and management processes and to permit flexible selection and assignment decisions to enhance the program's operation.

The third major area of district preparation involved the design of a comprehensive program of research, integrated into the implementation process. This research, supported by the Ford Foundation and involving both district personnel and researchers from the University of Pittsburgh, had three major components. One area of research focused on documenting the implementation process over the life of the program. The documentation research was designed to provide a basis for an "institutional memory" of the lessons learned through the experience that could inform future staff development efforts. The second research stream focused on formative evaluation activities designed to aid the center's leadership (faculty and administration) in understanding the status of various program components. This set of evaluation activities sought to generate information about mid-course corrections that should be considered to improve the effort. The third area of research involved a number of activities designed to assess the impact of the center in terms of changes in teachers' attitudes, knowledge, and behavior. (More details about this research program can be found in Cooley and Bickel 1986, Denton and LeMahieu 1985, Bickel 1985, LeMahieu et al. 1989).

The integration of this three-pronged research program was an important departure from the past district experience. Typically, under previous administrations, evaluation research (if done at all) came at the end of a program's first phase of implementation and was generally used only to ask impact questions. Given the scope of the staff development goals, the complexity of the effort, and the intent to drive the effort into other grade levels, there was a clear interest in capturing as much of the implementation experience as possible. The goals were twofold: to make the program as effective as it could be by continually shaping it through data-based management, and to glean the necessary lessons from the experience about what worked and why to inform future district staff development efforts.

The fourth area of enabling activity involved the preparation of district administrators to make an important and positive contribution to the staff development process. The focus on administrators had three phases. First, before the opening of the center, all district administrators received significant tutoring in the core instructional refinement concepts to be used in center programming. Working with the district's staff development team, administrators received comprehensive training in the district's instructional model. Also, specific training in instructional leadership responsibilities was added to the administrative training programs. Finally, school-based experiences at the center gave administrators an understanding of their responsibility regarding program "follow-through" in their own school.

As the center was planned, administrators were integrated within the elaborate subcommittee planning structure for input and for communication purposes. As pointed out above, when the center began operation, and as growing numbers of visiting teachers completed their experiences and returned to the home schools, principals and vice-principals were brought to the center to observe activities, participate in enrichment programs for themselves, and interact with teachers as they participated in the program. For principals, this on-site participation occurred in two blocks of ten days each during which they would be at the center.

The fundamental perspective here was that teacher renewal could only go forward in a system that was knowledgeable about and supportive of the renewal goals. The district must involve building administrators to help maintain and extend the gains made at the center as teachers return to their home schools. The preparation, training, and involvement of administrators in the implementation process had an important impact on the district's infrastructure, one necessary to enable the center to reach its systemwide goals.

In sum, reshaping existing and inventing new planning and implementation structures, recrafting personnel policies and practices, integrating a reflective management capability into the process through a multifaceted program of research, and working to involve administrators systematically in the effort were all critical features of the Pittsburgh Public School's effort to implement districtwide staff development. Each was necessary to the success of the Schenley High School Teacher Center.

Institutionalization

Purkey and Smith (1985) have noted that "genuine reform . . . is predicated on finding solutions to relatively complex problems and devising policies that will implant those solutions across a spectrum of schools that make up public education" (p. 353). The successful implementation of the staff development program at the center was a necessary precondition to the installation of comprehensive districtwide staff development. However, the renewal activities at Schenley alone were not enough to ensure that the goals of staff renewal would be transmitted to and sustained within the other high schools in the district.

Early in the center's history, the district's leadership began to address the issue of what would happen when the teachers returned to their home school. The level of attention, sophistication, and complexity in the district's response to the institutionalization issue increased over time. Beginning in the second semester of operation, the center incorporated an expectation that all visiting teachers would devise follow-through plans to be implemented when they returned to their home schools. The basic purpose of the plan would be to encourage teacher growth in some area of professional development initiated at the center. The teachers were to select the area of interest, using their CRT at the center as a consultant in the process if they so chose. This early, rather informal expectation grew over time to include more formal procedures, including the explicit involvement of the CRTs, meeting with one's principal before leaving the center to discuss follow-through goals, and eventually some activities (e.g., peer observation) that were mandated for teachers as a component of their ongoing professional development program.

The change to a more formal linking of the process to the CRT and the principal were responses to a growing conviction that comprehensive, long-term renewal of the professional staff required a persistent attention that was not envisioned in the original design of the center. In effect, the real challenge was to devise ways to help teachers, once they returned to their schools, to sustain and expand the professional growth begun at the center.

Initially, the focus was on the individual teacher, and what he or she could do to continue the process. However, this focus began to change as the program's leadership had more experience with the follow-through peer observations. After approximately two semesters of this effort, it was clear from research involving teachers that the implementation of the follow-through effort was uneven at best and that teachers were confronting a number of obstacles in their schools as they sought to continue their professional growth. These constraints included a lack of time, lack of on-site support, and lack of direct input into the decision processes in their buildings. Only once these issues were remediated would they be able to facilitate the development of ongoing professional growth activities.

The recognition of the difficulties confronted by returning teachers influenced the center's leadership to shift from a focus on the individual teacher to one that emphasized a renewal of the overall professional climate in each high school in the district. Building on the work already done with the district's administrators, this "phase two" of the center's staff renewal effort was created and is midway through its implementation.

This effort has several aspects to it. Each school faculty has been asked to develop a Center of Excellence (COE) project designed to improve some aspect of the educational environment of their school. In addition, each faculty has been encouraged to design a school-based program of related staff development activities. Each of these efforts has been implemented through an explicit process of shared decision making, replicating in principle the districtwide teacher involvement that characterized the development of phase one of the center.

To facilitate the school-based activity, the district's leadership has funded a phase-two facilitator position (the equivalent of a half-time teacher on special assignment) to work with colleagues on the school's COE project and the attendant program of professional development activities. In addition, the facilitators have been working with their school's instructional cabinet. These instructional cabinets have been the mechanisms through which the facilitators have sought to extend the capacity for shared decision making among the professionals in the building.

Supplementing the school-based activity have been a series of district-wide innovations negotiated with the local teachers' organization. These have sought to significantly increase the capacities of and resources available to district teachers as they work to continue their own professional development. For example, the district has recently instituted common departmental planning time within secondary teacher schedules. This facilitates intra-departmental planning and professional growth activity. In addition, the role of the traditional chairperson has been redesigned and is now called the Instructional Team Leader (ITL). The ITL role more closely resembles that of the original CRT at the Teacher Center. An important goal was to redefine the role and capacities of the ITLs in ways that would add to the support structures devoted to the improvement of the quality of instruction.

The institutionalization of the center has evolved dramatically over the life of the program, from initial informal encouragement of teachers to follow through on some of their renewal activities to a much more systematic attempt to build the capacity for professional development at the school level. This comprehensive effort aims at significantly enhancing the professional climate by altering the norms and expectations manifested in the workplace. Phase two of the center's work recognizes the difficult issues of building an infrastructure of resources that can give some hope to achieving these ends. As noted earlier, this effort is midway through its initial implementation phase. While definitive conclusions are premature at this point, early feedback indicates both the need for and the value of this effort to build school capacities for ongoing professional development; preliminary data also indicate how difficult such an effort will be. True institutionalization, which involves "the envisioned changes" becoming routine and established parts of the school's professional life, still awaits fulfillment. However, it is hoped that some of the "flywheel mechanisms" that Purkey and Smith (1985) identify as critical to the continuation of the change process are already in place.

Concluding Comments

Certain characteristics of the Pittsburgh staff development program have proven essential to the successes that have been realized. First and foremost, this effort has taken a systemic and comprehensive view of staff renewal as a fundamental instrument of educational improvement and an essential strategy for addressing this renewal goal. Critical to this approach has been the fact that the particular needs for staff development were rooted in a detailed analysis of the district's reform needs. The interest in staff development was derived directly from a districtwide needs assessment. It was manifest in the interest of board and district personnel in improving evaluation practices, in widespread concerns about student achievement, in the board's need to respond to pressures for and against school closings, and in the broad interest expressed by professional staff in increasing opportunities for professional renewal.

These efforts became part of a larger and comprehensive district reform effort, encompassing curriculum changes, school renewal strategies, and modifications in personnel practices and student achievement monitoring strategies, as well as other reform initiatives too numerous to review here. The development of a vigorous staff development program represented one key element in a systemwide commitment to follow through on recognized district needs. This process compares favorably to what is often the basis for educational improvement initiatives, namely, the latest reform fad or the good idea that is in the heads of the few that intend to improve the many.

The interests in staff renewal were formally ratified as a part of the board's priorities. An important result of this commitment was that district leadership worked closely through collaborative planning and formal agreements to integrate union leadership into the renewal process. These commitments of the board and the union were necessary conditions for mounting the sustained staff development program that was implemented over the eight-year period that is the focus of this chapter.

A second noteworthy feature of the Pittsburgh staff development effort concerns its ambition and scope. This can be seen in numerous ways: in the time allocated to the effort (in terms of both quantity and quality), in the complex curriculum implemented, and in the willingness of the system to extend the renewal effort to all teachers in the system (and recently, to new inductees to the profession as well). Perhaps it was most ambitious in the determination to mount such a program through the genuine participation of the teaching professionals of the district.

The participatory base of the program was evident in the early planning stages. More significantly, it was inherent in the basic design of the center. While the program drew upon the talents of many role groups within and beyond the district to enrich its efforts, the professional teaching staff at Schenley were at the heart of the renewal effort. They developed and delivered the rich clinical and seminar experiences that were the essence of the program. The district took the perspective that if this program were to work it would be through the interaction of teachers with their colleagues. The district was most ambitious in recognizing its obligations to the professional staff and in assuring its commitment to the transfer of the mechanisms for professional renewal to the professional staff. In many ways, this commitment anticipated much of the discussion of the teacher professionalism movement so prevalent in the current literature.

One final characteristic of the Pittsburgh staff development effort of particular relevance to this discussion of "district initiative" involves the "data-informed" management of the effort. This orientation can be seen in the original assessment context that helped to define the basic goals of the effort. It continued to be manifest throughout the implementation of the program, when numerous substantive changes were made based on data from participating teachers. The interest in data has more recently been an important element in the district's decision to implement phase two of the program. It established the need for the new direction and contributed to its definition as it implements in each school some of the basic renewal principles first manifested at Schenley.

The point here is that a comprehensive district commitment to professional renewal requires ongoing information on how its many components are faring. This information, in turn, becomes the basis for program improvement and for new initiatives. In this way, the system can pursue its systemic reform objectives over the long haul. Only through such comprehensive, sustained commitment to renewal can a district hope to achieve genuine educational reform.

References

Bickel, W.E., S.E. Denton, J. Johnston, P.G. LeMahieu, and J.R. Young. (1987). "Teacher Professionalism and Educational Reform." *The Journal of Staff Development* 8, 2.

Cooley, W.W., and W.E. Bickel. (1986). *Decision Oriented Educational Research.* Boston: Kluwer-Nyhoff Publishing.

Davis, L. (1983). "Improving the Performance of Teachers: The Pittsburgh Research Based Supervisory Model." Paper presented to the Annual Meeting of the American Educational Research Association in Montreal, Canada.

Denton, S.E., and P.G. LeMahieu. (1985). "Evaluation Research as an Integral Part of an Inservice Staff Development Center." *Evaluation Bulletin* 6, 3.

Hammond, P., P. LeMahieu, and R.C. Wallace, Jr. (1989). "Telling the Whole Story: The Educational Program Audit." Paper presented at the Annual Meeting of the American Educational Research Association, San Francisco.

LeMahieu, P.G. (1984). "An Assessment of the Needs of Secondary Teachers Relevant to Professional Development: A Story of Evaluation Use." Paper presented at the Annual Meeting of the American Educational Research Association in New Orleans, La.

LeMahieu, P.G., M. Piscolish, J. Johnston, J.R. Young, D. Saltrick, and W.E. Bickel. (1989). "An Integrated Model of Program Evaluation, Administration and Policy Development." Paper presented at the Annual Meeting of The American Educational Research Association in San Francisco, Calif.

Purkey, S., and M. Smith. (1985). "School Reform: The District Policy Implications of the Effective Schools Literature." *The Elementary School Journal* 85,3.

Wallace, R.C., Jr., J.R. Young, J. Johnston, P.G. LeMahieu, and W.E. Bickel. (1984). "Secondary Education Renewal in Pittsburgh." *Educational Leadership* 4, 1.

Wallace, R.C., Jr. (1986). "Data-driven Educational Leadership." *Evaluation Practice* 7, 3.

11

The Los Angeles Experience: Individually Oriented Staff Development

Robert T. DeVries
Joel A. Colbert

T his chapter describes the structure of the staff development program in the Los Angeles Unified School District, the second largest school district in the United States. The district has a diverse and well-developed, yet loosely coupled, staff development program involving personnel at many levels. We describe the population of the district, the organization of our staff development program, teacher training programs, administrator training programs, training programs for certificated support personnel, training programs for classified and paraprofessional personnel, and the successes, failures, and recommendations for the future.

Robert T. DeVries is Director, University/College Relations, Los Angeles, California, Unified School District. Joel A. Colbert is Associate Professor, California State University, Dominguez Hills.

The Los Angeles Unified School District

The Los Angeles Unified School District (LAUSD) is a microcosm of urban America, with 644 schools, approximately 600,000 students, and more than 28,000 teachers and 3,000 administrators. There are also 90 child development centers, 68 magnet school centers, and 21 regional occupational centers.

The district covers a total area of 708 square miles. The Los Angeles basin, and particularly the LAUSD, is a major port of entry for immigrants from throughout the Pacific Rim as well as Mexico and Central and South America.

Three quarters of the schools in the district operate on a traditional September-to-June calendar. The remaining schools, including 87 elementary schools, 9 junior highs, and 4 senior highs, operate on a year-round schedule because of overcrowding. For example, one year-round elementary school has 19 kindergartens. One of the year-round junior high schools is the largest junior high in the United States, and one of the senior high schools is the largest west of the Mississippi River.

The district is governed by an elected board of education, composed of seven members representing geographic regions. For administrative purposes, the district is divided into eight regions that include elementary and junior high schools and four districtwide divisions: the senior high schools, special education, adult education, and child development. In addition, there are support services and the central administration.

Many variables affect the district's structuring of staff development, which falls under the board of education's umbrella. The board is committed to improving instructional effectiveness, as evidenced by the soon-to-be-released LAUSD publication, "Priorities for Education: A Design for Excellence," which emphasizes the need to direct the energy of the district to the vital environment of the classroom so that the teacher can teach and the student can learn."

In addition to the centralized administrative office, we have decentralized management as well; each region operates with a degree of autonomy and its own management team, region/division superintendents, and staff. This structure can lead to conflicts between central support services and region operations since the needs and resources across regions/divisions vary greatly. However, in a district as large as the LAUSD, there is clearly the need for both central and regional management structure and function as well as a substantial degree of autonomy at the local school level.

District Organization for Staff Development

Policy and Governance

District policies on staff development are predicated on an array of local, state, and federal legislation and administrative guidelines. Schools receiving categorical funds, such as Chapter I and Bilingual/ESL, are obliged to provide six to eight two-hour staff development sessions each year on subjects cooperatively developed with staff and reflecting the purpose of the specialized funding. A district regulation enables schools to use a minimum-day configuration to provide a student-free period to conduct staff development sessions. Schools may schedule ten or more minimum days per year. Furthermore, the contract with the local teachers bargaining unit specifies, in detail, a number of conditions relating to staff development and salary advancement. Essentially, these conditions identify acceptable procedures and options for the accumulation of credits for salary advancement as well as scheduling, attendance, and reporting of program completion.

Roles and Responsibilities

Staff development is both a centralized and decentralized process in the district. We have a professional development branch that is responsible for coordinating, planning, directing, and conducting districtwide training programs. This office works cooperatively with other centralized functions to maximize the level of service and coverage to achieve a coordinated central office commitment to improving staff effectiveness.

A district director of university/college relations works closely with all district units as well as some 30 postsecondary institutions to expand developmental opportunities for both staff and students.

District, region, and division staffs have the responsibility for not only transmitting training emanating from central office sources, but developing and conducting training consistent with regional and local school needs.

Organizational Efforts to Coordinate and Collaborate

Several advisory and ad hoc committees facilitate internal coordination and maximize external collaboration. The Community College Consortium, which meets semiannually, has a membership consisting of the presidents and senior staffs of the nine greater Los Angeles community college campuses, and the district senior staff members. The Higher Education Consortium, which also meets semiannually, has a membership consisting of the 20 deans of the schools of education in the greater Los Angeles basin, and the district senior staff members. Consortium meetings facilitate linkage, strengthen relations, and provide access for specific program development activities for district staff and students.

Two additional external ad hoc committees further strengthen district staff development efforts. The Los Angeles Marine Studies Consortium has responsibility for operating an educational program and research center on a permanently leased military site. This consortium is composed of public agencies and institutions of higher education. A Human Corps Advisory Board coordinates an extensive program involving students who provide voluntary service. Recent postsecondary legislation in California, written by Assemblyman Vasconcellos, exhorts public postsecondary institutions to encourage students to volunteer 30 hours of public service per annum. This legislation has provided a substantive impetus for the expansion of student voluntary service programs.

Three major district internal committees provide coordination for staff development activities. The Inservice Advisory Committee, composed of region and division representatives and Professional Development Branch staff, provides direction for the identification and scheduling of district inservice classes. The Staff Development Council, which includes district personnel with instructional leadership functions, members of the Professional Development Branch, and other support personnel, provides direction for a variety of district curricular and instructional professional development priorities. The Future Teacher Preparation Corps Ad Hoc Committee is charged with the development and implementation of an educational career ladder for the district's 2,500 paraprofessionals, the initiation of future teacher clubs in the 49 senior high schools, and the implementation of an educational career ladder for classified and paraprofessional personnel.

Training of Teachers

As with the other major programs in the district, there are both centralized and decentralized staff development programs for teachers. This section is divided on this basis. The centralized portion is further subdivided into specialized training for new teachers, including both preservice and inservice, general inservice programs, training predicated on or mandated by legislation, and other programs that do not fall into the other three categories. The decentralized section includes training conducted by the regions/divisions, school-based programs, and specialized programs attributed to legislation and Board of Education directives.

It is estimated that the typical teacher in the LAUSD participates in the equivalent of ten full days of professional development activities per annum. This includes many of the programs described in the following sections.

Centralized Programs

Specialized Training for New Teachers. There are several basic specialized training programs for new teachers in the district. The first is the District Internship program, which is coordinated by the Professional Development Branch. Approximately 200 new teachers are initiated in this program annually. This program provides preservice and inservice training for teachers who enter the district without a teaching credential but meet the following criteria: a bachelor's degree in a district-identified teacher shortage subject area (i.e., science, math, language arts, and bilingual); a passing score on the California Basic Educational Skills Test (CBEST); and a passing score on the National Teachers Examination (NTE). When hired, these teachers are fully employed classroom teachers, working with an intern credential. They participate in both preservice and inservice training classes for two years, at which time they are eligible for their clear credential. They attend preservice classes prior to their initial classroom experience and meet once a week during the academic year for classes that include content methods, educational psychology, computer education, multicultural education, special education, and other subjects.

The second specialized training program for new teachers is conducted collaboratively with two local universities, the California State University, Dominguez Hills (CSUDH), and the California State University, Los Angeles (CSULA). It is also an internship program, but the target audience is emergency/provisional credentialed teachers who choose to complete their credential in a university setting. Over 1,000 teachers were initiated in this program annually over the past five years. In addition to coursework, participants are supervised by university faculty and can go on and pursue a master's degree. An example of one program in this area is the Mathematics and Enrichment Training for Inservice Teachers (MERIT) program at CSUDH. The MERIT program was developed jointly by the district, the university, and the Los Angeles County Office of Education for emergency and standard credentialed teachers who desired to add mathematics to their credential. Courses are taught by university faculty and district mathematics teachers in order to provide both the mathematics and the pedagogical content to participants. There is a shortage of mathematics teachers in Los Angeles; in addition, some teachers in certain subject areas (e.g., home economics and industrial arts) find it difficult to keep their positions due to declining enrollments and wish to add math to their credential to expand their employment potential. MERIT has been very successful at doing this.

The third special program for new teachers is of the inservice variety and is funded by the California State Department of Education and Commission on Teacher Credentialing. This program is conducted collaboratively by the district, the CSUDH, and the district's bargaining unit, the United Teachers of Los Angeles, and is called the California New Teacher Project. It is 1 of 15 such programs statewide to explore teacher induction models for the development of state policy regarding support for new teachers. The purpose is to provide support and assistance to probationary teachers (i.e., those who enter the profession through a traditional teacher training program and have their credential). Participants take classes in classroom management and cooperative learning at the university and receive support and assistance by lead teachers at their school sites.

At the California State University, Northridge (CSUN), there is the Teacher Institute, a collaborative project between the district, the CSUN School of Education, and the CSUN academic departments. This program is aimed at aspiring K-12 teachers and focuses on developing content area expertise in addition to pedagogical content.

In addition to these three basic programs, there are ancillary programs for new teachers and for those who desire to become teachers. For example, there are CBEST and NTE preparation workshops, special language programs for becoming bilingual, and collaborative programs with the community colleges for future teachers.

Inservice Education. The district's Professional Development Branch offers a wide range of inservice classes for teachers. These classes are taken for salary points, which can lead to additional salary increments. Examples include computer education classes, methods of observation and coaching, classroom management, cooperative learning, and subject-specific training. There are approximately 20,000 enrollments each year, with participants able to enroll in more than one class.

In addition, the district operates three teacher centers. These centers are open daily for teachers to work on lesson planning and instructional materials development, but inservice classes are also held on weekends. During the course of the year, the teacher centers hold weekend conferences on topics ranging from generic teaching strategies to subject-specific topics. During the summer, they conduct a wide range of inservice classes.

The Office of Instruction also conducts comprehensive inservice classes on a variety of topics. For example, as a result of National Science Foundation and other grants, inservice programs in science, health, social studies, language arts, and other subject areas are offered. Funding was provided by the Board of Education recently to develop a curriculum devoted to nuclear energy issues. The curriculum is interdisciplinary in nature, encompassing both science and social science issues. In order to disseminate the curriculum, inservice classes were conducted throughout the district to introduce the Nuclear Issues program and train teachers in its use. There have been many other inservice programs of this nature as well.

Legislated Programs. The District Internship Program was made possible by special legislation. This legislation was enacted in response to the teacher shortage in certain critical content areas, listed above. In addition, other legislation and policy decisions have resulted in specialized programs related to credential requirements in the state (e.g., multicultural education and computer education).

The Board of Education has also enacted policy-driven programs. For example, the district collaborated with the University of California, Los Angeles, to develop a supervision of instruction program. District staff met with UCLA faculty to design the program and train representatives from the regions/divisions in program content. The region teams then conducted their own supervision of instruction training to address the unique needs in their regions/divisions.

Other Training Programs. The following programs do not fall into the preceding categories.

1. The Future Teacher Preparation Corps is designed to provide training to paraprofessionals working in the district to prepare them to enter a college or university and to become teachers. This program will be discussed in greater detail later.

2. The Los Angeles Marine Studies Consortium, described previously, is a group of university faculty, school district staff, and private sector scientists planning the development of the LAUSD Marine Studies Center. This center will serve as a site for training students and teachers in all aspects of marine science.

3. The Model Teacher Training Schools, a collaborative venture between the district and the district's bargaining unit, the United Teachers of Los Angeles, are selected school sites in the district that will serve in two capacities. First, they will be teacher training sites for student teachers from each of the major teaching colleges and universities in the Los Angeles basin. Second, they will be demonstration schools for inservice programs to explore innovative instructional strategies and skills development and to apply emerging theories to pedagogy.

4. The Teacher Academy for Professional Development is a collabo-

rative effort between district staff, the United Teachers of Los Angeles, and the Graduate School of Education at UCLA. The purpose is to provide advanced training for teachers aspiring to move up the career ladder by providing training and development opportunities in specific areas (including school-based management and curriculum and instructional practices); by offering leadership development; and by promoting student achievement through the improved professional skills of staff.

5. There are numerous collaborative programs between local universities and the district to provide advanced degree programs for aspiring teachers. For example, there are four cooperative master's degrees/administrative credential programs; three master's degrees/pupil personnel credential programs; a special master's degree program for mentor teachers; and two cooperative doctoral cohorts, with another in development.

6. There is a substitute teacher training program, designed to provide assistance and training to the two to three thousand substitute teachers in the district. The staff of the Professional Development Branch offer a two-day program focusing on such areas as classroom management, lesson planning, and school operations.

7. The Office of Instruction implemented the Computer Education Program in 1984 to integrate microcomputers into instruction. As part of this program, a districtwide inservice program was initiated to familiarize teachers with computer-related topics. Every 5th grade classroom in the district received a microcomputer, printer, and inservice training, while every secondary school received a complete computer lab with inservice training.

Decentralized Programs

The ultimate responsibility for change and improved teaching effectiveness lies at the region and school level, where the most pressing needs can be addressed in an intensive manner.

Region/Division Training. Each region or division in the district receives an annual allocation to conduct training to meet the specific needs in that region. There is also a staff inservice advisor whose job is to organize and schedule inservice classes. For example, one of the inner city regions has targeted critical thinking skills as a high-priority area for the entire region and has been conducting very successful regionwide inservice classes for the past several years. Furthermore, every region/division conducts training for new teachers at the beginning of the school year, focusing on areas that have been designated high-priority areas for new teachers (e.g., classroom management, instructional strategies, lesson planning, and multicultural education). This teacher induction ranges from one to three days, depending on the region/division.

The region inservice advisors meet regularly with staff from the Professional Development Center to coordinate districtwide programs. For example, during the middle 1980s, the regions collaborated with staff from the Los Angeles County Office of Education, Teacher Education and Computer Centers and Professional Development Center, to design and implement computer education inservice classes in each region/division. Needs were identified by the inservice advisors and classes planned accordingly. In addition, to ensure that each region received consistent, high-quality instruction, a training-of-trainers program was conducted for two trainers from each region/division. After completing the program, they taught computer-related inservice classes in their home region/division. They also conducted mini-workshops at local schools as their schedules permitted, often working after school and on Saturdays to address topics related specifically to individual schools.

The regions also coordinate programs with local colleges and universities. An example is the Ten Schools Program. This program identified ten elementary schools, equally divided between two regions, which had the lowest student achievement scores in the district, with the goal of improving instructional effectiveness. Working with CSULA and CSUDH, the schools developed a master's degree program in curriculum and instruction for teachers. Participating teachers are then responsible for returning to their school site and conducting staff development sessions for the entire staff. Currently, there are 16 teachers in the CSULA program and 19 in the CSUDH program.

Other specialized programs are managed on a decentralized basis as a response to Board of Education directives and state and federal mandates. Examples include two state programs, AB 551 and AB 803. Although neither of these programs is still in existence, they had a significant impact on regions during the 1980s. AB 551 provided funds for staff development programs at individual school sites based on needs assessment data gathered from faculty. AB 803 provided funds for schools to integrate technology into their instructional plan. Legislation is pending that would restore a funding base for these programs and others like them.

School-Based Programs. Two types of staff development programs occur at each school site. Every school has its own staff development plan, based on needs, priorities, and district goals. These staff development sessions typically take place after school on Tuesdays, but they can also be conducted on minimum and shortened days—unique schedules for staff development purposes. Participants do not receive incentives for attending these inservice sessions, since attendance and participation are part of job responsibilities.

The other type of staff development program is categorical in nature; that is, it is based on federal and/or state legislation. Examples include two programs described previously, AB 551 and AB 803, which were state programs, and Chapter II, a federal program. Depending on the legislation and school plan, participants can receive either salary points, which lead to an increase in pay, or the district training rate, currently $8.00 per hour, for attending.

Training of Administrators

A variety of substantive training programs is conducted for district administrative personnel. These programs range from entry-level experiences through cooperative doctoral programs. Programs are conducted on a districtwide basis and in a decentralized manner by regions and divisions.

Districtwide Programs

Districtwide programs are coordinated by the Professional Development Branch through an administrator training center funded by the State of California and by the district's Director of University/College Relations when postsecondary institutions are involved.

Entry-Level Programs. Cooperative master's degree and administrative credential and/or pupil personnel credential programs are conducted annually with five postsecondary institutions: CSULA, CSUDH, Pepperdine University, California Lutheran University, and Mount Saint Mary's College. These programs reflect district career development and promotional examination requirements and focus on the application of theory to reality-based situations. Instructor assignments are cooperatively determined and internship supervision is provided by district staff. During the period from 1985 to 1987, approximately 1,300 members of the district staff participated in one of these programs, an average of 260 annually.

Additionally, when members of the district staff apply to participate in an administrative promotional examination, they attend a 16-hour orientation program. This orientation session reviews examination procedures, identifies district expectations for administrative service, and proffers simulated assessment activities.

New Administrator Training. All new administrators in the district participate in a three-year, ten-session-per-year program. This training is conducted through the district's Administrator Training Center, funded by the California School Leadership Academy. This training focuses on the instructional leadership role of the school site administrator as well as critical district developmental priorities, especially in the area of instruction. Over 125 administrators begin this program annually.

The State of California, through the Commission on Teacher Credentialing, has a two-tier administrative credential requirement. This program necessitates the completion of a second tier, entitled the Professional Administrative Services credential, subsequent to assignment as an administrator. In cooperative configurations with CSULA, CSUDH, and Mount Saint Mary's College, the new administrator training program satisfies one-half of the unit requirement for this tier of the credential. Approximately 50 administrators begin this program annually.

Experienced Administrator Training. Fifteen hundred experienced administrators in the district annually participate in a 16-hour renewal training program emphasizing the leadership role of the school administrator in supervising the instructional program. Furthermore, mentor principal programs operate in selected regions and divisions for newly assigned personnel and on an individual basis for experienced administrators in relation to need.

The district also facilitates the participation of experienced administrators in doctoral programs with Pepperdine University and the University of LaVerne. Currently, a cohort of 15 administrators is enrolled at each of these institutions.

Decentralized Programs

Regions and divisions in the district conduct an array of seminars and workshops for administrators, focusing on identified needs. These presentations range from knowledge-based sessions to extended sessions on skill development. More than 200 such sessions are being offered annually throughout the district.

Training of Credentialed Support Personnel

The purpose of training for credentialed support personnel is to coordinate the field testing, implementation, and dissemination of curriculum and instructional programs with the schools (i.e., to train personnel to become effective with a wide range of products and to disseminate these products to school sites). There are both centralized and decentralized programs of this nature.

Centralized Training

As new instructional programs and curriculum products become available, personnel such as the instructional specialists have to become knowledgeable if they are to introduce these products to the field. Conferences and conventions often serve in this capacity, but training may be more comprehensive as well. For example, textbook publishers, computer manufacturers, and curriculum developers often conduct training for credentialed support personnel to familiarize them with new products and services. Region advisers, staff with specific responsibilities for providing support and assistance to schools, also avail themselves of this type of training. Approximately 150 members of the district staff with instructional leadership responsibilities annually participate in the equivalent of five full days of training.

Decentralized Training

Once central office staff attend the centralized training sessions, their responsibility very often is to train region staff, who, in turn, service the schools in that region or division. Region advisors and other credentialed staff attend inservice workshops addressing such topics as computer education, legislation, compliance, and subject-specific topics in order to stay current with their fields and to eventually conduct their own inservice programs with the schools they serve.

Training of Classified and Paraprofessional Staff

The district has made a commitment to develop and implement both long- and short-term training and educational career developmental programs for the district's 15,000 classified and 26,000 paraprofessional personnel.

Districtwide Programs

Educational Career Ladder Program. The district, through the Future Teacher Preparation Corps Program, has established, in cooperation with the local community college district and CSULA and CSUDH, an educational career ladder. This activity facilitates participation in both Associate of Arts and baccalaureate degree programs for members of the district's classified and paraprofessional staff, which numbers over 15,000 classified, 12,000 teacher assistants, 8,000 education aides, and 6,000 recreation personnel. This educational career program is viewed as a potential source of new teachers for the district.

Inservice Education. A substantial number of 16- and 32-hour inservice classes are offered to classified personnel annually. These classes tend to be skill focused and emphasize such areas as clerical procedures, nutrition, bookkeeping, security, student discipline (for bus drivers), stenography, computer operation, crafts, and food services. Approximately 2,500 classified staff members participate in these programs annually.

Management Training. Specialized training programs are conducted for classified management personnel in both organization development and technical skill areas. Further, specialized master's degree programs in school business management are offered through CSULA and Pepperdine University. Two cohorts of 15 participants begin these programs annually.

Decentralized Programs

A number of classified units conduct short-term specialized training consistent with function. These programs essentially emphasize technical, legal, and safety considerations. Over 10,000 staff members participate in some form of decentralized training annually.

Retrospection

The size and magnitude of the workforce in the Los Angeles Unified School District mandates a loosely coupled approach to meeting staff development needs. Seven hundred physical locations, 28,000 teachers, 3,000 administrators, 15,000 classified staff, and 26,000 paraprofessionals impose an incredible training burden on a small, centralized staff.

A major consequence of the uniqueness of the district in terms of the size and magnitude of the workforce is the execution of a very substantial portion of the total staff development program on a voluntary and decentralized basis. Paradoxically, this training reflects several coherent staff development principles: needs-based, owned by participants, differentiated, experimentally/behaviorally based, cooperatively planned, individualized, and involved.

Selected elements of the district's staff development program for teachers appear to be effective, especially those that are voluntary and reflect the principles described previously. Standard off-the-shelf programs that offer minimal interaction and little ownership are poorly attended and only moderately valued.

Administrator training programs generally receive high marks for relevance and applicability. Programs emphasizing role playing, case studies, and problem solving receive high ratings. Input sessions receive much less support.

Classified and paraprofessional training programs are usually received as valuable. Primarily, such training efforts relate doubly to career and educational advancement and are abetted by the motivation related to promotion, as well as degree aspiration and skill development.

Coordination of staff development in the district is an incredibly complex task. The multiplicity of units conducting training programs exceeds 1,000. At best, central staff can establish staff development trainer guidelines, share priorities, provide training in facilitator skills, support subject matter needs, and coordinate programs with postsecondary institutions. The school administration, in cooperation with the school staff, remains the pivotal force in providing high-quality staff development programs.

Future Directions

As previously stated, it is an incredibly complex task to coordinate and manage the staff development programs in the LAUSD. The Professional Development Branch, working collaboratively with the central administration, regions/divisions, and schools, has been able to do this despite budget cuts and movement of personnel. Several areas need to be addressed if the district's efforts to provide a high-quality staff development program are to continue.

First, evaluation of staff development activities needs to focus on behavioral change. The standard one-shot inservice is most likely to effect little, if any, direct behavioral change in participants. Even when there are multiple sessions and follow-up activities, evaluation data are rarely collected to assess the change in behaviors after staff members participate in the program.

Second, every effort should be made for everyone who conducts staff development activities to receive training in such areas as adult learning theory, workshop design, evaluation, cooperative learning strategies, and other related areas.

Third, the Professional Development Branch needs additional support, both in funding and personnel, to expand programs currently being conducted and for developing new programs. Whenever a new priority or need that directly affects the Professional Development Branch is identified by the Board of Education, little additional funding or staff are provided. If this branch is to serve as the central coordinating unit for staff development in the district, it certainly warrants the budget and staff not only to maintain current programs, but also to develop state-of-the-art training as needs and priorities develop.

Finally, there needs to be greater recognition that staff development is an integral component in the professional growth of all district staff. It is not uncommon for staff development programs to be viewed as bothersome activities that do not directly affect instruction or professional growth, which, in fact, is far from the truth. That attitude has to change. The Board of Education and senior staff have to send a clear message to all district personnel that entering the teaching profession is but a first step in our commitment to continuing our own professional growth, and, therefore, the growth of our students.

12

The Lincoln Experience: Development of an Ecosystem

Betty Dillon-Peterson

An unknown sage once said, "We are never so independent as when we recognize and appreciate our dependence." In many ways, that statement characterizes the symbiotic relationship between the continued improvement of the individual and improvement of the organization we call the school. This chapter describes the characteristics of a comprehensive improvement process as an "ecosystem"—a complex of separate but dependent communities or groups that form a functional whole.

In this context, the staff development program operates as a part of a larger organizational improvement program. It has two basic components: (1) training related to accomplishment of the mission of the organization and the improvement of its overall organizational functioning and (2) training intended to improve individual job performance. Both components contribute to, and result from, a healthy organizational climate.

Betty Dillon-Peterson is Director, Curriculum/Staff Development, Lincoln Public Schools, Lincoln, Nebraska.

What is Meant by a "Comprehensive" Staff Development/Organization Development Program?

Traditionally, teachers have been the primary and often exclusive targets of staff development programs. Given the broader perspective used as the frame of reference for this chapter, many more individuals and groups should be involved. The comprehensive staff development/organizational development program focuses on at least the following categories of staff members in a school district: administrators at all levels, department chairs and team leaders, curriculum coordinators, veteran teachers (including special assignment staff on teacher salaries, such as counselors), beginning teachers, paraprofessionals, and classified staff (including custodians, clerical staff, food service employees, and bus drivers). In addition, school districts may provide inservice training for board members, PTA leaders, and community leaders.

A hallmark of quality, comprehensive, district-level staff development/organization development programs is breadth. For example, a narrowly defined inservice program for teachers would include only the training needed to ensure adequate delivery of a newly adopted curriculum. A program with more depth would also include study of current research about learning and how that applies to the curriculum and age level being taught. It would also take into account the participants' prior learning and the preferred method of instruction. A narrowly defined inservice program for bus drivers could be limited to such topics as vehicle maintenance, whereas a more comprehensive one might provide training in how to communicate better with hearing-impaired students.

Staff development/organization development activities for both certified and classified staff in a comprehensive program include those designed to affect the entire organization; those that are site- or job-specific; and those that are designed to meet a wide variety of individual needs.

Importance of Districtwide Development Activities

Much has been written and said about the importance of individual school effectiveness. Conversely, little has been noted about the importance of district support in regard to that effort. In fact, the relationship between the central office and the building or site is too often adversarial. This is unfortunate, because today's educational problems are serious enough to demand the best energies of all parts of our educational ecosystem. If that ecosystem is healthy, all individuals and groups are valued for their complementary contributions.

One could conjecture that this adversarial relationship may itself result from a lack of comprehensive staff development/organization development. A districtwide development program might have helped the staff members of various units of the organization to learn more about each other's contributions and difficulties. It might also have enabled them to acquire skills for improving the communication between and among all employees or employee groups within a school district in ways that would have fostered student learning.

Conventional wisdom tells us that people will be more productive when they are happy at their work and believe that they are contributing to a cause they perceive as important. To the degree that the comprehensive staff development/organization development program contributes to such a feeling, we may assume it to be valuable. Efforts in this direction should at least result in a better quality of life than would otherwise be the case.

Importance of Site-based or Unit-based Development Activities

Comprehensive staff development/organization development programs place significant emphasis on each unit where services are delivered. The individual school is the primary example, but the operations and maintenance department would be another, as would be the central office curriculum department. In a comprehensive program, development activities are provided that are exclusively designed to meet the unique needs of each unit of the district's operation. At the same time, each unit participates in some general activities designed to emphasize the relationship among and between all the individual units of operation as they cooperate to accomplish the ultimate goal—providing the highest possible quality instruction to students.

Importance of Individual Focus

Accompanying the whole-district and site-based (or unit-based) focus should be clear emphasis on the personal and job-related growth of the individual employee. This multiple focus typically provides people with opportunities to learn about and participate in (1) districtwide activities that enable all individuals to know about and make a contribution to the district effort; (2) site-based or unit-based activities focused on meeting needs identified at that level; and (3) activities focused on the needs of individual staff members.

This "individualized" approach takes two forms. In one, individual staff member needs that become apparent through the supervisory process are accommodated—even if only one staff member appears to have that need at the moment. For example, a teacher in a school may have classroom management problems for which he or she chooses to receive assistance from a helping teacher cadre member who specializes in classroom management techniques.

In the other form, individual opportunities for development are selected by the staff member from a variety of options, or they result from a staff member's initiative. Such a self-initiated activity might be a teacher's request to visit a colleague during the school day to see how she or he conducts a science lesson, with a substitute being provided by the district or by an administrator who temporarily takes over the teacher's class. Or a transportation supervisor may request the opportunity to participate in an assertiveness training workshop.

Activities designed primarily to serve one purpose often serve another as well. For example, teachers of behaviorally disordered students may participate in cooperative classroom training that enables them to work more effectively with these difficult students. If this practice is implemented successfully, it may also result in less stress for the teachers, thus enhancing their quality of life. Food service managers may learn communication skills to enable them to act as better liaisons between the central office and the building principal. These same skills may improve communication in their families.

Why Is a Comprehensive View Necessary?

All of us have experienced the surge of power that comes from being part of a group highly motivated to accomplish something—as members of a choral group that rose to an exhilarating finale conducted by a master director; when a powerful speaker adjured us to defeat a referendum potentially detrimental to our community; when a building staff determines through a "we agree" process to cut its drop-out rate by 20 percent. That there is psychological as well as actual strength in numbers is also true where developing staffs and organizations are concerned.

The "culture" of an organization, which is so emphasized today, is what is affected by appropriate staff development/organization development activities. Staff members are usually motivated to do better when the norm is understood and reachable and when everyone in the group accepts the need to do a better job. We cannot exert quality control on the type of student who comes to us, but we can, through concerted effort, keep raising our own performance standards with the firm intention of improving the quality of learning in our schools. Typically, as the norm of expectations is raised through majority consensus, detractors become more silent.

In addition, a comprehensive program can result in better use of resources. With economic constraints impinging on almost every part of our work, it is especially important to use our resources efficiently. Unless we look comprehensively at the development of the organization as a whole, as well as its component parts and the individuals in it, wasteful duplication of effort and funding of activities that may be at cross-purposes may occur. For example, two divisions within the same school district unwittingly scheduled the same out-of-state consultant for separate presentations twice within a three-week period. Not only would the departments have saved money had they consolidated their efforts, but they might have strengthened both causes had they collaborated on the presentation and follow-up.

Finally, a comprehensive view of staff development/organization development is more likely to ensure continuation of adequate support for this vital function. Because development has more indirect than direct influence on perceived school success, funding and staffing for it is more at risk than are other, more concrete, parts of the system, such as teacher salaries, textbooks, transportation, and fuel oil. In educational organizations, this function is most similar to research and development in industry; therefore, it is vital that it be perceived as integral and essential to the total school improvement process.

What Are the Key Characteristics of a Comprehensive Development Program?

Policy-Level Commitment

Obviously, a districtwide, comprehensive staff development/organization development program will not occur without the support of the local district board of education and key district administrators. It is essential that a continuous commitment to the program be written into district policy. Such a policy may be general, but it should clearly commit the district— ideally through the board of education's mission statement—to an ongoing program of staff training for all district employees; it should also include some reference to continuous, positive change.

Time should also be provided within the school calendar to enable staff members to deal with staff development/organization development issues. In the typical comprehensive program, a minimum of five regular contract days are set aside for this purpose. Ordinarily, these days focus almost exclusively on districtwide or building-specific activities, with much more diverse offerings available at a variety of other times throughout the year—at the end of the school day, in the evening, on Saturday, and throughout the summer.

Continuous Regular Budget Funding

All of us know that many of our priorities can be identified by where we put our money. The same is true of a comprehensive staff development/organization development program. If a district has no regular line item in its budget for staff development, its commitment to educational improvement is questionable, whether or not substantial monies are coming in from outside sources, such as federal funds. Long-term educators are aware of how ephemeral such outside funds are. Worse, they often create the illusion that the district has a commitment that it really does not have.

Appropriate Involvement of Representatives of All Target Audiences

The field of staff development now has ample documentation in its literature to underscore the need for genuine involvement of at least representatives of the target audiences in needs assessment, planning, execution, and follow-up of staff development/organization development activities. Nevertheless, these tasks are too often carried out (if they are implemented systematically at all) by someone other than the district employees for whom they are intended. Site- or unit-based activities are one means of making sure that appropriate staff members are involved in all phases of establishing the need for, planning, delivering, and evaluating improvement efforts. A strong cross-sectional, broadly based group representing all categories of district employees, however, helps to establish direction for districtwide staff development/organization development efforts.

Each such program also provides opportunity for, and encourages, individual teacher initiative, which may be totally aside from (but not in conflict with) site, unit-based, or districtwide emphases. For example, a group of elementary teachers prepares an individualized staff development plan in which they propose to use several substitute days to develop a student management system to help them implement the whole-language philosophy into their classrooms, although that may not be a current district or building emphasis.

Relating to an Institutionalized Change Process

All people who have worked for any time in the fields of staff development and organization development are aware of how difficult and how slow the change process is. They also know how important it is to help all those affected to accept the reality that change is an integral part of all our lives, regardless of how reluctant we may be to accept that fact.

Developers of comprehensive staff development/organization development programs purposefully learn all they can about how change occurs and how human beings react to it. Their shared insights can provide the basis for orderly, systematic change so that it may be perceived as beneficial by those involved in it. They do this by implementing ideas such as those described in the Stages of Concern of an Innovation and the Innovation Configuration tools developed by the R & D Center at the University of Texas under the leadership of Gene Hall.

Concern for Human Dignity

Although the emphasis in this chapter is on a comprehensive, district staff development/organization development process, effective, well-conceptualized efforts in this arena emphasize appreciating and protecting the professional autonomy of the individuals involved. Much of the criticism that has been, often justly, heaped on staff development efforts has been the result of paternalistic, top-down, do-it-to-'em determinations of what training others needed to make them more effective.

Nevertheless, sometimes a comprehensive program requires district-wide direction, such as that resulting from requirements placed on districts by PL 94-142. So a staff development program left solely to individual staff member choice is unrealistic, since individuals are part of a larger system with a different, sometimes broader, perspective. Nevertheless, even in instances where mandates are necessary, great care should be taken to respect the wants and needs of individual staff members. Ideally, individuals are enough in tune with the organization, because of having been treated with dignity and respect, that they feel some ownership and, consequently, are willing to work toward goals the district has declared as important.

What Steps Are Taken in Building a Development Program?

Key steps in creating a comprehensive district staff development/ organization development program include the following.

Determine Purpose

Without a clear statement of purpose, no effort is likely to be successful. Logically, this statement of purpose should begin with the mission statement of the board of education and should be a part of the mission statement of every site or unit. At the very least, planning for organization and individual improvement should be a part of every district's annual procedures. For example, the district and each of its natural subdivisions should all declare program improvement targets annually, based on appropriate data collection and determination of needs.

To complete the cycle, individuals should be encouraged to develop their own plans for personal and professional development in concert with— or aside from—site/unit or district direction. The relationship between formal staff evaluation and staff development continues to be an uneasy one, but in a climate where staff members at all levels trust each other and communicate well, supervisors and supervisees can cooperatively set job targets for improvement based on a nonthreatening analysis of needs. The successful marriage between collaborative formal evaluation and self-selected growth experiences for which support is provided has by no means been fully achieved, but progress is being made.

Develop a Flexible Structure

Just as we ask teachers to diagnose the needs of each student and provide appropriate instruction at the right level of difficulty, so, too, do we need to respond to the needs of each staff member who is a part of our ecosystem. At all times, staff development should exemplify the best of what we know about quality instruction—about diagnosing and meeting individual needs, about active participation, about guided practice, and about practice over time with feedback. In addition to having input into the planning and preparation for staff development, participants should have as many options or choices as possible out of respect to their adult status: type of sessions (lecture, small group, independent study); time of sessions (late afternoon, breakfast, summer); type of follow-up (small group seminar, demonstration, observation and feedback).

Establish a Comprehensive Program Improvement Planning Process

To be truly comprehensive, a program improvement process should have both a short-term (one-year) and a long-range (at least three to five years) component. It may include district-level emphases, goals, or objectives toward which all employees of the district should lend support over a period of several years, such as drug-free schools. The first year could be an informational year, with a total staff kick-off, a motivational speaker, and an explication of the specific objectives the district hopes to accomplish regarding that topic during the ensuing year. Each sub-unit could then be asked to develop a plan of support related to its responsibilities (e.g., individual schools, school nurses) but supportive of the total effort. In following years, a more careful analysis of the local drug situation could be made, and student and community groups could be enlisted, with goals being set for lowering the incidence of drug use and continuing to change attitudes.

In addition to the major districtwide emphasis, each site or unit would assess its other needs, establish its own objectives (short- and long-range), design a plan within funds allocated to it for that purpose, and carry out its own improvement activities. The staff development/organization development office or other departments could provide technical assistance. Although this process is consistent with the growing interest in decentralization of responsibility and "empowerment," it lacks the potential negative side effects of independent site operation, which can result in less efficient use of both human and economic resources, less equity of program from school to school, less sense of common purpose, and less psychological and technical support as groups experiment with new techniques.

Establish a Comprehensive Communication Process

Regular information flowing through an established source (such as district, division, building, or department publications) that notes progress and identifies problems contributes to the cohesion of the district and the "we-ness" that is an important part of organizational health. It helps to encourage everyone to keep working on the task by serving as a continuous reminder of the commitment. If this effort is managed successfully, failures can be accepted without undue discouragement, and successes can be used as stepping stones to the next level of achievement.

Evaluate Goal Achievement or Efforts Directed Toward the Emphases Declared

Too often, we set out with enthusiasm and high hopes, only to be distracted by the intervening pressures in our lives so that we fail to determine what we actually accomplished. District evaluation departments can provide invaluable help in clarifying goals at the outset, identifying what data to collect and how, assisting with data analysis, drawing conclusions, and writing the summary report. This information is extremely useful for establishing the next set of objectives or emphases.

If a district has no such specially trained individuals, staff members can still make sure that the expected outcomes of their efforts are as clear, simple, and reachable as possible. They can ask themselves what data they could collect to demonstrate whether or not they have accomplished what they set out to do. They can collect and interpret data to be used for

Figure 12.1
Number of times teachers participated in staff development activities over five years

	Teacher Level		
Staff Development Focus	**Elem.**	**JR**	**HS**
Content-related (including curriculum implementation)	66	1	25
Instructional delivery—general	17	3	2
Climate/environment/affective (including drug and alcohol)	25	4	8
Theory/current practice	5	0	1
Classroom techniques/organization	14	6	1
Student management/protection	7	1	0
Resource review/use	2	0	0
IEP, CPR, etc.	2	0	0
Technology	10	3	6
Special education (including at-risk and gifted)	23	3	2
Personal development	2	1	0
Thinking skills and processes	5	0	0
Organizational Development	0	3	1

Figure 12.2
Individual time invested in staff development by randomly selected staff members over five years

	Hours	**Years of Teaching**
Primary teacher #1	112.5	5
#2	140.0	12
#3	72.0	10
#4	154.5	12
Upper elementary #5	245.0	2
#6	291.0	5
#7	144.0	8
#8	91.5	28
Middle (counselor) #1	105.0	9
#2	13.5	22
Senior high #1	19.5	15
#2	138.5	29
Total	1,527	
Average per year	25.45	

reporting to appropriate audiences or for future planning. Many times, this process can be more important than knowing whether or not the hoped-for outcome was achieved.

Another nonquantitative, yet meaningful, assessment of the impact of a comprehensive staff development/organization development effort can be made by reviewing the record of participation. Figures 12.1 and 12.2 show the pattern of 12 educators' participation in district-delivered activities over a period of five school years. This random selection of educators comprised four primary teachers, four upper-elementary teachers, two middle-level staff members (one of whom is a counselor), and two high school teachers in a district with a well-established staff development/organization development program.

Summary

As we consider the serious business of improving our schools and our delivery of services to students, it is important that we look more broadly at how to do that. This chapter suggests that we should look at the whole as well as its parts—as though it were a true ecosystem. It suggests also that we are more likely to be able to make significant improvements if we more systematically apply what we know about human behavior and organizational behavior to our districts, to our schools or other working units, to our classrooms, and to ourselves as individuals. Use of this knowledge should result in a more open system, more action research and meaningful experimentation, and a more collegial approach to professional problem solving. Most of all, this knowledge should lead to meaningful changes in the institution we call the school and enable it to fulfill its awesome hope and responsibility.

13

An Experience in Anchorage: Trials, Errors, and Successes

Bill Mell
Carol Mell

The Anchorage School District is in many ways a typical example of a large public school system. It serves 40,000 K-12 students and exhibits traditional forms of instructional and administrative organization. Staff development is seen as an activity separate from school management and classroom instruction.

The staff development for the district has passed through the normal phases found elsewhere: (a) large group presentations by circuit riders, (b) massive groups of mini-courses presented by outside experts and some local helpers, (c) school-based activities selected by a variety of grassroots approaches, and (d) school board activities mandated by various legal requirements. District experience, particularly in the secondary schools, has shown that large group and mandated activities have had little effect on teaching. The grassroots approach has resulted in many trivial activities.

Bill Mell is Executive Director for Secondary Education, and Carol Mell is Assistant Principal, Bartlett High School, both with the Anchorage, Alaska, School District.

The most common activities have become modules easily plunked down in the time slot allocated for training. Often, no follow-up activity takes place in the classroom. For example, the most recent hot items have been first-aid training and staff wellness. Both are perfect staff development activities. They are dramatic, obviously important, and can be expected to have little impact on a classroom. They can use up development time for an entire staff without fear of criticism for improper use . They also do nothing to improve instruction directly or develop staff skills in the instructional area.

A key issue in educational administration is managing the change process. It is an area in which educational researchers are intensely interested. For the educational practitioner, however, it is more accurately a matter of life and death. Skill in managing the change process is essential if the character of the schools is to be developed to meet student needs.

In our society, change is tolerated and expected. Rather than being an overtly directed process, however, it is usually a naturally evolving event. It happens to us rather than being done by us. In the framework of change, ideas are assumed to have the power to convert and create change by their own strength. The correctness of an idea is judged in Darwinian terms: Bad ideas disappear; good ideas prevail. In the school setting, acceptance of this assumption is to invite failure.

The power of the social system within schools to maintain the status quo has overwhelmed most change attempts (Sarason 1971). The ambitious change efforts from curriculums of the 1960s to the more recent back-to-basics movement have not worked or have resulted in largely cosmetic results (Fullan 1982). If traditional efforts do not work, staff development programs must focus on methods that avoid the pitfalls of traditional practice. Peer coaching is the only research-based technique currently available that addresses the problem of transferring new teaching approaches into the active repertoire of classroom teachers (Joyce and Showers 1982). The data, as well as past experience, are convincing: Vast resources have been expended on staff development programs that have resulted in little or no classroom change. It is apparent that instituting peer coaching (called "teams" in this chapter) throughout a school can provide a framework for implementating changes within the unit. The power of this process lies in the fact that it is a radical departure from the way schools are currently organized. It also presents a problem. How do we make the first change—implementing instructional teams? Can a process be identified and implemented that has a high probability of success in the public school setting?

The Setting

The purpose of this article is to look at the conditions that determine the shape of such an effort and to discuss briefly a local attempt to produce a major change in a school district's pattern of staff development.

The history of failure of school innovation in our district has resulted in the comfortable notion that any new idea can be expected to pass away and, hence, can be safely ignored. The failure of many change efforts has, in the Anchorage School District, validated a tendency of teachers and other staff to give lip service to new programs and outwait the implementation process. Their cheerful contention that business-as-usual is just around the corner has been correct more often than not. In Anchorage, this historical tendency must be accounted for in any change effort. Our efforts must involve the right people at the right time and in the right way. The power of the idea is not enough.

Besides the change process, the nature of the school affects planning for change. Some of the common aspects of school nature are evident in Anchorage schools, as elsewhere. Goodlad (1984) described them in detail.

The aspects that most strongly affect the Anchorage School District are the following:

1. Schools operate at an automatic nonintrospective level. Events are a result not of careful planning, but of expectations. Commonly agreed to focuses in schools are exceptions and are often not educational in nature. Our football teams are a more common central emphasis than reading.

2. Schools are not naturally relevant to students. Students do not share common goals with other students or staff. The modern comprehensive high school in Anchorage, through the effort to reach all students, produced a wider rather than a more narrow focus. Staff meet the needs of students voluntarily. Focuses are not planned, and staff opt in and out at will. This makes any instructionally focused effort difficult to maintain because staff members can abandon a project if it is outside what is customary or is becoming uncomfortable.

3. In addition, school organization sets limits that control the types and depth of interpersonal relationships with other staff and students through time management and funding. Teachers tend to see students during class and are isolated from fellow teachers. It takes extraordinary effort to form close relationships. Teachers are expected to function unaided. Supervision is essentially a spot check on the teacher's ability to survive independently.

Any change effort requires components that will cause the teacher and principal to become introspective about their craft, focus on instruction and teaching as a major goal, reduce isolation, and put some control of time and resources in the hands of practitioners. This is a radical notion bound to generate resistance.

Secondary teachers themselves exhibit characteristics that increase the resistance to change. At this level, teachers see themselves as content area experts first and teachers second. As a group, they are limited in the use of varied teaching methodology. Teachers also view themselves as well prepared and their colleagues as competent. Any change effort aimed at improving them is not welcome.

Teachers' analyses of school problems consistently point away from themselves. Innovation, on the other hand, usually places the teacher at the center stage and incorporates new teacher behaviors as the critical feature of the change effort. There is an inherent conflict here. The initial stages of the change must be nonthreatening and of value to the teacher in the classroom. In Anchorage, change has been most accepted when it is viewed as making successful people even more successful.

Traditional teacher training processes for professional-level teachers in Anchorage have been the hit-and-run model. Our teachers report that this method has minimal influence on teaching. Prepared curriculums, student interest, and personal interest have a far greater impact. When this is added to weak teacher interaction and classroom autonomy, our potential for developing a realistic strategy for change is bleak.

Fundamentally, schools oppose change. The staff does not value change, and school organization naturally frustrates the transmission of ideas. Effective staff development requires a change in the system itself. The organization must be transformed to allow change before it can be made with any degree of certainty. Persons working in the area of staff development must find ways of creating a school culture that is able to:

• Tap the creative energy of the school staff.
• Value creativity in school staff.
• Make it safe for staff to propose and act on new ideas.
• Teach organization members the norms and behaviors necessary to support and be comfortable in a school open to new ideas.
• Provide resources of time and money to individuals beyond traditional patterns.
• Develop group consensus on ideas regardless of point of origin.

The Gamble

A blueprint for achieving this type of school culture does not exist. Nevertheless, an effort was made to attack the existing system at the following three points and capitalize on whatever fell out:

1. Break staff isolation.

2. Secure funding for open-ended school improvement efforts and protect the practitioners from the resistance as much as possible.

3. Invite school-level staff to design the shape of the school effort while providing training in areas of instructional methods.

In the spring of 1984, a central office administrator and a high school principal launched a project designed to revamp the staff development pattern in at least one school. The core of the effort was to change the style of professional interaction between teachers through the development of instructional teams. Teachers would work with each other to learn new methodology and help each other transfer it to the classroom. The structure of the project required extensive funding for substitute teachers to replace the participating staff members for a half day every two weeks throughout the spring semester. There was significant resistance to the project at all levels, which was dealt with by ignoring it.

It was felt from the first that providing time for staff to pursue professional growth would be powerful enough to sustain such growth through the early stages. However, it was recognized that continuation of the project would depend on adequate funding and acceptance of the process by teachers and principals. Methodological content would also have to have a real impact on classroom practice.

The process of implementation was designed to follow these steps:

1. Initiative pilot team concept at one school.

2. Use team members to support innovation within the pilot school and at other schools.

3. Set up team concept in other schools. While suggesting content and structure, leave final decision making at the school level. At this stage no idea was out of bounds.

4. Recruit and organize a districtwide steering committee composed of team members. Administrators attend only if they participate on a school team.

5. Provide content training in areas suggested by the schools. Stress a single theme but support other areas of interest. Use the steering committee to allocate training funds.

6. Develop cross-district training and sharing events designed to refine recurring themes of interest.

7. Promote change concept using team members to expand into nonparticipating schools.

8. Promote large-scale single theme training events outside of the school year. Use the steering committee to validate and communicate

decision process.

    9. Standardize team practice through district steering committee.

    10. Link team processes to job expectations, professional duties, status, and salary scale.

The Outcome

The district, as a whole, made it to a weak Step 8. Six high schools implemented instructional teams to some degree. Each high school was given the opportunity to develop its own instructional teams model and its own timeline for implementation of the model. Funding and other support were the same for each unit. The models varied from unit to unit, as did the degree of implementation.

Four out of seven junior high schools have done the preliminary work to begin the process in their schools. There is some interest in elementary schools, even though resources have not been allocated at that level. The process has been on hold for the past three years, due to loss of funding and changes in personnel.

Loss of funding has been the most critical. In each school some staff members were willing to resist the social pressure to cease instructional team activity because funding allowed administrators and teachers the time to avoid confrontation over traditional use of the school day. Cooperation of the rest of the staff was not required to make it work, and more staff became involved as time passed. With the drop in oil prices, the available funds for this type of activity dried up. Instructional teams were expensive and competed with powerful issues such as teacher salaries, class size, and funding for additional staff in traditionally important programs—namely, remedial classes and athletics. Instructional teams had not become part of the school culture before hard times hit. It cannot even be said that they competed for money. Instructional teams simply disappeared as a formal district program. Their disappearance was accompanied by a cry of dismay by participants and a much louder sigh of relief from staff who feared potential invasion of their private classroom autonomy.

Time to work together turned out to be a critical factor in maintaining the instructional team. While time was available and instructional teams were a sanctioned overt activity, a variety of approaches seemed to flourish and enjoyed different degrees of support. Four basic models were evident: the showcase, the flower child, the circus, and the study group. It is important to stress that each school started with the same funding and focused on the same instructional content. In each case, the unit administrator was the key player in the development of the character of the model.

The Showcase Model

In the showcase model approach, the school effort was organized to show the trappings of instructional teams. The numbers of teachers involved, meetings, classes observed, and release days used were given more attention than what happened instructionally. Excellent teachers were paired with poor teachers, and it was announced that the poor teachers would improve. In the school culture, the excellent teachers were chastened for being uppity while the poor teachers were viewed with sympathy for being singled out. All participating teachers were uncomfortable with the directed relationships. When time and funding disappeared, so did the instructional team. After all, it was really no team and filled no internal need for any team member.

The Flower Child Model

In the flower child approach, staff were presented with a variety of content and time to work together. They were encouraged to select any content and work out their own relationships. The team developed close personal relationships and became open to sharing classroom experiences and time. Teachers concentrated on refining skills already held rather than acquiring new ones. Where content areas were presented, teachers felt free to change the model to suit their own practice. As a result, content became a trivial feature of the team effort. When time and funding disappeared, the team did also. The teacher's normal school day militates against social contact between the teachers. In this case, the team was missed, but teachers had not built team activity back into their own available time. The team did not fill an internal need that could not be met in traditional school social settings.

The Circus Model

In the circus model approach, staff members were presented with content, release time, and resident teacher experts in the instructional content. The model was organized around massive presentation of the content to the staff in large groups and small-group minicourses. Administration served as facilitators to the process but did not take an instructional role. The model contained a high level of activity for the entire staff. It was fun. It closely resembled traditional inservice efforts and held a high level of comfort for staff. Its fatal flaw was in the release time process. The teacher expert on staff also substituted for the teacher who wished training in content. The experts were not able to work consistently with staff team members. When time and funding disappeared, the circus stopped and the experts became full-time teachers. The team was only a team when presenting inservices.

The Study Group Model

In the study group approach, the staff were presented with content and a model of interaction and observation that required using the content in the classrooms. As a result, the team was composed of teachers open to change and willing to try new ideas. The team was small compared with the others. Team members, however, were able to learn new skills that they found useful in the classroom. When time and money dried up, the team did not. The team sought alternative means to provide time and motivation. In place of team funding, an arrangement was made with the local university to allow the team to provide credit courses after school in the content area. The study group has continued to exist and has been able to recruit new members. It was a team that met internal needs of team members. It is the least flashy but most enduring of the basic instructional team types. Whether it can be exported to other schools or even to a significant portion of the staff at its own school remains a question.

As a result of these experiences, the following guidelines offer suggestions for avoiding major pitfalls:

1. If the school has a history of positive innovations and the staff see themselves as innovators, the culture of the school is obviously more apt to support the establishment of instructional teams. If the climate is less than ideal, the chief facilitator must decide whether it is wiser to invest time and resources to improve the school climate prior to implementing such a major change. An elementary principal who successfully established peer coaching teams in his school had worked for a number of years to foster the appropriate antecedent conditions (Grimmett, Moody, and Balasubramaniam 1986). However, if the chief facilitator is not in a position to carry out the changes necessary to make a significant improvement, a decision must be made as to whether enough other positive forces are operating to overcome this obstacle.

2. Change is a difficult and complicated process. A school faced with too many changes, particularly conflicting ones, may fail to implement any. On the other hand, some changes may work together to enhance each other. Determine if the other changes would be enhanced by the prior establishment of instructional teams or if the other changes would assist in making the implementation of instructional teams easier. Ensure that the other changes will not strain resources or drain staff energies. Make certain enough routines and procedures have been maintained to provide some stability. Aside from the real conflicts competing changes produce,

they also provide convenient excuses for staff members not to participate.

3. District-level monetary support is needed because the financial resources required at the onset of such a project are far greater than the discretionary funds usually available at the unit level. Central office conceptual support not only lends credence to the project, but helps to prevent teachers and administrators who would divert the resources to other projects from doing so. District-level support also makes it more difficult for an individual to undermine the project and provides a focus for the hostility of the opposition forces. The district-level support can also be helpful in working with union leaders to enlist their endorsement or, at the very least, to prevent organized opposition.

4. Teachers who express the need for a new challenge or indicate they are experiencing some sort of difficulty in reaching a particular group of students are usually more willing to try instructional teams. The successful teachers who have spent years teaching the same courses to the same types of students are less willing to change. They indicate that there is no need for improvement in their pedagogy, and they do not wish to jeopardize their success. The most helpful way of dealing with them is to enlist the support of at least one highly regarded, long-tenured teacher. This person's enthusiasm will sometimes help to encourage others. The political and opinion leaders within a unit are not necessarily the staff members most open to change. Look for the omnivores, the people who are "orientated toward growth rather than [being] possible impediments to it" (Joyce, Hersh, and McKibbin 1984, p. 164). This is the group most willing to try new ideas and bring some of their active consumer colleagues along. As a next step, consider the teachers new to the building. They are not yet entrenched in the social system and are often more open to change.

5. Be prepared to deal with turf battles, and do not underestimate them. Determine which individuals or groups within the unit, formal or informal, have traditionally made the decisions in this area. Decide whether it is possible to bring them into the process or if they will work to oppose any idea that did not originate among its members. Try to bring at least some member of this group into the process as soon as possible. Petty jealousies or power struggles often make it more or less desirable for certain individuals to be associated with the project initially. Determine where the central office staff, particularly staff development, fits into the plan.

6. The introduction of the instructional teams concept is important. Keep in mind that when the presenter of a new practice is a successful practitioner, credibility for the program is greatly increased (Crandall 1983, p. 6). Although the chief change facilitator will usually not be a teacher (it

is difficult for teachers to obtain the necessary resources), it is important for teachers to become the spokespersons for the program as soon as possible. Teachers who had decided to become involved in the program spoke with all building teachers on a conference period basis to explain why they had decided to participate, why they felt it was important, and to invite others to participate. This program will not be successful unless teachers feel it belongs to them. The chief facilitator must be willing to share power and control.

7. Assess whether staff members will readily accept outside consultants or dismiss them as ivory tower theoreticians. In some situations, you may wish to have the outside consultants introduce the concept. In others, you may wish to use outside consultants only with small groups or not at all initially. The stronger the political power base of the chief facilitator, the easier the implementation.

8. Adequate discretionary resources are essential. Release time is expensive but necessary for the program to function effectively. Initially, large blocks of time are needed for planning and determining how the groups will function, as well as for training purposes. This process is repeated as new members are socialized into the group. The need for release time decreases as the program progresses. Although teachers continue to use time to observe others, they use it more effectively. Much of the pre- and post-observation planning and debriefing tends to take place during lunch or conference periods or before or after school. Also, shared videotapes are used more than actual classroom observation. Materials such as books and demonstration tapes are initial costs, as are video cameras, recorders, and tapes.

9. Parental understanding is a prerequisite for parental support. If parents are supportive of the program, they cannot be enlisted by groups opposed to it. One tactic opposition forces tend to use with parents is to decry the amount of time teachers will be away from their students for training or other activities. Parents can also be useful in dealing with another pressure group—the students. As teachers develop new techniques that place greater responsibility for learning on the student, the students will often push for a return to the more comfortable methods of the past. Involving parent representatives of the school parent advisory group in some of the training prevents problems from developing in this area.

10. Instructional teams involve time and effort on the part of the participants. Although some writers have indicated that the desire to become a better teacher is the primary motivator for most staff development (Guskey 1986), it is helpful to allow for personal and professional gain

whenever possible. Providing teachers involved in instructional teams with opportunities for special workshops and courses is helpful. Arranging for teachers to act as trainers or training facilitators, particularly at other schools or districtwide, has also been viewed positively. Modifying existing evaluation procedures so that they recognize and encourage this type of endeavor also promises to be useful.

Reflections

Where do we go from here? The district has a new superintendent. Elections scheduled soon may radically change the composition of the school board and the way in which it is selected. Five of the six high schools have different principals from when the program began nearly five years ago. Declining enrollment and retirements have also resulted in the loss of some teachers who were involved in the program. Both the state and the city are in the midst of an economic change. As resources become more scarce, competition for them grows. Taxpayers do not view staff development as a necessity, but rather expect teachers to have all needed expertise when they are hired. On the positive side, each of the schools involved has a group of teachers who express a desire to recapture the feeling of instructional teams. They miss the time to talk shop, to work together as learners, and to pursue instruction as an intellectual process. New efforts will have a far richer soil in which to grow than did the initial change effort. The experience has taught several hard lessons:

1. Outcome goals are essential. Any route will do only when no destination is in mind.

2. Limits to the types of activities to be allowed are necessary. The means used to achieve the goals has a profound effect on outcomes.

3. Unlimited funding is no panacea. Unlimited options are no substitute for clearly understood goals and means.

If the district turns again to a large-scale effort to introduce new instructional methodology, we will attempt to learn from our mistakes. Our mistakes suggest a model of action with four essential components: the content expert, the process expert, the leadership group, and the peer coaching relationship (see Figure 13.1).

The model requires an expert in the content of the goals. The expert can be internal or external, but he or she must be recognized as able to transfer content and pass judgment on the validity of the transfer to others. The content expert also serves to anoint the others as experts in working with new staff.

The process expert and content expert may be the same. However,

Figure 13.1

**Process Model for Introduction
of Instructional Methodology**

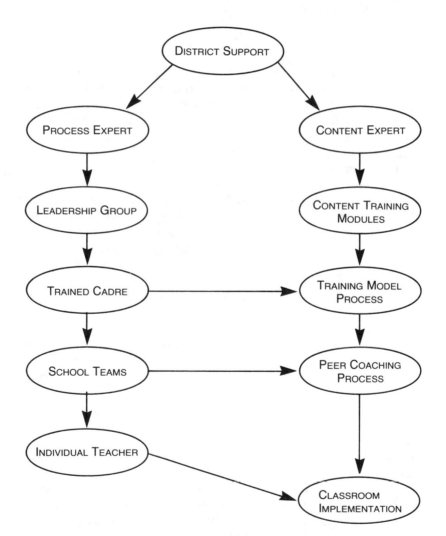

the process expert must be on site regularly. For this reason, the process leader should be internal or on hand continuously. The process expert performs the same function as the content person: blessing proper conduct and redirecting improper behavior. The process expert guards against the domestication of the implementation model itself; ensures the validity of training; selects who trains; insists on the use of the peer coaching relationship; and, in the end, validates that the behavior sought in the classroom is in fact reaching the level of classroom practice.

The leadership group is essential for several reasons. First, it is composed of respected members of the target group and supports the change as a valuable idea. Second, it is trained in content and process and thereby is able to function as both content and process expert for change sub-groups. They reach into the target group on an instant-by-instant basis and guard the models' integrity. Third, the group assumes a stance as instructional leader and learner that is accessible to all staff and provides role models. The process expert and leadership group must be able to change the normal time relationships for staff. Teachers must be free from class responsibility. This can be done through organization of the school day, buying substitute teacher time, and working at non-school time. The leadership group will often volunteer time. Beyond the group, some scheme that frees up classroom time or commits teacher time outside of school is essential. Creative use of credit courses can help, but at some point, in order to penetrate beyond the leadership group, some investment in funding for staff development will be necessary. The most effective use of the money would be in development of a school organization that continually provides time for staff to work together as a normal expectation of the school process. Continuous use of release time from class is not recommended because both teachers and the public will object to time missed with students.

Finally, the model requires the insertion of peer coaching as a normal professional relationship. Peer coaching as a concept will have to be taught and practiced along with the content. It is the core of the process expert's job in managing this change effort.

These essential components are all represented graphically in the figure included here. It is important to note that the idea of the change may be initiated at the top or at the grassroots, but our experience tends to suggest the whole structure must be in place for the change process to work.

References

Crandall, D. (1983). "The Teacher's Role in School Improvement." *Educational Leadership* 41, 3: 6-9.

Fullan, M. (1982). *The Meaning of Educational Change.* New York: Teachers College Press.

Goodlad, J. (1984). *A Place Called School.* New York: McGraw Hill Book Co.

Grimmet, P., P. Moody, and M. Balasubramaniam. (April 1986). "A Study of a District-Wide Implementation of Peer Coaching." Paper presented at the annual meeting of The American Educational Research Association in San Francisco, Calif.

Guskey, T. (1986). "Staff Development and the Process of Teacher Change." *Educational Researcher* 1, 5: 5-12.

Hall, G., and S. Hord. (April 1986). "Configurations of School-Based Leadership Teams." Symposium conducted at the annual meeting of The American Educational Research Association in San Francisco, Calif.

Hall, G., and S. Loucks. (1978). "Teacher Concerns as a Basis for Facilitating and Personalizing Staff Development." *Teachers College Record* 80: 36-53.

Joyce, B., R. Hersch, and M. McKibbin. (1983). *The Structure of School Improvement.* New York: Longman, Inc.

Joyce, B., and B. Showers. (October 1982). "The Coaching of Teaching." *Educational Leadership* 40, 1: 4-10.

Lieberman, A. (1986). "Collaborative Work." *Educational Leadership* 43, 5: 4-8.

Sarason, S. (1971). *The Culture of the School and the Problem of Change.* Boston: Allyn and Bacon.

Epilogue: The Curious Complexities of Cultural Change

Bruce Joyce and Carlene Murphy

This ASCD yearbook is a compilation of essays written independently by authors from four countries. Given the relative newness of staff development as a field, it is surprising how consistently the authors perceive its central mission as one of generating a change in the very culture of the school. The authors go far beyond the concerns that preoccupied the field 15 years ago—a search for inclusive governance structures, content that could improve instruction, and more effective training models (see Joyce, Howey, and Yarger 1975).

Whether they were writing from a research, shareholders', or national and local initiatives' perspective, the authors have unearthed a mission for staff development that was implicit in initial efforts to develop human resource development systems in education—that is, to create conditions in which education personnel can grow productively and school improvement

Bruce Joyce is Director, Booksend Laboratories, Eugene, Oregon, and Carlene Murphy is Director of Staff Development, "Adopt-A-Schools," and Public Relations, Augusta, Georgia.

is an embedded feature of collegial life. This mission, the authors agree, requires a major restructuring of the workplace. Furthermore, this restructuring is seen as much more than quantitative increases in instructional leadership, collegial activity, or amounts of high-quality training. Rather it involves a transformation of the roles of all personnel and a reorientation of the norms of the workplace, including how the educator's job is construed and how teachers, administrators, and service providers relate with and perceive one another. The challenge is to create an ethos that is almost an inversion of the one Lortie so accurately described in *Schoolteacher* (1975). That is, vertical and horizontal isolation and separation of roles will be replaced by integration and collaboration. Anti-intellectualism and protectionism will be replaced by thoughtful inquiry, inclusiveness, and an overlapping of roles.

It is too mild to say that such a proposal is ambitious. To suggest cultural innovation is outrageous. We must ask whether any reasonable person can seriously suggest that members of a society set out to change the norms of the enterprise of schooling, which hitherto has been devoted to the preservation of the status quo and has in many ways been organized to ensure that cultural change will be *prevented*. Yet, all these authors are practitioners, even those who make their primary living as scholars, and they know our schools. They write reasonably, even calmly, of the unthinkable. They think it can be done, must be done, and will be done, albeit not without difficulty. How can this be?

Perhaps it is because we live in an era where so many cultural changes have been recorded. We have watched Japan move, in only 40 years, from a condition where relatively few individuals received formal education to a completely educated society with the most efficient schooling system in the world. Likewise, India, starting from a condition in 1947 where fewer than one percent of the population received *any* schooling, has created a society that contains twice as many middle-class families as reside in the United States. We have watched desert nomads wire their tents so that their computers and facsimile machines can control their vast holdings in the urban centers of a hundred countries. And communism may have been disliked, but it was not closely watched until the day Sputnik rose to announce that feudal Russia had been transformed into a formidable technetronic power in only half an average lifetime.

Or perhaps cultural lag is finally catching up with education. Until a hundred years ago, societies managed with only a few educated persons, and then, until very recently, by providing a low-quality education to more and more of their members. We are now in a world where the quality of a person's education and the vigor of a nation's educational system will make more difference than ever before, but we possess an educational system that has been almost impervious to efforts at modernization. The difficulties inherent in that situation are beginning to be apparent in the undersupply of educated persons needed to service modern commerce and industry and the oversupply of citizens who cannot fend for themselves because they have not been sufficiently educated to be economically viable, let alone forage for quality in their lives.

So we will begin the effort to create a system for the revamping of our educational system, recognizing that the initiative will be regarded by some as a product of arrogance and by others as a sure sign of lunacy, but above all, that job will be hard.

How hard will it be? Where are the chief obstacles?

We don't know. But we will try, in the next few pages, to squeeze from our own work some of the more obvious lessons that we are being taught.

We are both technicians of staff development. One is an organizer and the other a trainer and researcher of training and teaching. We have combined our skills and those of some of our colleagues to build a staff development system in Richmond County, Georgia (Joyce, Showers, Murphy, and Murphy 1989). We did not intend to get into the cultural change business. All we wanted to do was apply some of the results of research on training and teaching to help teachers engage in the study of teaching. But as Fullan pointed out in Chapter 1, if we don't deal with the program in terms of cultural change, the results of our efforts will have a very short half-life.

Our setting has been able to support a major project. Twenty-six schools are involved thus far, with about 10 to be added annually until all 50 are connected and the district administration has easily handled conflicts, logistics, and the procedures for orienting personnel. Nearly a thousand teachers are regularly using research-based models of teaching that were completely new to them. Cooperative learning pervades the schools that have been involved for a year or more. Implementation has been substantial enough that in some areas there is evidence of notable increases in student learning. Yet the district is largely urban and has severely limited resources. Its personnel are typical of the nation's teachers. It is Southern, but there are few aspects of its operation that are distinctly different from those of any other region of the United States.

We have selected, for discussion, four of the features of the project that illustrate areas where we have flirted with changing the culture of the school and have been able to observe reactions in terms of norms of decision-making, beliefs about research and scientific inquiry in general, ideas about the nature of students and the efficacy of schooling, and ideas about relationships with colleagues.

Norms of Decision Making

Schools were accepted into the project on the condition that all faculty participate. The schools competed to be accepted. To qualify, building administrators had to describe the project to the faculties and receive written assurance from 90 percent of the staff that they would participate fully for at least two years. Also, the entire faculty had to understand that *all* personnel would have to participate if the school were accepted.

The "whole-faculty" notion definitely scraped the nerves of the prevailing norms. Although the program did not lack applicants, the idea that 90 percent agreement committed the entire group challenged the norm of autonomy by suggesting that the school behave in a traditional democratic manner. Schools generally do not have a process for commitment that involves less than 100 percent agreement. That is, under existing norms, there is no "body politic." Most faculty see themselves as autonomous operators who can refuse to participate in projects even when overwhelming majorities approve and want them. *However, this violation of the norms produced no stiff opposition.* It turned out that, at least in our setting, most people could see the sensibility of developing democratic procedures and realized that general school-improvement projects involve compromise and negotiated agreements. Most people reacted initially with shock, were flabbergasted as the "follow-up" training began (they did not believe that promises of follow-up were real), began to accept, and emerged with a certain pride and a great deal of pleasure in the increased collegiality. A few people screamed, stamped their feet, and predicted dire consequences for the children, but gradually quieted down. We were surprised and pleased. We hypothesize that the change to democratic processes was navigated with reasonable ease *because the lack of consensual governance procedures in schools is actually at variance with the basic norms of the society*. In other words, education personnel have the cognitions with which to engage in democratic procedures. Even though it is a change, establishing democratic governance in schools does not challenge societal norms.

Ideas About Research and Scientific Inquiry

Participation in the project included training in several models of teaching, as well as organizing the faculty into study groups who would work together to implement the content of the training and generate initiatives of their own for improving the school. Data were to be collected on effects and fed back to the faculties for their use in reorienting their efforts.

At the outset, most of the teachers did not believe that research relevant to teaching actually existed. As they studied the research, they also voiced the belief that the findings were probably peculiar to the settings in which the research had been conducted and that it probably would not apply to their setting. In other words, typical of educators (Lortie 1975), many did not believe that there can be generalizations about teaching and learning, but that knowledge is specific to individual teachers and learners. From this position, educational research as a scientific activity would actually be impossible.

The fact that teachers experienced positive results by using research to guide their teaching did not change this position significantly. After learning to use the first teaching strategies and finding that, to their surprise, they worked, most greeted the next strategies with the same skepticism with which they had welcomed the first ones and, again, expressed surprise when they garnered positive results. Two years and a half-dozen teaching strategies later, this cycle is still repeating itself. Furthermore, the faculties of neighboring schools tend to believe that the factors that have improved these schools will not work for them. Each new faculty accepted into the project is astonished that their trainers are going to teach them to use practices based on research (read "ivory-tower nonsense").

It is not news that many teachers are unaware of educational research and skeptical about it. However, unless the belief system about the possibility of a scientific base for education is changed, connecting research to educational practice will be very difficult. This may be a tough nut to crack. This may be because society as a whole is ambivalent about science, supporting it with one hand but maintaining suspicion of intellectuals with the other.

Views of Students and Learning

A real anomaly appeared with the use of data to judge the success of the schools and guide planning. At the beginning of the project, we believed that increases in student learning could be relied on to increase teachers' and administrators' commitment. For this reason, care was taken to collect data and make them available to all personnel. Despite some rather dramatic effects (one school increased its promotion rate from 30 to 95 percent) some teachers and administrators expressed the hope that reports of success would signal the *end* of the efforts and a return to normal practice. ("We've shown we can do it, so can we stop now?") This produced a schism between the teacher leaders, who were ready to add the next innovation to their repertoire, and the ones who hoped the project was over.

The reaction of administrators in non-project schools and the central administrators of the district was mixed. Some teachers and administrators organized their schools to join the project. Some others sought actively for reasons why the findings might be spurious. ("Let's see what happens next year." "Can they do this with high-SES kids?" and, "I bet they brought smart kids into the school.") This last type of comment brought to the surface a belief among many of the teachers and administrators that home background and inherited ability overwhelm curriculum and teaching as factors in learning.

The frustration in Ron Edmonds' famous question, "How many do you have to see?" may point to some of the real issues in the struggle to change the culture of the school. School improvement efforts depend on the belief that curriculum, instruction, and social climate affect student learning. If the culture of a school is permeated with a belief that the causes of student learning lie largely *outside* the school, in the genes and social background of the students, school improvement efforts may appear hopeless and even ridiculous. Stevenson, Lee, and Stigler (1986) and others (as Holloway 1988) believe that one of the reasons for the impressive recent record of Japanese schools may lie in the belief in Japan that achievement is a product more of effort than of talent, allowing teachers to believe that *their* effort to increase student learning can make a difference. If it turns out that many teachers in Western society believe that student talent, rather than the learning environment of the school, is the critical variable, the job of restructuring the culture of the school may well be a deep social process rather than a matter of reorganizing personnel and permeating the environment with opportunities for teachers and administrators to study and improve their craft.

Relationships

Finally, the development of the cadre of teachers who now provide the training, organize the study groups, and reorient the building administrators to new functions has produced its share of interesting reactions. Importantly, it has developed a community of teachers who study teaching continually and are learning to help others learn to innovate. This community has a powerful cohesiveness and is generating norms of experimentation and collegiality that appear sturdy at this point. And the group is determined to make a difference in the district. These teachers adapt to their new roles quickly and appear unperturbed by reactions to their peculiar beliefs and manners.

We are neither the first to develop such little communities of leaders nor the first to note how rapidly and satisfyingly they can create a different and productive normative structure. It encourages us just as it has encouraged others to realize how rapidly segments of the population can change. However, the group does not find that their role as teachers gives them added "credibility" as they work with their colleagues. Their colleagues greet them with the same attitudes toward children, learning, research, and collegiality with which they face trainers who are not teachers. The group is even resented by some because they have received recognition. They have broken the norms of anonymity as well as those of autonomy.

In the same vein, establishing functioning study groups did not involve the learning of particularly complex behaviors. It involved shared planning of lessons and development of materials, which makes the work of the individual teachers actually easier, though it challenges the individualistic norms of the workplace and takes a long time to get rolling. Even after two years, the system depends on the leadership of a very few teachers and is fragile enough that it would disappear in any one setting if only a few teachers were to leave at the same time. Even highly satisfying study groups depend on harmonious interpersonal relations. Unfortunately, these are subject to internecine rivalries and jealousies that are not particularly dysfunctional in the normal isolation of teaching. Also, the teachers who emerged as leaders were liable to criticism and had to resist ostracism by their colleagues. Many fine teachers avoid overt leadership activity because of this. We have been successful in solving most of these problems in the short run and can establish and nurture collegial groups, but we have not learned how to institutionalize them in such a way that they will be a regular feature of the workplace, even in middle schools where nominal "teams" have been in place for several years.

The chief norm-related problem that has emerged in the council of district administrators involves customs of bureaucratic empire-building and turf-protection. Although the changes in the schools and the development of the cadre should make all district initiatives for school improvement easier to bring about, several department heads treat the program as competitive. These department heads refuse to use the cadre as a channel for innovations they generate, and would cheerfully excise it. At this point, its success could not protect it were the top leadership to change. Many district administrators are as disbelieving of a science of education as are their teachers. Their history of isolation in the classrooms has not prepared them for collegial interchange in the executive suite. The culture of the policymakers and chief executives will surely be another concern as the change process continues.

* * *

On balance, our experience leaves us optimistic. There are problems, but not insurmountable obstacles. The system tolerates a great deal of change and many of the personnel are very able to build and maintain new norms. Teachers and administrators are sturdy enough to learn new patterns without disintegrating under the burdens of change. There is no easy path, however.

The challenge of our authors is a serious and subtle one. Most staff development personnel are by now very accustomed to conducting assessments of needs, searching for good content, finding training for their trainers, and battling for more resources and time—more priority for their work. They are in the process of learning how to apply training and organizational research to create better training designs and improve the social climate of their schools. They are now being asked to study cultural change seriously and plan to orient their efforts to impact the normative structure of schools. We forecast an interesting and productive future.

References

Holloway, S. (1988). "Concepts of Ability and Effort in Japan and the United States." *Review of Educational Research* 37: 408-412.

Joyce, B., K. Howey, and S. Yarger. (1976). *Issues to Face*. Syracuse, N.Y.: National Dissemination Center, Syracuse University.

Lortie, D. (1975). *Schoolteacher*. Chicago: The University of Chicago Press.

Joyce, B., C. Murphy, B. Showers, and J. Murphy. (November 1989). "School Renewal as Cultural Change." *Educational Leadership* 47, 3: 70-77.

Stevenson, H., S. Lee, and J.W. Stigler. (1986). "Mathematics Achievement of Chinese, Japanese, and American Children." *Science* 231: 693-699.

ASCD Board of Directors

as of November 1, 1989

Executive Council 1989-1990

President: Patricia Conran, Superintendent, Eagle County Schools, Eagle, Colorado

President Elect: Donna Jean Carter, Jostens Learning Corporation, San Diego, California

Immediate Past President: Arthur L. Costa, Professor of Education, Department of Administration, Counseling, and Policy Studies, California State University, Sacramento, California

Cile Chavez, Deputy Superintendent, Littleton Public Schools, Littleton, Colorado

Ann Converse Shelly, Director, Teacher Preparation Programs, Bethany College, Bethany, West Virginia

Bob Valiant, Assistant Superintendent, General Administration, Kennewick School District, Kennewick, Washington

Barbara Jackson, Executive Assistant to the Superintendent, District of Columbia Public Schools, Washington, D.C.

Luther Kiser, Associate Superintendent for Curriculum and Instruction, Ames Community Schools, Ames, Iowa

Charles Patterson, Superintendent, Killeen Independent School District, Killeen, Texas

Everette Sams, Professor of Education, Middle Tennessee State University, Murfreesboro, Tennessee

Francine Delaney, Elementary School Principal, Asheville Alternative School, Asheville, North Carolina

Delores Greene, Assistant Superintendent for Elementary Education, Richmond Public Schools, Richmond, Virginia

Arthur D. Roberts, Professor of Education, University of Connecticut, School of Education, Storrs, Connecticut

Board Members Elected At Large

Carl Glickman, Department of Curriculum and Supervision, University of Georgia, Athens, Georgia

Evelyn Holman, Superintendent, Wilcomico County Board of Education, Salisbury, Maryland

Blanche Martin, Superintendent, E.S.R. Winnebago/Boone Counties, Winnebago County Courthouse

Robert Walker, Program Coordinator, District of Columbia Public Schools, Washington, D.C.

Marilyn Winters, Sacramento State University, Sacramento, California

Alice Bosshard, Director of Instruction Resources, Valdez, Alaska
Rita Dunn, Professor, St. John's University, Jamaica, New York
Anne Price, Assistant Superintendent, St. Louis Public Schools, St. Louis, Missouri
LaVae Robertson, Principal, Oak Elementary, Albany, Oregon
Phyllis J. Hobson, Director, Parental Involvement Programs, District of Columbia Public Schools, Washington, D.C.
Elizabeth C. Turpin, Principal, Lansing School District, Lansing, Michigan
Beverly M. Taylor, Director of Professional Growth, Curriculum Design for Excellence, Inc., Oak Brook, Illinois
David Robinson, Superintendent, Sheridan Public Schools, Sheridan, Arizona
Alex Molnar, Professor, Department of Curriculum and Instruction, University of Wisconsin-Milwaukee
Susan E. Spangler, Director of Elementary Curriculum, Millard Public School, Omaha, Nebraska
Hilda Young, Principal, Fisk-Howard Elementary School, New Orleans, Louisiana
Linda O'Neal, Staff Development Division, North East Independent School District, San Antonio, Texas
Yolanda M. Rey, Director, Staff Development, El Paso, Texas
Belinda Williams, Martin Luther King School, Paterson, New Jersey
Harriett Arnold, San Jose, California

Unit Representatives to the Board of Directors

Alabama: Brooks Steele, Supervisor, Monroe County Schools; Horace Gordon, Birmingham; Annette Y. Cox, Anniston City Schools, Anniston
Alaska: Mary Francis, Wrangell City School District, Wrangell; Don McDermott, Anchorage
Arizona: Al Slawson, Consultant, Tucson; Larry M. Bibs, Arizona Department of Education, Phoenix
Arkansas: Steve Brown, Sheridan Public Schools, Sheridan; Gordon Floyd, Arkansas Department of Education, Little Rock
California: Bob Garmston, California State University, El Dorado Hills; Doug McPhee, Teacher, Del Mar; Harriet Arnold, Sequoia High School District, Redwood City; Loren Sanchez, Upland Unified School District, Upland; Ruben Ingram, Fountain Valley School District, Fountain Valley; Joanna Kalbus, San Bernardino County Office, San Bernardino; Lyn Perino, Ventura County Schools, Thousand Oaks
Colorado: Deborah Lynch, Aurora Public Schools, Aurora; Ann Foster, Poudre School District R-1, Fort Collins; Kay Shaw, Aurora Public Schools, Aurora
Connecticut: Roberta S. Ohotnicky, Torrington Public Schools, Torrington; Thomas Jokubaitis, Wolcott Public Schools, Wolcott; Christine Roberts, University of Connecticut, Storrs; Edward H. Bourque, Fairfield Public Schools, Fairfield
Delaware: Gary Houpt, State of Delaware, Department of Public Instruction, Dover
District of Columbia: Joan Kelley, Tyler Elementary School, Washington; Romaine Thomas, Ketcham Elementary School, Washington

Florida: P.C. Wu, University of West Florida, Pensacola; Virgil Mills, Ellenton; Jill Wilson, Elementary Principal, Pembroke Pines; Donna Miller, Orlando

Georgia: Kathy Carter, Floyd County School System, Rome; Gary Walker, Cartersville; Robert Clark, Marietta

Hawaii: Diane Gibbons, University of Hawaii, Honolulu

Idaho: Jerril LeFevre, Mountain Home School District, Mountain Home

Illinois: Karen Prudik, Frankfort Square School, Frankfort; Sheila Wilson, Forest View Educational Center, Arlington Heights; Fred Osburn, School District #117, Jacksonville; John Godbold, Illinois State University, Normal; Michael Palmisano, School District #643, Park Ridge; Richard Hanke, Thomas Junior High School, Arlington Heights

Indiana: Daniel Spangler, Southwick Elementary School, Fort Wayne; Ken Springer, North Adams Community Schools, Decatur; Leo Joint, Valparaiso

Iowa: Warren Weber, Council Bluffs Community School District, Council Bluffs; Douglas Schermer, Briggs Elementary School, Maquokita; Arthur Huinker, Western Dubuque Community School District

Kansas: Gary Marshall, Superintendent, Sublette; Jim Jarrett, Director, Secondary Education, Kansas City; Tom Hawk, Director, Secondary Education, Manhattan

Kentucky: Ann Evans, Hancock County Board of Education, Lewisport

Louisiana: Marjorie Herberger, Instructional Specialist, New Orleans; Julianna Boudreaux, New Orleans; Kate Scully, New Orleans

Maine: Ken Murphy, Yarmouth School Department, Yarmouth; Leon Lebesque, S.A.D. #52, Turner; Phyllis Deriagis, Division of Curriculum, Augusta

Maryland: Toni Worsham, Howard County Public Schools, Ellicott City; Joan Palmer, Howard County Public Schools, Ellicott City; Richard Williams, Towson State University, Baltimore

Massachusetts: Andy Platt, Educational Consultant, Acton; Isa Zimmerman, South Hamilton; Lyun Huttunen, Randolph

Michigan: Patricia Vickery, Livonia Clarenceville Schools, Livonia; Lenore Croudy, Flint Public Schools, Flint; Marilyn Van Valkenburgh, East Grand Rapids Public School, Grand Rapids; Erma Coit, Pontiac Public Schools, Pontiac; Leonard Murtaugh, Flint Community Schools, Flint

Minnesota: Kathleen Jorissen, Anoka-Hennepin Public Schools, Coon Rapids; Merill Fellger, Minnesota Center for Arts Education, Long Lake; Joan Black, Bloomington Public Schools, Bloomington

Mississippi: Nancy Bramlett, West Point Separate School District, West Point

Missouri: Sandra Braithwait, Clinton Public Schools, Clinton; Cameron Pulliam, Shrewsbury; Geraldine Johnson, St. Louis; Sandra Gray, Springfield

Montana: Beverly Flaten, School District #2, Billings; Tim Sullivan, Butte

Nebraska: Keith Rohwer, Fremont Public Schools, Fremont; James Walter, Center for Curriculum and Instruction, University of Nebraska, Lincoln; Ron Reichert, Scottsbluff Public Schools, Scottsbluff

Nevada: Joyce Woodhouse, Clark County School District, Las Vegas

New Hampshire: Ruthanne Fyfe, Jaffrey Grade School, Jaffrey; Carl Wood, Greenland Central School, Greenland

New Jersey: Marie Adair, Vineland Public Schools, Vineland; Paul Lempa, Bayonne Board of Education, Bayonne; Fred Young, Hamilton Township Schools, Hamilton; Ruth Dorney, Meddham; Richard Grandey, North Hunterdon Regional High School, Annandale

New Mexico: Mary O'Hair, New Mexico State University, Las Cruces

New York: Lynn Richbart, State Education Department, Albany; Donna Moss, Syracuse; John Glynn, Rockville Center; Robert Plaia, Massapequa; Dena Claunch, Rochester; Marian Schoenheit, Oswego; Mary Tobi, Bayport; Bette Cornell, Fayetteville

North Carolina: Judy Novicki, Camp Lejeune Schools, Camp Lejeune, Robert Hanes, UNCC, Charlotte; Larry Liggett, Asheville

North Dakota: Ann Wills, Williston

Ohio: Elaine Trivelli, Perry Local Schools, Massillon

Oklahoma: Sharon Lease, Oklahoma State Department of Education, Oklahoma City; Ken Baden, Lawton Public Schools, Lawton; Blaine Smith, Broken Arrow Schools, Broken Arrow

Oregon: Lee Wick, Beaver Acres School, Beaverton; Ardis Christensen, Oregon Department of Education, Salem; Carl Black, Medford

Pennsylvania: Leo Gensate, Hollidaysburg Area School District, Hollidaysburg; Lloyd Ruoss, Eastern Lancaster County School District, New Holland; John Gould, Eastern Lancaster County School District, New Holland; Jack Jarvie, Northwest Tri-County Intermediate Unit 5, Edinboro; Doug Macbeth, Hamburg Area School District, Hamburg

Puerto Rico: Jaime Vega, Inter American University, San German

Rhode Island: Bernardine DiOrio, Coventry Public Schools, Coventry

South Carolina: Myra Reynolds, Socastee High School, Myrtle Beach; Edith Jensen, Lexington School District Five, Ballentine; Nancy Smith, School District of Aiken County; Paul Prichard, Morrison Elementary School, Clemson

South Dakota: Robert Neely, Aberdeen School District

Tennessee: Judy Flatt, Cumberland University, Lebanon

Texas: Bonnie Fairall, Curriculum Director, El Paso

Utah: Sharon Griener, Sunrise Elementary School, Sandy

Vermont: Ray McNulty, Franklin Northeast Supervisory Union, Richford; Darlene Worth, South Burlington School District, South Burlington

Virginia: Walt Gant, Assistant Superintendent of Program Services, Grafton; Robert Hanny, College of William and Mary, Williamsburg; Judith Bell, York County Public Schools, Grafton; Ben Troutman, Virginia Beach City Public Schools, Virginia Beach

Virgin Islands: Sandra Lindo, Department of Education, Charlotte Amalie

Washington: Marge Chow, Richland School District, Richland; Judy Olson, Federal Way; James Barchek, Enumclaw; Richard Wolfe, Gonzaga University, Spokane

West Virginia: JoAnn Litton, Kanawha County School, Charleston

Wisconsin: Nancy Blair, Cushing Elementary School, Delafield

Wyoming: Scott Wegner, Campbell County School District, Gillette

Alberta, Canada: Richard Wray, St. Anthony's Teacher Center, Edmonton

British Columbia, Canada: Jacquie Taylor, School District No. 34, Clearbrook

Germany: Michael Shelley, Branch Coordinator PPS/TAG, DoDDS, Germany

Netherlands, Antilles: Reynold Groeneveldt, Island Department of Education, Philipsburg, St. Maarten
United Kingdom: Karla Stark, London Central High School, London

ASCD Review Council

Chair: Mitsuo Adachi, University of Hawaii, Honolulu
Donna Delph, Department of Education, Purdue University Calumet, Hammond, Indiana
Dolores Silva, Temple University, Philadelphia, Pennsylvania
Benjamin Ebersole, Hershey Public School District, Hershey, Pennsylvania
Carolyn Hughes, Oklahoma City Public Schools, Oklahoma City, Oklahoma

ASCD Headquarters Staff

Gordon Cawelti, *Executive Director*
Ronald S. Brandt, *Executive Editor*
Diane Berreth, *Director, Field Services*
John Bralove, *Director, Administrative Services*
Marcia D'Arcangelo, *Manager, Media Production*
Paula Delo, *Manager, Public Information*
Helené Hodges, *Director, Research and Information*
Anne Meek, *Managing Editor,* Educational Leadership
Michelle Terry, *Director, Professional Development*

Maria Acosta
Francine Addicott
Teddy Atwara
Sylvia Bayer
Vickie Bell
Carol Bennett
Kimber Bennett
Sandy Berdux
Jennifer Beun
Karla Bingman
Sandra Boemerman
Joan Brandt
Breena Brooks
Dorothy Brown
Kathy Browne
Robert Bryan
Jeff Bryant
Colette Burgess
Angela Caesar
Gail Cales
Sally Chapman
John Checkley
R.C. Chernault
Sandra Claxton
Carrie Conti
Elaine Cunningham
Keith Demmons
Becky DeRigge
Sheila Ellison
Gillian Fitzpatrick
Delores Flenoury
Christine Fuscellaro

Dorothy Haines
Vicki Hancock
Ned Hartfiel
Dwayne Hayes
Julie Houtz
Angela Howard
Harold Hutch
Arddie Hymes
Jeanne Jackson
Jo Ann Irick Jones
Teola Jones
Van Jones
Mary Keen
Michelle Kelly
Leslie Kiernan
Lynn Klinger
Lars Kongshem
Terry Lawhorn
John Mackie
Indu Madan
Sally Margolis
Janice McCool
Ralph McGee
Joyce McKee
Clara Meredith
Susan Merriman
Ron Miletta
Ginger Miller
Frances Mindel
Nancy Modrak
Cerylle Moffett
Simeon Montesa

John O'Neil
Jayne Osgood
Millie Outten
Patricia Ouzts
Kelvin Parnell
Jayshree Patel
Margini Patel
Judith Patrick
Sydney Petty
Geri Pieron
Carolyn Pool
Jackie Porter
Ruby Powell
Janet Price
Lorraine Primeau
Gena Randall
Melody Ridgeway
Mickey Robinson
Gayle Rockwell
Cordelia Roseboro
Beth Schweinefuss
Bob Shannon
Carolyn Shell
Lois Smith
Lisa Street
René Townsley
Diana Vipond
James Warren
Al Way
Scott Willis
Carolyn Wojcik